Routledge Revivals

Injustice, Inequality and Ethics

Abortion, distribution of wealth, civil disobedience, reverse discrimination, sex-role stereotyping, censorship – what does philosophy have to contribute to these practical moral issues? In this important book, first published in 1982, Robin Barrow argues convincingly that the capacity to make fine conceptual discriminations is crucial to an informed response to such issues, and he alerts us to the degree to which this ability has been lacking in much previous philosophical thought.

The author presents a series of formidable arguments regarding the more controversial social and moral issues of our time, and in doing so he gives the general reader and the student of philosophy a clearer appreciation of the nature of the philosophical contribution.

Injustice, Inequality and Ethics
A Philosophical Introduction to Moral Problems

Robin Barrow

First published in 1982
by Wheatsheaf Books Ltd

This edition first published in 2015 by Routledge
2 Park Square, Milton Park, Abingdon, Oxon, OX14 4RN
and by Routledge
711 Third Avenue, New York, NY 10017

Routledge is an imprint of the Taylor & Francis Group, an informa business

© 1982 Robin Barrow

All rights reserved. No part of this book may be reprinted or reproduced or utilised in any form or by any electronic, mechanical, or other means, now known or hereafter invented, including photocopying and recording, or in any information storage or retrieval system, without permission in writing from the publishers.

Publisher's Note
The publisher has gone to great lengths to ensure the quality of this reprint but points out that some imperfections in the original copies may be apparent.

Disclaimer
The publisher has made every effort to trace copyright holders and welcomes correspondence from those they have been unable to contact.

A Library of Congress record exists under LC control number: 82001603

ISBN 13: 978-1-138-92568-7 (hbk)
ISBN 13: 978-1-315-68360-7 (ebk)
ISBN 13: 978-1-138-92571-7 (pbk)

Injustice, Inequality and Ethics
A Philosophical Introduction to Moral Problems

Robin Barrow

First published in Great Britain in 1982 by
WHEATSHEAF BOOKS LTD
A MEMBER OF THE HARVESTER PRESS GROUP
Publisher: John Spiers
Director of Publications: Edward Elgar
16 Ship Street, Brighton, Sussex

and in the USA by
BARNES & NOBLE BOOKS
81 Adams Drive, Totowa, New Jersey 07512

© Robin Barrow, 1982
Reprinted 1983

British Library Cataloguing in Publication Data

Barrow, Robin
  Injustice, inequality and ethics: a
  philosophical introduction to moral
  problems.
  1. Ethics
  I. Title
  170   BJ1012

  ISBN 0-7108-0165-3
  ISBN 0-7108-0170-X Pbk

Library of Congress Cataloging in Publication Data

Barrow, Robin.
  Injustice, inequality, and ethics.

  Includes bibliographical references.
  1. Social ethics. 2. Social problems. I. Title.
  HM216.B17   170   82-1603
  ISBN 0-389-20269-X   AACR2

Photoset in Great Britain by
Rowland Phototypesetting Ltd
Bury St Edmunds, Suffolk
and printed by The Thetford Press Ltd
Thetford, Norfolk

All rights reserved

When people say that life is rough
I wonder compared to what.

> Glenn Martin, *I'm Just Me* (song)

Contents

	Acknowledgements	ix
	Foreword	xi
1	Discrimination	1
2	Utilitarianism	12
3	Dogmatism	23
4	Freedom	44
5	Feminism: Language and Thought	56
6	Feminism: Sex-Role Stereotyping	67
7	Reverse Discrimination	77
8	Abortion	91
9	Equality and Wealth	106
10	Democracy	129
11	Civil Disobedience	141
12	Animals	156
13	The Arts	169
14	Education	188
	Bibliography	199
	Index	203

For Alexandra, with love

Acknowledgements

I am extremely grateful to Sue Bird for her calm and patient typing of the manuscript, and also to Molly Clitheroe, Shelley Heighton-Towers, Elaine Humphries, Marjorie Richardson and Denise Spence for their generous assistance.

Foreword

My first, working, title for this book was *Moral Problems and Philosophy*, for that is what it was and is concerned with: the examination of some particular problems that require moral reasoning rather than technological know-how, if we are to come up with an answer to them. At an important stage of composition (after the first draft was completed), the title became *The Ethics of Discrimination*. That remains my own preferred title, for a central theme running through the separate chapters is that the ability to perceive and think in terms of clear and specific concepts, and to discriminate between matters that are superficially similar but nonetheless distinct, is crucial to a coherent response to any moral problem. Not only is this ability to discriminate important, it is also rather rare, for it is an integral part of the ability to philosophise, that most respected but least understood or practised of arts. Even very clever people persist in handling issues on the basis of faulty analogies and clumsy categorisation (for example, Northern Ireland is Britain's Viet Nam; the monarchy is merely an authority figure; women are an exploited group in the same manner as blacks). Even well respected figures can still build their reputations on little more than the art of mesmerising with misused words (for example, the conscious decision to take one's own life is not suicide, when it is harnessed to some cause; initiating violence is countering violence when the victim is an ideological enemy). This book is about the need to discriminate sharply and the need to accomplish the parallel task of devastating thought-crippling ideology; it is also an attempt to engage in discrimination in relation to the particular topics selected.

However, and I say it with no malice or bitterness, this is a predominantly commercial age, and publishers and editors, even excellent ones like my good friend Edward Elgar, though they might want their books to be worthy, most certainly require them to sell. In this case my publishers felt that my title was not so much appropriate as dull, not so much quite neat as totally un-mind-grabbing. The problem (for I am an accommodating sort of fellow) was to come up with an alternative. Several were tried. Now the utilitarian angle of the book would be stressed; now the marked shift towards liberalism and away from the totalitarian sympathies of some of my earlier books would be referred to; now the practical value of philosophy would be emphasised. But nothing was acceptable to all parties.

Finally, I found that the book was complete and we still had no agreed title. *Injustice, Inequality and Ethics* was proposed to me. Well, the book is certainly concerned with injustice, because it is concerned with avoiding injustice, be it to animals, to art or to each other in various ways. Some of it is directly concerned with equality (for example, of wealth, of treatment for animals), and most of it is clearly concerned with the closely related principles of impartiality and fairness. Of course it is concerned with ethics. It was not, as you see, my first choice of title, but it seemed churlish to refuse it, particularly since my publishers kindly agreed that I should write this brief explanatory foreword—this mild disclaimer?

The main message of the book remains: though there are many discriminatory practices that are to be deplored, we must cease to let that fact unconsciously persuade us that we should not discriminate in the sense of recognise differences. Whether we should act differently to different people in the light of their differences is a further question (often encountered in the course of this book). But we must certainly begin by reviving the art of perceiving and acknowledging differences that we are capable of discerning.

1 Discrimination

> If we want to *understand* and not just to paste labels, unfavourable and favourable as the case may be, we shall certainly begin and end with discrimination.
>
> John Dewey, *Liberalism and Social Action*

Our knowledge and understanding of the world owe a lot to man's ability to see differences or to discriminate. To many people there is a nasty ring to the word 'discrimination'. The context in which we most frequently encounter it is that of racial discrimination, and 'racial discrimination' is generally taken to mean something like 'treating people differently simply on the grounds of their racial differences'. As such it is generally, and quite rightly, regarded as objectionable. But what is wrong here is the particular practice of excluding a group of people from various advantages simply because of their race. It is racial discrimination in this sense that is morally repugnant, not discrimination itself in any shape or form. The connotations or overtones of undesirability that cling to the word discrimination are in fact quite unwarranted, arising out of this particular, and possibly other, examples of unjustified discrimination.

In origin 'discrimination' simply means 'the act of differentiating or distinguishing'. The verb 'to discriminate', coming obviously and directly from the Latin *discriminare*, means either (intransitively) 'to constitute a difference between' or (transitively) 'to perceive a difference between'. So, in the first sense, we may say that there are certain physical characteristics that discriminate between men and women. In the second sense, we might talk of discriminating between sheep and goats, meaning by that taking notice of, or drawing a distinction between, the two types of animal. Not only is 'the power of observing differences accurately or of making exact differences' the original meaning of discrimination, it is also, despite the connotations of a phrase like 'racial discrimination', still its essential meaning today. In other words, although people may sometimes use words like 'discriminate' and 'discrimination' in a way that implies *unfair* differential treatment, the fact remains that such words may be, and very often are, used quite simply to refer to the making or observing of differences that are there to be made or perceived. In this latter sense most of us spend most of our day discriminating. We discriminate amongst members of our family when buying clothes, we discriminate amongst competing goods in the shops, we discriminate between the serious and the trivial at work, and so on. Discrimination in this sense is unavoidable. There just are differences to be noted and distinctions to be made in life. It is also, on the whole, eminently desirable that they should be made.

It is with discrimination in the sense of making (whether constituting or perceiving) distinctions that this book is to a large extent concerned. It is concerned with arguing for the importance of discrimination in general, with arguing for various particular acts of discrimination, and with arguing for the moral importance of certain particular examples of discrimination.

The art of discriminating is essentially philosophical. One of the philosopher's main concerns is to try and refine his conceptions until he knows precisely what his ideas of, say, God, justice or education amount to, with the consequence that he is in a position to discriminate between God and a ghost, justice and equality, or education and training. He will also want to discriminate between similar looking, but subtly different, forms of argument, between apparent analogies that are not in fact analogous, and so on. And despite the recurrent myth that philosophy is impractical, a subject fit only for day-dreamers and idle theorists, this philosophical task is of crucial and enormous practical significance. Of course it has practical significance whether people can differentiate between cause and responsibility, for instance. For, if they cannot, then they will fail to distinguish between a person being the cause of a state of affairs and a person being responsible for a state of affairs, and they will start treating clumsy fools in the same manner as homicidal maniacs. Of course it is a matter of practical significance whether or not people have a crude conception of love, undifferentiated from lust and attraction, for on that may to some extent depend their chances of happiness. Of course it matters that people should be able to see the differences between an individual robbing a bank and the Ford Motor Company producing some shoddy cars, despite the fact that some would lump both together as acts of exploitation, for, if we are not prepared to make such distinctions, all manner of criminal activity would be rife, and justifiably so. Of course it is of practical value that people should be able to differentiate between indoctrination and instruction, otherwise we should have to treat teaching the multiplication tables and inculcating a political ideology as indistinguishable, which they are certainly not. Indeed, the idea that philosophy is impractical could itself only be entertained by those who lack discriminatory ability. No doubt senses may be given to the word in which philosophy is 'impractical'. It is not, for example, a manual activity, and it isn't very well paid! But assuming that 'practical' means something like 'having value for everyday life' conceptual discrimination is evidently of great practical value, if not for the agent himself, at least for the rest of us. The man who can't tell a spade from a shovel is, perhaps, more of a nuisance to the rest of us than to himself. But he is nonetheless a nuisance.

It should be noted however that discriminating is not simply a matter of seeing differences that are there to be seen. It may also be more or less a matter of judgement. Some distinguishing features of things present themselves directly to our senses and are hard to miss. Cows and chickens are transparently different. But even here a minimal amount of judgement is involved, for, after all, red cows and red chickens have their colour, the possession of two eyes and one or two other things in common, and it might conceivably have served our purpose to locate a class of red, two-eyed creatures. It is not written in the stars that we should make the classifications that we do, although some limits are set upon possible classifications by the facts of nature. We tend to classify people automatically by sex, when we might easily have chosen to make more of age, and could, as far as logic goes, have classified by reference to hair colour. In most people's view there is probably good reason to classify more by reference to sex than age; the point is merely that things could have been decided differently. In other cases distinctions that we commonly rely on are much more obviously based on judgement: for example, our tendency to note differences of accent and to ignore differences of stature is curious. And the way in which we have chosen to draw broad divisions in the worlds of music and literature seems, to say the least, negotiable. Some people have overstated the case and tried to suggest that all differences lie in the eyes of the beholder, rather than in the world. I am certainly not maintaining that thesis. There are obviously differences between things, regardless of who, if anyone, is looking at them. But I am underlining the point that the classifications we make use of are to some extent a matter of choice and judgement.

Much of this book is concerned with conceptual discrimination, because many moral dilemmas are inextricably bound up with questions of discrimination. If you want to decide whether a work of art ought to be censored on grounds of obscenity, you *have* to have a clear idea of art and obscenity. In considering the question of abortion, we need to ask what differentiates the eight month old foetus and a baby born one month prematurely. Is a foetus a person? We live in a democracy and often make appeal to the value of democracy, but what exactly is it that constitutes democracy and differentiates it from other forms of government? Must every issue be decided on the basis of one man one vote, or is it perhaps something to do with safeguarding minority interests? and what is the nature of the connection between democracy and various freedoms? If we turn to the domain of schooling, what, we need to ask, is this thing intelligence, on the basis of claiming to recognise which we make so many judgements? How is it that we think we can recognise it, and yet can scarcely explain what it is? How do we distinguish between intelligence and cleverness or wisdom? On a similar subject, how would one discriminate between merit and innate talent? What we need in answer to these kinds of question is not simply definitions, but definitions that are precise, coherent and revealing. It is no use just saying 'what I mean by a "person" is a "being with a soul" ', for that leaves questions such as whether a foetus or an animal is a person no further forward. We need to understand what you mean by 'a being with a soul'; we need a definition of 'person' that makes some sense to us.[1]

However, the ability to discriminate, though vital, is not sufficient for solving all our problems. Assuming that we have precise conceptions, we move into a position in which we are ready to make reasoned decisions. But to have a clear idea of what something is, and to perceive what differentiates it from other similar things, is not sufficient to enable one to decide how to treat it, and, in particular, whether to treat it differently from those other similar but not identical things. To discriminate, in this new extended sense of 'treat differently', requires that we know not only what differences there are, but also which of those differences matter for what purposes. Nobody can deny that there is a difference between black men and white men. The question is whether that colour difference justifies different treatment in any respects. Similarly, once we are clear what a foetus is, and in what respects it can be distinguished from a newborn baby, a seed, a person with severe brain-damage and so forth, the question remains whether abortion can be morally justified. The conceptual clarification makes it clear what we are talking about—in the abortion example whether aborting is or is not an instance of killing a person—but it will not settle the question of what is justifiable. To take another example, consider the problem of euthanasia. Here also there are conceptual questions to be examined: what constitutes being a person? what constitutes being dead? The recent argument as to whether the British Medical Authority has adequate criteria to prevent organs being removed from living patients for transplant, and to know when it is appropriate to switch off life support systems, involves at rock bottom not a medical question but conceptual ones. We do need to know certain medical facts, of the order of what the physiological significance of this or that phenomenon may be. But the central question remains: do we count somebody in such and such a state as dead or not? However, my immediate point is that even with a clear conception of death, we are left with the evaluative question of whether or when we should allow people, or even help them, to die.

It may be felt that in some cases what one ought to do is rapidly apparent from an adequate conceptual grasp of the situation. To appreciate what democracy is is to perceive readily enough that it is morally desirable, it may be said. But, if there are any such cases, that is accidental. If people sense the moral rightness of democracy as soon as they know what democracy is, that is only because democracy happens to enshrine values they hold. It remains true that in all cases the question of what something involves and the question of whether it is morally desirable are logically distinct. The former, conceptual, question is necessary to the latter question of justification, but it is not a substitute for it. Having a clear grasp of what abortion involves (let us say, for the sake of example, killing a human being) does not automatically reveal whether it may be morally justifiable.

The question, therefore, remains: do the various differences that we may be able to discern demand different treatment in various respects? Certainly animals differ from human beings in various ways, and no doubt those differences constitute good reasons for not providing animals with state-subsidised schooling. But do any of them justify the practice of vivisection? Women and men differ, and will continue to differ, in various ways, but do any of those differences justify the different roles we expect them to play? What, if anything, justifies differences in wealth? Here again it is not difficult to pinpoint differences between at least some people who have wealth and some who don't. Some are born rich, some have rare ability, some work hard. But do these or any other differences justify discrimination in this respect?

There is one principle to which we all necessarily subscribe and which is of some importance in the context of trying to answer such questions. It goes by many names, but may well be called the principle of impartiality. This principle states that no difference of treatment should occur without a relevant reason for such differential treatment being cited. And it has more force than is sometimes recognised. In the first place much of our behaviour, being arbitrary or inconsistent, runs foul of the principle, and in the second place the principle has negative significance in that it clearly implies that we should not always treat all people in the same way. (I should perhaps explain why I say that we all necessarily subscribe to this principle, while admitting that much of our behaviour is not in accord with it. We may fail to abide by the principle, but we cannot sensibly repudiate it. For to be concerned with reason at all, as we all maintain we are, is to be committed to having good reasons rather than bad, and the principle of impartiality arises out of that basic commitment.)

To assert so early in the argument that we are against treating all people the same may seem rather curious, for, it may be felt, many people have thought that everybody should be treated the same. But although some people have indeed expressed that view, it must surely be doubted whether any of them meant to espouse it literally. It seems more likely that the equivocal nature of the word 'equality' has caused confusion. Without doubt a great many people expressly assert that they are in favour of equality or equal treatment, without qualification. But it is scarcely credible that any of them should mean by that 'similar treatment for all, without qualification', so that every man, woman and child would ideally be provided with exactly the same food, work, social environment and so forth. Surely no sensible person really believes that both champion wrestlers and babies should have two pound steaks set before them, as if there were no differences between them that warranted different treatment. Presumably what those who claim to believe in equality, without qualification, really mean to advocate is one of the following three positions.

Firstly, they might want to insist on exactly similar treatment for all, but restrict it to certain broad, as yet unspecified, respects. Perhaps they are concerned to argue that when it comes to certain important things such as wealth or living space every man, woman and child should have the same. Whatever our reaction to this limited kind of demand for identical treatment, it is at least coherent. (A modification of this view would confine its application to all adults, in which case, *prima facie*, it would be easier to extend the range of similarities in treatment demanded.) Secondly, they might mean to champion a very different view, namely that everybody should have equality of opportunity. This is a widely held view, particularly in the Western democracies, and is sometimes more specifically expressed as the view that every individual ought to have the same opportunity to fulfil himself or to live well. The upshot may be that certain particular types of treatment have to be identical for all, in order to ensure such equal opportunity. But there is no necessary incompatibility between equality in this sense and many specific differences of treatment in a society. Thirdly, they might mean by the demand for equal treatment what might be more explicitly expressed as equal concern for all people, regardless of any recognisable differences between them.

Any of these views would represent an advance on the view that all people should literally receive the same treatment in all respects in all circumstances. Nonetheless, each of them has its problems. Clearly the plausibility of the first view will depend upon the respects in which it is argued that people should receive the same treatment. The second view raises the problem of what is to count as fulfilment or well-being, as well as the question of how far a community should be expected to go to ensure equal opportunity. One readily sees that equality of opportunity demands some form of adequate schooling for all. Does it not also demand the provision of adequate homes for all? And how is one to determine when to stop? The third view raises the question of what showing equal concern for everybody actually amounts to (besides, incidentally, raising the question of why we should unhesitatingly assume that equal concern should be shown for all humans, and no animals except humans).

At this stage, therefore, it would seem unwise to commit ourselves to more than something like Aristotle's statement of the principle of fairness or impartiality.[2] No distinction ought to be made between those who are equal in all respects relevant to the kind of treatment in question, even though in some irrelevant respects they may be unequal. On the other hand, in any matter in which they are in relevant respects unequal, they ought to be treated in proportion to their relevant inequalities. One immediate problem that we therefore face is that of trying to determine what makes a difference a relevant difference. That there are differences between people is self-evident, but which of them, if any, are relevant to a question such as who should make political decisions? That there are respects in which *Fanny Hill* differs from *War and Peace* few would deny, but how are we to determine whether those differences are relevant to the question of censorship? That there are differences between a foetus and a baby is clear, but are they relevant to the decision to terminate life? What factors are relevant to the question of whether a situation justifies civil disobedience?

8   Injustice, Inequality and Ethics

A partial answer can be provided fairly easily. Why is it that we see at once that intelligence is relevant to academic concerns and physical strength to football, while hair colour is relevant to neither? It is surely that in the first two cases there is some kind of conceptual tie-up. Academic concerns and intelligence have something in common, as do football and physical strength. I am not suggesting that relevant factors must necessarily have a conceptual or logical tie up with the matter in question. But there does have to be some kind of connection, whether logical or contingent, direct or indirect, for a difference to be a relevant difference. When the connection is logical it tends to strike us as self-evident, as in the case of the relevance of physical strength to football; whereas, very often, when the connection is contingent, one has to use reasoning to show that there is a connection. For example, I would think that personal appearance might be a relevant reason for appointing one person rather than another as a shop assistant. It is not the case that comely appearance has any logical connection with the idea of a shop assistant. (There is no logical oddity in the idea of a slovenly shop assistant.) But it is not difficult to establish a connection nonetheless. One might argue that the shop assistant has to sell goods, that customers by and large respond to neat appearances, and that it is therefore a relevant consideration that an individual should have a neat appearance.

An important point implicit in the last example is that the relevance of factors depends to some extent upon one's objectives. Neatness becomes a relevant consideration because of what we want the shop assistant to do. It might cease to be relevant, if we want the shop assistant to mind the stores at the back of the shop, rather than serve customers. (The situation is essentially the same in the case of the tighter logical kind of connection: physical strength is part of what is involved in being a rugby player, which entails that it is part of what we want or are looking for when we select people to play.) Reasons can therefore become or cease to be relevant as we change our objectives. Lack of ability in a subject such as the study of English literature would seem on the face of it to be a relevant reason for discontinuing the study, but it is so only given certain presumptions, objectives or preferred states of affairs. Obviously it is a relevant consideration on the usual assumption that classes in English are for making academic progress in the study of literature. It would not be necessarily, if you thought the main purpose of such classes should be to promote social harmony or to familiarise everybody with a similar cultural background.

A relevant reason, then, is one that is connected to the object of the exercise, either directly or indirectly. This means that an important part of what we need to do when we examine specific issues is to consider the implications of taking some reason as relevant. If we presume that the fact that humans have reasoning ability is relevant to discriminating between them and other animals, that is to presume that the object of life is something like contentment for the rational. In which case there may be awkward questions to face such as whether, in consistency, we should not treat severely brain-damaged people as comparable to animals. If we argue that some works of art should be censored on the grounds of obscenity, we are revealing something about our preference for a world without obscenity.

However, to determine whether a reason is relevant or not to an issue of differential treatment is not the end of the matter. Usually we need to consider not only whether there are relevant reasons for discrimination, but also whether those reasons are compelling. This is a straightforward distinction, sometimes overlooked. It is also obscured by the equivocal phrase 'good reason' which might mean either 'relevant reason' or 'overriding reason'. Many forms of discrimination may be shown to be legitimate or fair, in the sense that they are based on relevant reasons, but they might nonetheless be felt on other grounds to be unjustifiable. Differences in intelligence are obviously relevant reasons for differential schooling, and it is certainly not self-evidently unfair to engage in differential schooling. On the other hand one might reasonably argue against it. The most obvious kind of case is where more than one conflicting practice can be shown to be fair in itself, but one has to make a choice between them. More often we will be faced with a conflict between different objectives, as between those who see schools as primarily there to advance intellectual development and those who see them as there to promote social harmony.

At this point one is forced into consideration of the wider question of what ethical theory is to guide us. For, in the end, particular judgements about what we ought to do, how we ought to treat each other and in what respects it is morally acceptable to treat different groups differently, depend upon clear conceptualisation, noting differences and linking them to objectives, and rank-ordering those objectives. Some practice that involves differential treatment which is agreed to be based on relevant or even good reasons might nonetheless be regarded as immoral, just because it runs counter to some fundamental moral tenet. Thus one might wish to bypass discussion of whether there can be factors that are relevant to distinguishing between people when it comes to taking life, such that euthanasia might sometimes be justified, on the grounds that killing is always under any circumstances a moral wrong. (Such views are quite rare, just because of what they commit one to. In this case consistency would demand that anyone who held such a view should refrain from and deplore even killing in self-defence or to protect one's family from being tortured. Nonetheless such a position might be held.)

It is certainly possible to approach the particular issues with which this book is concerned without having any general ethical theory in mind. There are even certain possible advantages in so doing. One avoids the danger that if one adopts a particular theory of what makes acts morally right, one will not be very imaginative or critical in approaching specific issues, but will simply let the theory dictate the answer. If I am committed to the view that the ten commandments enshrine the whole of morality, then my answers to particular questions are fairly predictable. I shall in fact have some strongly critical remarks to make about those who interpret all events in terms of some one unquestioned theory in Chapter 3.[3] But it is important to distinguish between reading off the solution to a problem from a particular theoretical position, and being aware of what one's theoretical position is. The truth is that, however one approaches the matter, some theoretical position is an integral part of taking a stand on particular issues. To interpret a particular case in a particular way logically presupposes a theory, so that if I say, 'do not abort foetuses because they are persons', I implicitly commit myself to some theoretical stance on the need to treat persons in certain ways. One of the dangers of approaching each issue on its own merits, without having given any thought to one's overall moral position, is that one may end up with a number of clear answers to particular problems that are logically incompatible.

In the next chapter, therefore, I intend to explicate the utilitarian moral theory, since I regard it as the only satisfactory moral theory. This will enable readers to be alert to some basic assumptions that lie behind and explain certain things I say. But having done that, it is not my intention to approach every issue from a utilitarian point of view. That, as I argue in Chapter 3, would be the antithesis of true intellectual enquiry. Rather I shall approach each issue by focussing on the issue itself, seeking to discriminate, to clarify, and to reveal the implications of adopting various positions. It is my belief that this approach tends to confirm the plausibility of a utilitarian viewpoint, but that is not my main concern. Only occasionally does a view on a particular issue crucially depend upon some aspect of the utilitarian perspective. In many cases quite different moral theories may lead to the same substantive conclusions about particular practices.

NOTES

1 I have gone into the difference between verbal definitions and conceptual analysis in more detail in my *The Philosophy of Schooling*.
2 Aristotle, *Nicomachean Ethics*, 5.6; *Politics* 1.2; 3.1.
3 In Chapter 3, however, I am primarily concerned with explanatory theories, which differ in important respects from prescriptive moral theories.

2 Utilitarianism

> Yet what is human society, but one great family? What is moral duty, but that precise line of conduct which tends to promote the greatest degree of general happiness?
>
> Thomas Love Peacock, *Melincourt*

Utilitarianism is probably the most widely subscribed to and practically significant ethical theory in the Western world. That is not to say that most people would claim to be utilitarians. In all likelihood very few would. But many people who would not see themselves as utilitarians effectively behave as if they were. Many arguments, public and private, unconsciously take utilitarianism for granted, and many of our social, legal and institutional arrangements presuppose utilitarianism. But I spell it out, not for those reasons, but because I believe it to be by far the most plausible ethical theory there is.

Two quotations from two of its founding fathers will serve to introduce both the theory and most of the main problems that have been found in it. According to John Stuart Mill, 'the creed which accepts as the foundation of Morals, Utility or the Greatest Happiness Principle, holds that actions are right in proportion as they tend to promote happiness, wrong as they tend to produce the reverse of happiness. By happiness is intended pleasure and the absence of pain; by unhappiness, pain and the privation of pleasure.'[1] Jeremy Bentham even more starkly remarked, 'Nature has placed mankind under the governance of two sovereign masters, pain and pleasure. It is for them alone to point out what we ought to do, as well as to determine what we shall do. On the one hand the standard of right and wrong, on the other the chain of causes and effects, are fastened to their throne.'[2]

These quotations convey admirably the essence of utilitarianism. It is that theory which estimates right and wrong by the principle of utility. Despite the common use of the word 'utility' as a synonym for useful, sometimes with overtones of economic usefulness, the principle of utility in this theory is solely concerned with happiness, pleasure, pain and unhappiness. What ought to be done is whatever is most conducive to happiness in the world. But there are undoubtedly some problems already lurking even in this skeletal account.

A very obvious problem arises with the key term happiness. What exactly is happiness? Is it a sensation or a state of mind? Should it be identified with something akin to ecstasy or contentment, or neither? Can we accept Mill's succinct identification of it with pleasure and the absence of pain, and are those terms not also more problematic than either Mill or Bentham here seem to allow? The quotation from the latter also raises a rather different kind of problem, for he seems concerned to make two quite distinct points: first, that as a matter of fact we are only motivated by considerations of pleasure and pain, and, second, that what we ought morally to do is promote pleasure. But is the first, empirical, claim in fact true, and how important is it to the second, moral, claim? In the passage quoted from Mill the at first sight innocent phrase 'tend to' is not entirely unproblematic. What exactly is its force, and does Mill mean to refer to the tendency of each particular act, or to the tendency of types or classes of act? Finally, the notion of the Greatest Happiness Principle itself needs a certain amount of explanation and spelling out. Can it reasonably be paraphrased as the view that the Greatest Happiness of the Greatest Number should be pursued, and, if so, what if anything does this principle imply for particular conflicts between short- and long-term happiness, or between the intense happiness of a few and the milder happiness of many?

In what follows I shall attempt to offer some kind of answer to most of these questions. (I shall not attempt to answer the conceptual question of the nature of happiness, which I have dealt with elsewhere.)[3] But I shall pursue the matter without particular reference to the texts of Mill, Bentham or anyone else. I am not concerned with textual questions or questions about interpretation of what particular people were trying to say, but with outlining an account of what makes actions right and wrong. Perhaps I should add that this is quite distinct from trying to establish how in fact people do form their moral views. Just as the physical sciences seek to explain what actually is going on in various situations, as opposed to what the casual observer may think is going on (which may or may not be compatible with the deeper scientific account), so I am seeking to elucidate what we are saying about an action, if we correctly say that it is a right or a wrong action, as opposed to what we may think we are saying.

Let us start again from the beginning and consider the range of alternative accounts of morality available to us. A broad division can be made between what are sometimes called deontological theories and consequentialist theories. Deontological systems are those that hold that an action can be right or wrong, regardless of consequences. A religious ethic embodying principles such as that adultery is always morally wrong, no matter what the circumstances, or a secular intuitionist ethic that held that telling a lie could never be right, would be examples of deontological systems. Consequentialist theories, of which utilitarian theories are examples, as the name implies, involve the assumption that the rightness or wrongness of an act depends upon its consequences. This entails that an act might be right today and wrong tomorrow, and this has sometimes been urged as a criticism of consequentialist views. But it surely isn't a very strong criticism. It certainly doesn't amount to a charge of inconsistency, as some would imply, since by definition the act that is right today differs from the act that is wrong tomorrow, because the circumstances are different. And that is something that generally seems proper to us. We do, for example, feel that the fact that this act of killing is engaged in out of self-defence, while that is engaged in to further a political end, might make a morally relevant difference. There is besides a major weakness in deontological theories (apart from the point that there are many rival theories competing with each other, and no obvious means of judging between them), and that is that we surely do not feel that, if an action that was nominally right was known to be the cause of widespread misery, it would still be right to do it. Even supposing that we believed keeping promises a good thing in itself, surely we can conceive of circumstances where the keeping of a promise would have such appalling consequences that we would think it wrong to go on keeping it. To concede as much, is to accept some version of consequentialism.

All utilitarian theories are consequentialist, but there are nonetheless different utilitarian theories. The major division here is between ideal utilitarians, who believe that various end states, such as beauty and truth, may be good, and acts therefore right insofar as they tend to promote any of those ends, and hedonistic utilitarians, who regard happiness alone as a good in itself, and acts as right only insofar as they promote happiness. It is hedonistic utilitarianism that I am concerned with.

The most important thing to be considered is the rival merit of adopting an act-utilitarian or a rule-utilitarian position. The difference is between holding that one should judge the rightness or wrongness of every individual act by reference to its consequences in terms of happiness, and holding that one should judge the rightness of adopting certain rules by reference to the consequences of so doing, and then stick by the rules, regardless of consequences in particular cases. It has been argued that the difference between the two is a distinction without a difference. The two, it is argued, collapse into each other, because the precise formulation of a rule depends upon calculation of the consequences of different practices. The rule-utilitarian thinks there should be a rule against killing, except in self-defence. But how did he arrive at the clause excluding self-defence? By deciding that on balance the interests of happiness are best served by allowing killing in self-defence. Then why doesn't he just say that the rule is 'don't kill except where to do so would be in the interests of happiness'? And in that case, it is concluded, he is indistinguishable from an act-utilitarian.

But fairly clearly that line of argument is inadequate. Even if a rule-utilitarian adopts a rule with a qualificatory clause, such as 'never kill, except in self-defence', that is still distinct from arguing that each case should be decided on its merits. The former involves abiding by the rule, even when to break it in a particular instance would cause more happiness. A similar response must be made to R. M. Hare's view that act-utilitarianism amounts to rule-utilitarianism, on the grounds that if one ought to do any particular act, one ought at least to do any other act exactly like it, and therefore one is effectively acting on the rule do such and such a kind of act.[4] But this is to ignore the crucial point that in life we never know all the conditions and consequences of actions, so there is a very real practical difference between a theory that says, 'Do this action always in precisely similar circumstances', assuming you can ever discern them, and a theory that says, 'always do this', (even when 'this' has specific qualifications built in). Whichever way you look at it, there is a difference between saying each individual ought to do that which on any occasion would most promote happiness (act-utilitarianism), and saying each individual ought to abide by certain rules, regardless of the advantage or disadvantages in so doing on particular occasions (rule-utilitarianism). (Incidentally, where he sees no case for a rule, the rule-utilitarian does proceed as an act-utilitarian.)

This brings us to the important question of whether we should espouse act or rule-utilitarianism. J. J. C. Smart, in an attempt to push the claims of act-utilitarianism, has argued that the same kind of consideration that inclines one to reject deontological systems (namely that it is counter-intuitive to conclude that it would be right to do something regardless of the overwhelming misery it caused), must lead one to abandon rule-utilitarianism. The rule-utilitarian, he asserts, 'is open to the charge of preferring conformity to a rule to the prevention of unhappiness', which, if true, would be more than merely counter-intuitive in the case of the utilitarian.[5] It would be a nonsense, since the basis of his position is the supreme importance of happiness. But Smart has clearly made a mistake. The rule-utilitarian does not prefer conformity to a rule to preventing unhappiness. On the contrary, he believes that conformity to a rule will, on balance, promote more happiness. The difference is that he takes a more long-term view of the situation. The act-utilitarian says, 'but look, killing this man will make a lot of people happy now'. The rule-utilitarian replies, 'I know. But once drop the rule against killing and accept a state of affairs in which every individual has to make up his own mind on every occasion as to whether to kill someone, and the resulting fear, uncertainty and unfortunate decisions will cause, in the long run, even more unhappiness than that admittedly caused by refraining from killing this man now.' Indeed, it is this very line of reasoning that establishes that, if we are going to be utilitarians at all, we have to be rule-utilitarians. For utilitarians want to promote happiness, and therefore we ought to adopt rules in those cases where we believe that to do so would itself be in the interests of happiness. In fact Smart effectively, but unwittingly, concedes as much, when he admits that for practical purposes even act-utilitarians have to work with some rules of thumb. What leads him to characterise them as 'rules of thumb', rather than straightforward rules, and hence to misclassify himself as an act-utilitarian, is his entirely correct observation that, as time passes, we may come to see that a rule we had adopted should be dropped. But that is quite a different point. Of course it is conceivable that circumstances may change, or our perceptions change, to such an extent that, whereas it seemed yesterday that it was imperative to set up a rule, 'Do X, except when A or B' in the interests of our happiness overall, today it seems better to drop that particular rule, and to let individuals determine for themselves whether they ought to do X or not, when the question arises. All the rule-utilitarian is committed to, and the significance of being a rule-utilitarian, is the view that, where there is reason to think that leaving a particular decision to individual choice would cause more unhappiness than adopting a rule, there one should adopt the rule.

The points to be made in favour of adopting utilitarianism are fairly straightforward and even obvious (though it must be remembered that we are not engaged in the task of finding advantages to be had from acting as if one were a utilitarian, but of producing reasons for regarding this account of what makes actions morally right as more plausible than alternatives). Firstly, happiness has a unique status amongst human values in that it would be logically inconceivable to deny that there is any value in happiness, and, since that is not true of anything else, it is the only thing that everybody does in fact recognise as valuable. Naturally, we are aware that many people would claim to value other things, such as freedom or equality, more than happiness. But it is not logically odd to assert that one doesn't value equality or freedom, as it would be to say that one sees no value in happiness. And although it would be a mistake to deduce from the fact that people do value happiness that they are right so to do, it surely is a point in favour of an ethical theory that what it regards as the central pivot of morality is something that all the world regards as having moral value. Secondly, it appears to be the case that people have a feeling of generalised benevolence, such that they do acknowledge as a test of moral behaviour the question of whether people generally are the happier for it. When rival political creeds are tearing each other apart, for instance, whether in word or deed, there is none who dares to assert that the well-being of people in general is neither here nor there. On the contrary, all parties to such disputes are at great pains to say, however implausibly, that, were it not for resistance to them, they would produce a pleasanter world for all. Once again this does not prove that it is correct to place great emphasis on happiness, but it suggests mankind's understanding of morality is in fact grounded in belief in the importance of happiness. At the very least, therefore, one need feel no shame in regarding a theory that makes happiness central as more plausible than others. The third consideration, which is really the reverse side of the previous two, is perhaps in the end the most telling. Nobody disputes that many individuals have sincerely and strongly held non-utilitarian views. But how is somebody who holds a particular moral view that is not generally acknowledged going to persuade the rest of the world of its correctness? Without a doubt, basic moral principles are not the kind of thing that one can demonstrate as valid beyond reasonable fear of contradiction. What has not been stressed often enough is that the strength of utilitarianism lies in its very limited claims. Other theories say, 'we intuit this and that', or 'God ordains this and that'. They are, without exception, long on detailed prescription, and short on reasons for believing. With utilitarianism the reverse is the case: the explicit demands are minimal;

the reasons for accepting them are relatively persuasive. One good reason for adopting utilitarianism, then, is that there seems no reason whatsoever to adopt any other theory, whereas nobody has ever seriously challenged the importance of utilitarian considerations. They have merely asserted that there must be more.

However, no account of utilitarianism would be complete without some consideration being given to the standard objections that have been raised against it (and that are still trotted out, despite the fact that all have been successfully met).[6] One favourite line of attack is to say that utilitarianism depends upon calculating the consequences of various acts in terms of happiness, but that this cannot in fact be done. One cannot be sure that one's predictions will be accurate, one cannot in any case measure things like the intensity of people's happiness, and, even if one could, one could not conceivably weigh that against, say, the extent of a lesser degree of happiness amongst another group of people, since that would involve weighing two incommensurables, rather like trying to weigh the juiciness of some pears against the crispness of others. Now the points made here are in themselves quite correct. But the line of attack is quite irrelevant. It is quite true that for these reasons and others, utilitarians cannot be sure what it is right to do on all occasions. But utilitarianism is not, and does not purport to be, a moral geiger counter that will enable one to read off the right action. It is an attempt to explain what makes actions right and wrong. Insofar as it is an acceptable account, it has the very important practical consequence that it tells us what we ought to consider, if we wish to do what is right. That is what moral theories are for. To criticise it on the grounds that it does not also make it easy for us to know what we ought to do, is to misunderstand the nature of moral theory. It is about as silly as criticising a railway timetable for not telling us which journeys to make.

Another criticism is likewise based upon a correct observation. It will readily be seen that utilitarianism ignores entirely questions of motive and intention, whereas, generally speaking, people think of these as rather important in assessing moral conduct. And of course they are important, if what we are concerned with is attributing praise or blame, and determining whether somebody is behaving as a moral agent. Certainly, doing what happens to be right, because you think it will bring you a handsome profit, is not to deserve moral acclaim. But once again it can hardly be an objection to utilitarianism that it does not take account of motives and intentions, since it was not supposed to. It does, of course, presuppose that the question of what actions are right can be divorced, theoretically at least, from the question of what intentions make for morally praiseworthy conduct. But such a divorce surely can be made, and indeed *is* made by almost all of us practically every day of our lives, when we make judgements along the lines of the 'right thing, but the wrong reasons'.

A rather more important criticism in my view is the suggestion that there is something essentially unfair inherent in utilitarianism, since it might in principle lead to the sacrifice of innocent minorities for the sake of the happiness of the majority, or certain unjust institutional arrangements, again in the interests of majority happiness. There is a subsidiary reason for taking this objection seriously, which takes us back to one of the problems noted earlier in this chapter. Everybody knows that utilitarianism is in favour of happiness: everyone knows too that, since in realistic terms we cannot expect complete happiness for all, some formula has to be adopted to express the utilitarian strategy, given competing claims. And so arises talk of the Greatest Happiness Principle, maximising happiness, the greatest happiness of the greatest number and so forth.[7]

None of these has ever seemed to me to be entirely satisfactory. Certainly it is they that give rise to this particular problem of minority scapegoats, and yet I am far from convinced that any of them adequately summarises a utilitarian position. To be sure, if you say that you want the Greatest Happiness of the Greatest Number, and say no more, it would seem to follow that a social arrangement whereby a few miserable souls toiled, in order to make the rest of us supremely happy, would be acceptable. Or, to take a popular example, an innocent party might be rightly executed to assuage fears in certain circumstances—if, for example, the state had reason to believe that a wave of terror was over, but felt the need to reassure everybody by producing a guilty party they did not in fact have. But is it correct to say that utilitarians want the greatest happiness of the greatest number? Bentham, for what it is worth, was careful to gloss the phrase 'principle of utility' as 'that principle which states the greatest happiness of all those whose interest is in question . . .'[8] which, though it is somewhat equivocal, suggests something slightly different. Certainly, utilitarianism as I am trying to expound it would be more accurately represented as the view that ideally everybody's happiness should be maximised equally. I should therefore prefer a formula that built in the assumption that all count equally (assuming they do not forfeit their right by some act of theft, etc.), and that nobody's claim to happiness can simply be ignored, though in an imperfect world a policy may have to be adopted that brings little happiness to particular individuals. This could be done, I believe, by adopting a form of wording that owes something to John Rawls' formulation of the principle of justice:[9] in practice one should aim at the greatest happiness of the greatest number, provided that no policy is adopted that either ignores the claim to happiness of any individual or would make some happier at the expense of others (always excepting those who forfeit their rights to some extent by criminal acts). That is to say, in striving to ameliorate the human condition, it would be legitimate to act in ways that disproportionately increased happiness, provided that everybody's happiness was to some extent thereby increased. Naturally, where possible, one should still opt for courses of action that provide more happiness for more people, since the sum total of happiness would be increased thereby.

Having said that, which is sufficient to dispose of the charge that utilitarianism would sanction the sacrifice of some in the interests of others, it is worth adding a further riposte to the innocent scapegoat charge. If one studies the examples produced to support the charge, they are invariably either very far-fetched or extreme. We are invited, for example, to imagine a fat man accidentally blocking a cave-mouth under circumstances whereby, if four of his friends in the cave behind him don't blow him up, they will all die. Or it is presumed that a scientist, who has a cure for cancer up his sleeve, and a car-dealer, who has little to offer, are starving on a raft, and we are asked whether the scientist should kill the car-dealer in order to survive. There is nothing wrong with fanciful examples as such, when the object is to examine points of logic rather than fact. But it does seem worth pointing out that, by and large, the circumstances opponents of utilitarianism are driven to depicting, in order to suggest that the theory might sometimes sanction killing an innocent person, are so dire and improbable, as to make it unclear that the terrible things the theory might in such circumstances allow represent much of an objection. After all, if a group of people are in such a predicament that it really is a question of taking one innocent life or losing five, is there any moral theory that can unequivocally state that the innocent life should not be taken? Added to which we should note that in real life the people in the cave never could be sure that their only hope of survival lay in blowing up the innocent. (It should be stressed too that such examples do not necessarily constitute any problem for the rule utilitarian, since his rules outweigh even the most dramatic of particular situations.)

There is, finally, another quite interesting objection to utilitarianism that requires a little sorting out. It may be asked whether, if one ought to promote happiness, one ought therefore to take active steps to increase the sum, by having a great many children, refusing to accept abortion and such like. A variant of the same point involves arguing that according to utilitarianism we must always be doing less than our moral duty, because, almost certainly, we could always find something to do other than what we are doing that would make a greater contribution to human happiness.

Neither the suggestion that as a utilitarian I ought to have lots of children nor that I ought to be helping the homeless in Kampuchea instead of mowing my lawn strike me as at all plausible, but they do need to be explained away. There are various points one might make. Firstly, without modifying or further explaining utilitarianism at all, one might try to argue that the world would in the long run be a less happy place, if people insisted on having many children, on refusing to countenance abortion, on taking on the big moral problems to the neglect of their personal family role, and so on. And it must be said that there is something in that line of thought. The mowing of lawns, so to speak, is a minute part of a great pattern of living that in itself accounts for much human happiness. Secondly, at any rate on the point that one could almost always be doing more than one is to promote human happiness, we could concede the point, and merely observe that nobody ever lived up to any moral code entirely. 'Yes', we could say, 'people ideally should be helping the poor, when they're washing their cars. That shows we are not perfect utilitarians; it doesn't show that utilitarianism is implausible.' Another possibility is to redraft utilitarianism in negative terms. It might be argued that the essence of morality is diminishing misery and suffering, rather than promoting happiness, and that it therefore does not follow that one has a moral duty to procreate and increase the number of beings on earth. But my own preferred response would be to make it clear that utilitarianism offers an account of what makes actions right amongst those who are affected by them. It is not, in other words, strictly speaking true to say that utilitarianism demands that we promote happiness (at any rate, not as that phrase might be understood). It does not enjoin us to produce beings in order that they may be happy, as some religious views do enjoin us to produce beings in order that they may rejoice in the Lord. It enjoins us to act with a view to the happiness rather than the reverse of those beings there are. Similarly, it does not require us to plan our lives doing large-scale happiness-promoting social work (quite apart from the fact that a world in which all tried to function in that manner would probably be solemn, dour, chaotic and counter-productive). It requires us to live our lives in ways that spread happiness rather than misery to those with whom we come into contact (though that should cover indirect contact too). There is nothing anti-utilitarian about a reclusive life-style.

I conclude by pointing out that a large part of the significance of utilitarianism is negative. Rather as the interesting thing about the dog in the Sherlock Holmes story was that it didn't bark in the night,[10] so a significant point about utilitarianism is that it denies that there is a number of types of behaviour that are always and necessarily obligatory or forbidden. It is sometimes said that utilitarianism on closer inspection turns out to be of no use, for it doesn't clearly tell us what to do: it will be difficult to calculate whether, say, the practice of euthanasia is good or bad, because it will be difficult (for logical and contingent, empirical, speculative and conceptual reasons) to work out the consequences. But utilitarianism is not something designed to be of use at furnishing determinate rules of conduct. As I have said, it is a view about what in principle makes actions right and wrong. It may be that its greatest strength is that it forces us to face up to the fact that there aren't many determinate rules of conduct, and that those who dogmatically assert that there are, are the ones to be suspicious of. But that requires another chapter.

NOTES

1 John Stuart Mill, *Utilitarianism*, ch. 2.
2 Jeremy Bentham, *The Principles of Morals and Legislation*, ch. 1.
3 Robin Barrow, *Happiness*.
4 R. M. Hare, *Freedom and Reason*.
5 J. J. C. Smart, 'Utilitarianism', in *The Encyclopedia of Philosophy*, Vol. 8.
6 See, for example, J. J. C. Smart, *An Outline of a System of Utilitarian Ethics*; A. Quinton, *Utilitarianism*; Robin Barrow, *Moral Philosophy for Education*, ch. 6 and *Commonsense and the Curriculum*, pt. 2.
7 The phrase, 'the Greatest Happiness of the Greatest Number', appears to originate, in print, with Francis Hutcheson (1694–1746).
8 Jeremy Bentham, *The Principles of Morals and Legislation*, ch. 1.
9 John Rawls, *A Theory of Justice*. For further reference to Rawls, see below Chapter 9.
10 A. Conan-Doyle, *Silver Blaze*.

3 Dogmatism

> Only the better ideas turn into dogma, and it is this process whereby a fresh, stimulating, humanly helpful idea is changed into robot dogma that is deadly. In terms of hazardous vectors released, the transformation of ideas into dogma rivals the transformation of hydrogen into helium, uranium into lead or innocence into corruption. And it is nearly as relentless.
>   The problem starts at the secondary level, not with the originator or developer of the idea but with the people who are attracted by it, who adopt it, who cling to it until their last nail breaks, and who invariably lack the overview, flexibility, imagination, and, most importantly, sense of humour, to maintain it in the spirit in which it was hatched.
>
> Tom Robbins, *Still Life with Woodpecker*

In the first chapter I pointed out that approaching particular issues with a prior commitment to some theoretical position can impair rather than aid one's thinking. It can inhibit rather than liberate, still less enhance, one's powers of discrimination. Now that in the second chapter I have outlined something like a theoretical position of my own, it is necessary to elaborate on that point by drawing a distinction between rationalism and dogmatism, and explaining the limited function that my reference to utilitarianism is to be allowed to have. Dogmatism in any case is one of the real evils of our time, and one of the most potent sources of injustice.

The word itself may not be the most appropriate for what I want to describe. Trying to decide on the best word to use was surprisingly difficult. Terms such as 'doctrine', 'ideology', 'credo', and 'faith', which fall in the same broad area as 'dogma', all had some things to be said in their favour and some against. Usually, the main thing to be said against them was that they had another well-known usage with connotations unsuitable for my use here. I have chosen to talk of 'dogma' and 'dogmatists' because these terms seem less associated with any specific usage and consequent connotations than others. But nothing that I wish to say hangs upon the terms used, provided that my account of what I mean is understood. In a nutshell what I mean by a dogmatist is one who subscribes to, and acts upon, an explanatory theory that encompasses a wide range of human activity, that is based on one or more unproveable and/or contentious premise. (That is what some would regard as subscribing to a 'doctrine', and my outline departs slightly from a typical dictionary definition of 'dogma'. But I want a less familiar term than 'doctrine' and I want something of the overtones of blindness, arrogance and speculativeness that 'dogma' carries, especially through its connection with 'dogmatic', because, as I shall explain, the dogmatist is necessarily somewhat arrogant, blind and speculative.)

It is now necessary to further elucidate some of the elements in that definition. The inclusion of the phrase 'acts upon' is crucial, because what I mean by a dogmatist is somebody who, to a marked extent, actively makes use of his explanatory theory or doctrine, and not merely somebody who, if pressed in an academic context, would claim to subscribe to such a theory. There may be a number of doctrines that an individual regards as more or less plausible, and to which to some extent he is inclined to commit himself intellectually. Thus, I might be inclined to take Freudianism and Catholicism quite seriously. But there is an important distinction between the man who has personal faith in the doctrine of the Catholic Church, and the man who approaches every event with the conviction that a Catholic orientated explanation is necessarily the only one that is called for. To believe that there is something in Freudianism is quite distinct from wishing to explain events exclusively in Freudian terms. By a dogmatist, I mean somebody with the latter tendency to confront experience with doctrine.

Secondly, what is meant by an unproveable premise must be made quite clear. Traditionally, it is a premise relating to which we lack agreement about what would settle the question of its truth or falsity. It is not merely a premise as to which we dispute whether it has been established as true or not. The basic theist claim that God exists will serve as an example here, in contrast to a claim such as that snakes can swim. Both claims may conceivably be true, but not known to be true to a particular group of people. But there is not likely to be much doubt about what would establish the truth of the latter, whereas it is far from clear or agreed what should count as evidence for or against the former. Believers and non-believers are not essentially divided on questions such as whether there is evil in the world, whether various individuals sincerely claim to have had certain spiritual experiences or whether the world seems to have some kind of overall design. They are divided on whether such points are or are not relevant to establishing that God exists. In addition to unproveable premises in that sense, it is important to note here a further group of postulates that involve empirical claims the evidence necessary for which is not in principle in doubt, but which, for a variety of reasons, is not in fact likely to be available. There is no problem in principle about how one would ascertain whether a particular social policy would make people more self-reliant, but it may just be far too complicated a matter to hope to establish one way or the other. Propositions of this type are often to be found at the basis of economic and political theories. They are not unproveable in the sense defined so far, which implies necessarily unproveable, because there are no criteria for deciding what counts as proof, but they are at a given time contingently unproveable, and I intend the phrase 'unproveable premises' to cover them too in this context.

Thirdly, the qualificatory expression 'a wide range of human activity' should not be taken as a sign of weakness or uncertainty on my part. One sometimes encounters objections to this kind of phrasing along these lines: 'if you merely say a "wide range" nobody can judge how much is enough'. Such objections miss the subtlety of the phrasing, common figure of speech though it may be. Strictly speaking no definition can have a qualification of degree, though it may have of range. That is to say, happiness, love, democracy or what you will, are what they are, and, insofar as some alleged instances of any of them fall short of the ideal, they are to that extent imperfect and less than true love, happiness or democracy. As far as this goes, Plato was clearly correct in his view that conceptions, or what he called forms, are more perfect, more real than physical instances.[1] No physical table is perfect, in the way that the idea of tableness, democracy or happiness may be. No person is without qualification perfectly happy. So when it comes to applying words to instances, we introduce the notion of degree. We are prepared to label things as tables, democracies, happiness and so forth, provided that they approximate significantly to our idea of tableness, democracy or happiness. What I mean by a dogmatist could have been stated more starkly and simply as 'one who subscribes to and acts upon an explanatory theory of human activity based on an unproveable premise'. The modification gives warning that, there being thankfully no actual examples of anybody quite so tunnel-visioned as that, I shall apply the term to anybody who is markedly dogmatic.

Fourthly, the inclusion of the word 'contentious' is important. What is logically unproveable might conceivably never change, but what is unproveable in my extended sense (which includes what is in practice unproveable) clearly could. There must have been a time at which the idea of there being life on other planets would have seemed plainly false, because other planets were thought to be near but small. Then, at a period when they were recognised as being far away and large enough to support life, but the notion of space travel appeared fanciful, the idea would have seemed in practice unproveable. It is now evidently proveable, both logically and practically. That being the case, at any given time what appears to be unproveable might in fact not be so and vice versa. Proponents of a doctrine, therefore, might try to deny that they are dogmatists by presuming that their premises are proveable. But it is of no less concern that people should cling too desperately to what at any given time appears unproveable. Hence my inclusion of the word contentious, in the specific and limited sense of supported by contentious evidence.

Fifthly, by 'a wide range of human activity' I mean to include reference to how one lives one's life, one's interpretation of natural phenomena, and one's factual and evaluative beliefs.

Finally, by 'based upon' I mean to suggest that any particular question or challenge about life could, if pressed hard enough, be shown to tie up with the premise or premises in question.

It should be clear that on this account such diverse theories as theistic religions, Marxism, Freudianism, a Leavisite theory of literature, or a Friedmanite economic policy are all doctrines that could be entertained in a dogmatist manner. To be a dogmatist is to act and think with unquestioning commitment to some such doctrine. That God exists, that the mode of production is ultimately responsible for the form of all social phenomena, or that repressed sexual desires lie behind all human actions, are classic unproveable claims. But to recognise that each of these claims might prove illuminating in trying to understand or explain a particular incident is one thing. To proceed to interpret the world, live one's life, exhort, advise and abjure others in the fixed light of one of them, whatever is to be said for or against such a practice, is quite another. My neighbour with his quiet faith is quite a different animal from a raving and ranting Luther. My neighbour who considers a Freudian explanation for a problem he faces, is quite distinct from the man who assumes all problems are to be explained in Freudian terms. My neighbour who comes to the conclusion that a particular problem is indeed essentially the outcome of a capitalist form of society is to be sharply distinguished from the Marxist who takes it for granted that all problems are to be so explained.

At this point let me introduce and explain the term rationalist, for subsequently I wish to compare dogmatism and rationalism.

Rationality I take to consist essentially in the giving of good reasons. A person exhibits rationality, shows that he is rational or behaves rationally insofar as his thinking or conduct are directed by or based upon good reasons. Sometimes isolated arguments or pieces of behaviour may be described as rational, but when the term is applied to a person it has a dispositional force. To assess somebody as rational is to attribute to him the tendency or disposition to proceed in a rational manner. (For just as there are no perfect examples of dogmatists so there are no perfect examples of fully rational beings.) Here too that initial account needs further elucidation in order that it may be properly understood.

First, to describe somebody as rational is not in itself to say anything about their passions or emotions, or their lack of the same. The opposite of being rational is being irrational rather than being non-rational or not being rational, just as the opposite of moral is immoral and not non-moral. The judgement that somebody is moral says that he does what is good rather than what is bad, when the question of moral choice arises. It does not deny that much of his life may be spent outside the moral sphere. Describing someone as moral does not imply that he is forever making everything a moral issue. In the same way judging somebody to be rational suggests that, when the question of looking for reasons is to the fore, he looks for good rather than bad reasons. It does not imply that he lives permanently in the rational domain. There are obviously many aspects of our lives that are non-rational. The lover does not require rational responses. There is no obvious objection to pursuing one's hobby fanatically rather than rationally. Rationality does not seem much to the point as one relaxes in a deck-chair on a summer evening. Possibly there are some areas of life or situations where the very decision to treat them as non-rational could be criticised as irrational. Nonetheless, to describe someone as rational is to say something about his tendency and capacity to engage in good reasoning or well-reasoned behaviour, when it is appropriate to engage in reasoning or reasoned behaviour. The question of capacity cannot, of course, be ignored. For although people may proceed irrationally out of cussedness, laziness, emotion, stupidity and many other things, they may also do so as a result of a lack of ability to do otherwise.

There are certainly problems about rationality, but they are not about its meaning, as has often been suggested. It is, for example, sometimes extremely difficult to tell whether somebody is being rational or not. It may be difficult to tell at a quite ordinary level, because motivation can be a complex business, with the result that we are not sure why a person is doing something, or, at a deeper level, because we cannot in the nature of things be sure of his subconscious motivation. Then again, we may be unclear how to characterise a situation, uncertain what somebody is actually up to. Daft looking behaviour often enough turns out to have been perfectly rational, and vice versa. But problems about being able to recognise instances of something are not necessarily an objection to the delineation of the concept. The fact that no circle is perfect does not lead us to amend our conception of circularity. The fact that it's hard to tell a donkey from an ass doesn't invalidate the distinction. And the fact that it is sometimes hard to tell whether people are educated or not is not evidence that our idea of education is unclear. There is a sense, as I noted above, in which every conception is an idealisation, and the fact that there is no justice in the world is no reason for denying that we can formulate a clear idea of justice. A theoretical distinction can be drawn between rational and irrational people, which is quite untouched by these observations about the difficulty of detecting the difference in practice. Furthermore, whilst acknowledging that such a difficulty may exist, let us not forget that even in practice some distinctions are fairly clear: some people and actions are manifestly more rational than others.

It is evidently of considerable importance that we should discriminate between the rational and the irrational, both in theory and so far as is possible in practice. The value of rationality cannot be coherently denied, for its value is presupposed by a philosophical inquiry such as this, or any other kind of intellectual inquiry or purposeful endeavour. Commitment to such diverse activities as science, playing football or philosophy presupposes a commitment to the search for, and to acting in the light of, good reasons (although the nature of the good reasons may change). The football manager no less than the physicist wants to know for what good reason X did not do Y at time T. Not only is the value of rationality implicit in most of what we do, but it would be incoherent and illogical to deny that it had value. The very notion of argument presupposes its value. If you want to argue me out of my commitment to rationality or convince me that there is no good reason to value it, not only are you going to have to use rational procedures yourself, but your very concern indicates that you think a distinction can be drawn between good and bad reasons, and that it should be. In other words, you yourself are committed to rationality.

Occasionally, nonetheless, people do declare themselves to be against rationality. In such a case one must presume that one of the following explanations applies. Firstly, and very likely, such a person has not really thought about or understood what he is saying. Perhaps what he really wishes to declare is that he doesn't like engaging in abstract theory or intellectual inquiry, or more sweepingly, that he is content to spend most of his life on a non-rational level. Whatever we may think of them, these claims make perfectly good sense. But what they do not do is suggest that rationality in itself has no value. They suggest, whether convincingly or not, that there is often no cause (no good reason, one might say) to worry about the reasons for one's behaviour and beliefs; but that is another matter. Secondly, a person might, in seeming to set his face against rationality, be confusing it with rationalisation. The latter involves the offering of fictitious or false reasoning in an attempt to justify behaviour that really has some other explanation, as when someone rationalises his failure in an exam by saying (falsely) that he wasn't concerned about it. But clearly to be committed to rationality is not to be committed to rationalisation in this sense. Thirdly, a person may be guilty of the confusion (already noted) of identifying rationality with a cold, emotionless, automaton-like Dr. Spock of Star-Trek. But a disjunction from human emotions is no more necessarily implied by describing someone as rational, than sentimentality is necessarily implied by the term love. People may be both rational and extremely emotional in temperament. Fourthly, the person may be sincerely and coherently denouncing rationality, as he would have us believe, provided that he does not self-contradictorily try to argue that he is correct to do so or that other people ought to. If he simply proposes to opt out of rational thought and behaviour, and confines himself to announcing that he may in future proceed quite irrationally, it is not clear to me that we can satisfactorily prove that he ought not to. But we can observe that nobody ever has opted for this extreme position, and point out the likely consequences of doing so.

The value of rationality then can scarcely be doubted. What next need to be considered are the implications of a commitment to it. If one is committed to rationality, one must prefer good to bad or specious reasons. This claim does not involve going back on the admission that many areas of life may lie in the non-rational domain. Falling in love, for instance, would be generally conceded to be a non-rational matter. Occasionally, somebody might commit himself to a partner of proven unsuitability and that might count as irrational, but for the most part we assume that people's emotional relationships are simply outside or beyond reason. What the commitment to rationality involves is not an attempt to make everything subject to the rule of reason, but a rejection of bad reasoning when encountered, and a preference for reasoned behaviour over non-reasoned behaviour, where good reason can be given for such a preference.

There is also necessarily an element of autonomy in the concept of rationality. Autonomy involves appealing to oneself as the final arbiter or determining agent, rather than to somebody or something outside oneself. The heteronomous man bows to authorities. The autonomous man is his own boss. No doubt one may sensibly enough sometimes autonomously choose to follow the advice of others in particular matters. Autonomy is not co-extensive with wisdom and it would be exceedingly foolish for somebody like me to act autonomously when it came to making financial investments. One remains autonomous to the extent that one remains the ultimate judge of what one should do and think, including decisions to trust the advice of others. The rational man is necessarily autonomous, because he seeks to do what there is good reason to do, rather than what he is told to do or what authorities tell him to do. Here again, naturally, there is a question of degree. It is no more rational to ignore expertise in areas where one is ignorant than it is to enslave oneself to authority. Rationality does not commit one either to following or rejecting authority as such. It commits one to doing what one sees good reason to do, and that may vary from person to person and place to place. But rationality cannot encompass any wholesale surrender of autonomy. Circumstances might conceivably make it rational to surrender one's autonomy to party, to state or to another. But though it might be rational to make such a surrender, it would involve the surrender of oneself as a rational being. For although the rational man may make use of authorities, he can never regard the authority as being final. To the rational man authorities are always open to challenge.

It is an essential part of being rational that one keeps one's options open, and takes each case as it comes, or at least preserves the right to opt out of any commitment previously rendered. Ideally the rational man takes each case on its merits, because, until he has checked it out, he cannot be sure that a new case, a given instance, is not unique, or the exception that is mysteriously said to prove the rule, rather than an instance of the rule in operation. That remains an ideal, because the demands of living up to it are too great, and we do have good reason to believe in the efficacy of many of our general rules, our authorities, and our systems of classification. So we regard it as quite rational for people to relinquish the job of making a fresh rational appraisal of every situation. It would, given our experience, be irrational to stand in the path of an oncoming lorry on the grounds that it might be a hallucination, because, although it might be, we have good reason to suppose that it probably isn't. In the same way, it would be irrational to ignore the lead given by accredited experts. But what must be appreciated is that we are dealing here with the point that it may be rational to trust rules and authorities. Once one has handed oneself over to them, one ceases to be rational. The rational man must always be ready to challenge the stratagems, classifications and theories, the rules, the sources and the authorities that he often makes use of to make his thinking easier. And herein lies the great difference between the rationalist and the dogmatist. The former is piecemeal and provisional, while the latter is wholesale and uncritical. It is on that note that we must turn to pinpointing some of the shortcomings of dogmatism.

The danger starts when we adopt some overall explanatory theory and seek to apply it to all cases. Any such overall theory will necessarily be very general, otherwise it is inconceivable that it should cover all cases. Its basic assumptions will also almost invariably be unproveable, such that explanations will ultimately be in terms of something like God's will, repressed desires, male conspiracy or historical necessity. But we have now entered the domain of doctrine, and what the dogmatist does is cling unquestioningly to his unproveable premise and generalise from it. The belief that God exists becomes the unyielding assumption that everything is to be explained in terms of God's will. The belief that particular social features have an economic cause becomes the rigid conviction that the entire superstructure is exclusively explicable in terms of the economic substructure. The belief that sexual desires may become repressed becomes adherence to the doctrine that all human behaviour is only explicable in terms of repressed drives. Once the unproveable premise has become the idée fixe, a surrounding superstructure can be built up. These superstructures are often extraordinarily sophisticated, as indeed they should be, since they arise out of the ingenuity of a large number of hard working zealots, anxious to meet and render the doctrine impregnable against objections. They thus become part of the doctrine themselves. Thomist theology will serve as a reasonable illustration of the point: St. Thomas Aquinas grows up committed to a doctrine that invites much opposition and many questions. He therefore lends his agile mind to the task of explaining, elaborating, and subtly reinterpreting the received faith, so that, for many, his attempts to interpret themselves become part of the received wisdom or doctrine. Just so do generations of Freudians or Marxists seek to formulate more and more precise accounts of their doctrines, with the result that the original hypothesis of a Freud or a Marx becomes more and more rigid and pervasive. Once the doctrine is sufficiently developed and embracing it becomes possible for adherents or disciples to interpret a wider and wider range of activities in its light, until, in extreme cases, every aspect of life is covered by it. Finally, as if from nowhere, some evaluative element emerges. Up until this point the various doctrines have been presented and refined as explanatory or descriptive theories, purporting to tell us how things are or how things work, whether the reference be to God's mysterious way, economic necessity, historical inevitability or sexual frustration. Then suddenly the doctrine includes the presumption that we should worship God, welcome the inevitable or value highly the way things are, even to the point of working to help advance the will of the omnipotent and inevitable. Now we are truly dogmatists.

Needless to say, the above is not supposed to be an account of the historical stages in any particular transition from a fresh insight to a hidebound dogmatism, nor do I wish to suggest that faith in a doctrine is equivalent to dogmatism. I have merely identified some of the key features in a position that I am choosing to label dogmatist. There is no suggestion here that religious believers, Marxists and Freudians are all dogmatists. As to that, the individual must try on the shoe for himself and see whether it fits. My concern is only to identify a particular kind of doctrinal commitment, which I am calling dogmatism.

And there is a great deal that is objectionable about dogmatism in this sense. There is obviously nothing inherently wrong with an unproveable proposition: it might well be true, it might turn out to be proveable, and even if it is false or is finally shown to be false, it might still have proved a fruitful hypothesis in various ways. But something begins to go wrong, if one becomes too firmly, too intolerantly, attached to an unproveable proposition. After all, it might equally well be false. The idea that the economic base might be extremely significant in explaining various social phenomena is, when first considered, of extreme interest, and it is important to give full rein to it. But blind adherence to the validity of the hypothesis has nothing to recommend it. Things get worse when a particular suggestion is generalised, or the range of the hypothesis is extended. If it remains possible, but uncertain, that we can explain a particular pattern of behaviour in terms of repression of desires, it may well be worth exploring the same hypothesis in relation to other similar patterns of behaviour. But to begin instead to assume that the same (unproven) explanation holds good across the board is risky, to say the least. Creating a web of surrounding superstructure is the most dishonest part of the whole business, for it is, almost confessedly, an attempt to *make* the doctrine work. Instead of counting objections to the thesis as objections, means are found to protect the thesis against them. But why do that? For example, whatever the truth in the contention that riots by predominantly black youths in an area with high unemployment are caused by resentment of the police, when it is suggested that the problem might be exacerbated by the unwillingness of small businesses to invest in the area, why not consider that as a possible qualification to the initial hypothesis? Why, instead, protect the hypothesis by asserting that the media invent that suggestion at the behest of the police? And, again, why assume that an explanation, unproveable at bottom, and already unbalanced by defensive tactics, proposed for a particular range of situations, must apply to all? Is it particularly likely that all events from the falling of a meteor to the ploughing of a field, from a racial riot to a preference for football over cricket, from the splitting of the atom to a splitting toothache are to be explained in the same way? Finally, the transition from explanatory theory to theory of value is quite simply unacceptable. Nothing in the various attempts to establish God's existence would, if convincing, establish that we ought to worship God. Nothing in the thesis that the classless society is inevitably coming would entitle us to conclude that that is good, or that we should try to forward the day. Nothing in the thesis that a lot of our behaviour is the result of repressed desires allows us to conclude that we should not repress desires.

But what is perhaps even more to be deplored than the various suspect moves in the creation of these ingenious systems is the phenomenon of unswerving commitment to them, for that is the antithesis of true imaginative and critical thought. (I ignore the social danger of those who think they know how to explain everything, who are far more to be feared than those who actually don't know and know they don't, and of those who are drawn to dogmatism out of a psychological need for controlled, stable situations and extremely clearcut, simplified explanations.)

So far I have been concerned only to delineate two contrasting casts of mind, the rationalist and the dogmatist, and to indicate the value of the former and the drawbacks of the latter. At this point, lest it be thought that dogmatism does not really exist, it is necessary to introduce some examples of it in action, in purportedly scholarly contexts. The examples are deliberately chosen from contexts that will be examined further in subsequent chapters.

It has long been appreciated (since the time of Plato at least) that the concept of poverty is relative.[2] What counts as poverty varies from culture to culture and from time to time, because expectations, estimates of necessities and relative wealth vary. Many poor people in England today would pass as rich in certain parts of India. Now, one could perfectly well recognise that point, but nonetheless believe that poverty in Britain is substantially less today than it was in Victorian Britain. (Whether that view is true is not of immediate concern, which is only that it is a perfectly coherent and intelligible view, even granting the undeniable point that poverty is relative.) Some Marxists, however, do not wish to accept even the possibility of such a conclusion, because the mere idea of it runs counter to the received doctrine, which says that during that period the lot of the poor would necessarily deteriorate in advanced industrial societies. They therefore attempt to define trouble away. Just as 'omnipotent' has sometimes been redefined by theologians in such a way as to allow that there are some things that an omnipotent God cannot do (such as the logically impossible), some Marxists argue thus: any society will have a standard view of what counts as a minimally decent life, and very often this will be identified with the sort of life a person of average income can afford. Provided that we define poverty in terms of having an income below that required for the appropriately designated minimally decent life, we have saved our doctrine with its claim that the poor cannot have improved their lot since Victorian times. For what we have done is defined poverty as less than average income. In that sense of poverty it is inconceivable that poverty should disappear until we have flat equality of income. The doctrine is preserved, but the price was high. For, of course, it was not poverty in that sense that most of us, including Karl Marx himself, had in mind. (It should be noted that my concern here is not with Marxists as such, but with certain Marxists who in their determination to make the facts of life fit their doctrine become dogmatists.)[3]

Hardly different in technique is the attempt by Lenin to confirm the doctrine of the inevitability of the classless society. Lenin, in line with Marxist orthodoxy, foresaw a period during which the capitalist exploiters would be crushed, following which, 'when the capitalists have disappeared . . . [and] the state ceases to exist', 'it becomes possible to speak of freedom' and we get what the doctrine regards as real democracy. Lenin concedes that even then there will probably (he seems to feel certainly) be some troublemakers, but these he assures us will be 'individual persons' rather than a class.[4]

All of that is very important, because the doctrine holds quite explicitly that the state will wither away, there will be freedom, and the classless state will inevitably come. And that is a significant view, if taken at its face value. But one has only to scrutinise the detail of Lenin's rhetoric to see that he has either defined anything that obstructs out of his way, or presumed that it will be physically ousted. Naturally, if you physically destroy capitalists, call whatever is left 'working class', ignore troublemakers as a serious phenomenon, while again physically crushing them and calling them 'individuals', and define freedom in terms of freedom from capitalism, you get a picture of the free, classless, stateless state. (Though incidentally, even on this scenario, you don't inevitably get it, and the fact that something like this will, I believe, come about, is no evidence that it was inevitable.) What you certainly don't get is what ordinary people thought they were being promised: an end to class antagonism, an end to state bureaucracy, and an increase in actual social freedom. Anybody but a dogmatist knows that Marx's vision was to some extent misplaced, while Lenin's vision will come about, if it does, not because of Marxist laws, but because of Marxist agency.

The dogmatist bypasses the normal reasoning process by refusing to discriminate. Another perfect example is to be found in Kai Nielsen's argument surrounding the proposition that socialists should only engage in 'revolutionary violence . . . in response to counter-revolutionary violence.'[5] This, when it is fully explained, turns out to mean that physical violence may be engaged in by our side in opposition to aspects of the other side's policy that we don't like. Nobody who understands the game being played will be surprised to find Nielsen innocently admitting that that means 'when the time is ripe'. In short, 'a pre-emptive strike *will not count* as initiating violence'.[6]

The central objection to the above examples is not to the views embodied in them, at any rate not to some of the ideals that the dogmatists in question may happen to hold. What has to be heroically resisted is the way in which language, argument and ideas are refashioned to preserve the sanctity of the doctrine, rather than the doctrine reshaped in the light of experience and argument (and consequently less blindly worshipped). Marx saw the poor being grievously exploited. He believed that the economic organisation of society explained a great deal of apparently non-economic social phenomena. He further opined (whether more as a battle cry or a description, it is not always easy to tell) that inevitably the poor would become more and more exploited, until the point at which they threw off their chains and got rid of their masters. But some of this is certainly wrong, and to try and retell history, in order to make it seem as if it wasn't, is not to engage in rational thought at all, but to exercise ingenuity in ritualistic interpretative exercises. Furthermore, the greater the extent to which this sort of thing goes on, the less we are being told. As God is further and further redefined to meet commonsense objections to the idea of his existence (he cannot be seen or touched; he isn't anywhere specific), he suffers 'death by a thousand qualifications'.[7] Given today's conception of God, to tell a man that his roof falling in was an act of God is to tell him nothing. Everything is an act of God. What he wants to know is why or how it was *his* roof that fell in and not someone else's. He wants to discriminate between the multitude of God's acts. If all human behaviour is to be explained in terms of repressed sexual desires, how helpful or significant is it to tell a man that that is why he hates his boss? Maybe so, but then why didn't he hate his previous boss? If there is a sense in which everything to do with the superstructure of society depends upon the organisation of the economic substructure, then there is a sense in which that becomes of secondary importance. Granted that, how comes it that this situation differs markedly from that?

There is a danger that at this point the dogmatist will assert that the 'capitalist class will not be persuaded by reason',[8] and will revert to what Newton Garver has depicted as a variant of the Freudian rebuff, which consists of suggesting that the very vehemence of your denial shows how deeply repressed are your desires and, therefore, how right the theory you question is. Thus, it may be said, 'it is because of your class standing that you have [the critical view you present here], and if you deny that the class standing is influencing you in that way, your very denial shows how deeply you are imbued with the obfuscating ideology.'[9] Or else it may be suggested that one's consciousness needs raising (a patronising way of saying that one has got it wrong), and that one does not appreciate that there is no one reality against which to measure theories, only a host of rival ideological realities. The point of such ploys is to discredit the rationalist, as opposed to the dogmatist, approach. They are an essential part of the doctrinal superstructure, rehearsed moves designed to beat off critical inquiry, comparable to the rehearsed answers to doubts about God's existence instilled in some Catholic seminaries.

It is often argued by dogmatists that their correct view of the world is rejected by others because they are unable to see it. They are in a state of false consciousness, and once their consciousness has been raised they will see things differently, clearly and properly, after the manner of the prisoners in Plato's cave 'who need to be turned away from a world of shadows and brought to gaze on reality.'[10] Thus some feminists will assert, in reply to the claim that many women like being the way they are, that that is only because such women are in a state of false consciousness. They would not be content, it is said, if they could see things properly. The dogmatist sees his task as being to shed light in order to raise consciousness. There are aspects of this line of thought of which straightforward sense can be made. Many of us, in many respects, do not think things out, and it seems quite reasonable to use the phrase 'raising somebody's consciousness' to mean making him become aware or making him think. To be specific, no doubt many points in a typical feminist viewpoint are not appreciated by some because they have never thought seriously about the issues. (Perhaps those who lack appreciation here are dogmatists in respect of the traditional view of women's role.) No doubt also there are ways whereby awareness, in the sense of sensitivity to features of a situation, can be heightened, so that sometimes people may be brought to see points that they will not come to see through reasoning. The problem, then, does not lie in the idea of people sometimes being unconscious of the true state of affairs. It arises when the phrase 'false consciousness' is wheeled out as a stock response to any failure to follow the party line. The notion of false consciousness derives its meaning from a contrast with consciousness of what is the case. Usually one discerns it by means of pinpointing inconsistency: everything about a man seems straightforward except that he thinks women necessarily ought to maintain their traditional role. We can't dismiss him as a stupid man, because we know in general he isn't. We can't say he has never been invited to think about the matter, because he has. On this one issue he appears to have a mental block. So we might choose to say he is here, for whatever reason, in a state of false consciousness. But the dogmatist, by loosely using the phrase of anyone who does not agree with his doctrinal position, takes the force out of it. He simply begs the question, for there is no test of *bona fide* consciousness other than agreement with his position. He may in fact be correct in his views, and those who dissent from them may indeed be in a state of false consciousness, but merely to claim as much when faced with a challenge to the doctrine is to ignore the challenge rather than to meet it. (Note also the implications of 'false' as opposed to 'un' consciousness, which latter term seems to me generally preferable. False consciousness suggests a thought-out position. The former therefore makes a much more stringent charge and, incidentally, as

I shall point out below, carries it with it the implication that there is a real and correct viewpoint.)

It is important in this context to distinguish between people's beliefs, wants and needs, for the idea of false consciousness fits more readily with some things than others. So far as beliefs go, obviously people may be mistaken. It is conceivable that they may be mistaken about their own needs too, but it should be noted that what a person needs is to some extent tied up with what he wants. (If it is beyond question that I want X, then my need for Y becomes a matter of fact about which I may be mistaken. But if there is no dispute that Y is a necessary means to X, then whether I need Y becomes essentially a matter of whether I want X.) When it comes to wants, it is arguable that the agent cannot be mistaken. At any rate if we distinguish between primary wants ('I want a fix of heroin now') and secondary wants ('I want to give up being a drug addict'), it is difficult to understand the suggestion that a person might be mistaken about his primary wants.

Clearly it is reasonable to suppose that a person might have particular beliefs that need rectifying. A person might also have mistaken views about what he needs. But dogmatists go way beyond that. They have a doctrine that involves completeness, unverifiability and a set of values. This leads them to assert that even people's wants may be unreal, that their whole view of life may be mistaken. But that again is to beg the question. To assess competing world views we have to consider particular issues, without relying on the views themselves. That is the rational procedure. The dogmatist procedure is to settle particular issues by appeal to the doctrinal answer book, which is absurd. Of course, from the point of view of the Catholic, the rest of the world has got it wrong and, for instance, has an unacceptable view of contraception, because they do not take the Catholic view of sexual relations. The question is whether the Catholic view on this issue can be rationally defended, and whether, if the sole ground for accepting it is that it is the Catholic view, that should not count as a possible objection to Catholicism. Of course, from the point of view of some feminists, some women need their heads examining. But what has that to do with what? To say that the reason such women do not see the truth of a particular brand of feminism is that they need their consciousness raising, is simply to say that they see things differently and/or want different things. What is required, in place of taking cover behind a phrase like 'consciousness-raising', is a reason why they shouldn't see things their own way.

Sometimes the matter takes a more intense form and it is

suggested or implied that one is not really oneself, one is in an inauthentic quasi-clinical state. This seems to me grievously mischievous. As a rule clinical states are defined by their oddity, and it is doubtful whether it makes a lot of sense to dismiss whole segments of humanity as inauthentic and hence odd. Be that as it may, the notion of there being a real-self distinct from my actual-self is very hard to swallow. Even if I am clinically mad, there is a lot to be said for facing the fact that this mad person is me, rather than hiding behind misleading colloquialisms to the effect that I am not myself. If I become mad for a day, there is some sense in saying I am out of my mind or suchlike. And if I become mad, it makes sense to say I am not the same old me. But generally speaking one's identity is tied up with one's mental and physical continuity. I am the being with my memories, beliefs, physical body and outlook on life. So if, in unexceptional circumstances, somebody suggests that my opposition to fascism is not really me, but the product of my environment or a state of false consciousness, I would be inclined to reply that I am that product, I am the person with this state of consciousness. I may have acquired my views from somewhere else and they may be incorrect. But they are my views and I am the being with these views. Even if I were to accept a theoretical distinction between the me I am and the real me, I fail to see why or how anybody else should feel able to determine which was which. Once again it is clear that those who pontificate on the authenticity, reality and genuine consciousness of others do so in order to preserve their doctrine, and yet are doing no more than begging the question of their doctrine. They are dogmatists.

It has sometimes been maintained that the rationalist presupposes some objective reality, waiting to be explained, whereas there is no such thing. (It will be recalled that this move is not open to those who talk of false consciousness in others, notwithstanding the fact that many contemporary doctrines do inconsistently preach relativism and the objective truth of their own doctrine.) The view that there is no reality, but only points of view, interpretations and subjective impressions, is either true but trite or significant but false, and either way it fails to make any serious inroads on the case for rationality. That our beliefs and judgements are vulnerable can readily be conceded, and that they are usually, possibly always, more or less tinged and modified by our standpoints, prior sets of beliefs and ways of looking at the world is obviously true. But that, far from being a blow against the rationalist position, is one of the reasons for adopting it. It is precisely because our judgements should be held in a provisional spirit, that one objects to sweeping dogmatism and wants to look at each case on its merits. On the other hand, there is no obvious sense in which any of us is going to accept that everything is a matter of opinion. One is not free to believe anything one likes, if one expects to deserve respect for one's beliefs. There is very obviously a reality in the sense of a world of physical entities, human experiences and actual occurrences, to be contrasted with dreams, false impressions, guesses and imaginative ideas. And rationalists, in trying to distinguish between the real world and the world of opinion, are engaged upon a perfectly feasible, if exceedingly difficult, task. Once again, the trouble begins when people feel the need for grand comprehensive accounts of the world and all its ways. If one deals with particular issues, nobody would be tempted to deny a real world independent of ideological perspective. (Who ever heard anybody in a pub declare that the lorry running down the hill was a social construct?) It is only by insisting that we talk in doctrinal terms that the dogmatist can get himself taken seriously in the first place: world views possibly do inevitably end up being relative to time and place. The moral would seem to be to take world views less seriously.

One need have no hesitation, then, in saying that there are some truths about the world, and that we may hope to have access to some of them, notwithstanding the fact that any claim to truth had best be held provisionally. What we had therefore best do, as rationalists, is eschew dogmatism. In subsequent chapters I shall not look at the various issues that arise from the point of view of any doctrine. Needless to say the task would be easier if one were a dogmatist, for a doctrine would furnish an answer. That is what they are designed to do. Take most of the issues discussed in this book, and it would not be difficult to read off the Marxist, the Freudian, the Catholic or what have you account. So too could they be explained in terms of the Greek Gods or the philosopher's stone. But the dogmatist approach is non-think. It is a crude, untesting and soporific procedure. The only ingenuity comes with the desperate attempt to shore up the banks of the argument. Some doctrines may be true or contain some truth, but the only way to find that out is to examine particular issues without prior reference to them.

One appreciates that many people are psychologically drawn towards the certainty and direction that doctrines provide. There is comfort and security to be derived from being a Catholic or a Marxist. Nor have I said anything to suggest that one should not adhere to these or any other doctrine. My argument is not that one should not be, but that one should not examine contentious issues as, a Marxist, a Catholic or adherent of any other doctrine. We should seek to explain the particular, and work outwards towards formulating general conclusions. We should try to understand the nature of what we observe, and to locate immediate causes in an ever expanding circle of outward ripples.

It should be clear that the importance of rationality lies in it as both a procedure and a state of mind. It is therefore necessary to conclude this chapter by raising the questions of whether belief in rationalism, and belief in utilitarianism, do not themselves involve a dogmatist element, for are they too not doctrines?

The brief response to the suggestion that rationalism is a doctrine no less than, say, Marxism is to point again to the need for discrimination. Isn't a dog an animal?, it might be asked. To which the reply might be, 'Yes, indeed. But don't confuse it with an alligator.' Whether rationalism is classified as a doctrine, a faith or a set of procedures is of little importance, provided that it is recognised that the rationalist position differs in important respects from that of the dogmatist approach, as defined.

If one regards commitment to any belief or set of beliefs as holding a faith, a creed, a doctrine or a dogma, then the rationalist has a faith, for he has commitment to the belief that one should seek to be rational. The only real difference here between rationalism and other faiths is that almost everyone shares the rationalist faith. But this is not a dogmatist faith: there is no set of interrelated beliefs, based on unproveable premises, designed to explain all things. Marxism, Catholicism and all other doctrines differ from rationalism in having an account to give of the kind of reasons that are good reasons. But the essential point about the rationalist position is that there is no prior commitment to any particular mode or type of explanation of events or issues. It involves commitment to a procedural rule only. All other doctrines add a theory of explanation, and the dogmatist adds to that a closed mind on the subject. (In a feeble echo of the Freudian rebuff, the dogmatist may retort that all minds are closed minds. If appeal is made to the idea that no mind is free of environmental influence, the point may be conceded. But if open-minded means uncommitted to a particular kind of explanation, then some minds are quite obviously more open than others.) It is occasionally claimed that rationality varies from culture to culture. But that is not true. Views as to what constitutes a good reason or a good explanation change with different cultures, and consequently what is regarded as an instance of being rational may change. In the light of different information it may also seem more rational to believe something in one setting than in another. But neither of these points shows that the idea of rationality undergoes any change. (Indeed there is an incoherence in the very idea that it could. Words can change their meaning, so that what people mean by 'rationality' might change. But ideas are what they are. Our view or idea of something might change. But the idea itself, the concept, is what it is. Roundness is roundness is roundness.) What the explanation of an event is does not change with one's cultural perspective, although how we explain it may. What is logically possible and impossible is not a matter of cultural preference, although again, how logical people are capable of being may show cultural variation. What rational people look for is an explanation or a justification that is logical, sufficient and necessary, couched in straightforward and precise terms. One of the features of doctrines is that, precisely because they have been relentlessly worked on to keep them in business, they are generally capable of offering a sufficient explanation of an event. The point is that a sufficient explanation is not necessarily the necessary one, or the best available one.

The matter is slightly different with utilitarianism. It is not in fact a doctrine, as defined, since it is not an explanatory theory and makes no claim to being an overall theory. It is, much more specifically, a theory about how one should determine the value of ways of behaving. Nonetheless, it has in common with doctrines a basis of unproveable proposition and it would be as dogmatistic to read off the utilitarian answer to each of the following problems as it would be to read off the Marxist answer. The only purpose that could possibly serve would be to provide some glimpse of what being a utilitarian commits one to. It would not serve to establish the plausibility of utilitarianism, and it would not constitute an attempt to show how one ought to resolve the issues in question. My procedure therefore, having outlined utilitarianism, will be to examine each issue without reference to utilitarianism in the first instance. Sometimes it will prove possible to resolve the issue without any appeal to utilitarianism. On other occasions the argument will lead us directly to some point where being a utilitarian has direct relevance. (For example, it may be that a particular policy will cause more widespread suffering than it could possibly save.) At such moments, I shall not seek to use utilitarianism as an argument, so much as acknowledge that a utilitarian would accept the point as decisive. The main thing is to approach the various issues with an open mind as to what should be done, being prepared even to find oneself arguing that one might do something that utilitarianism would oppose.

NOTES

1 See Plato, *The Republic*, esp. 472 ff.
2 Strictly speaking, we should say that conceptions of poverty vary. See below, this chapter.
3 This particular point will be encountered again, and the more subtle variant of Bernard Gendron be considered, in Chapter 9.
4 V. I. Lenin, *State and Revolution*.
5 Kai Nielsen, 'On justifying revolution', *Philosophy and Phenomenological research*, Vol. 37, No. 4, June 1977.
6 *Ibid.* (my italics).
7 The phrase is taken from Antony Flew's contribution to 'Theology and falsification: a symposium', in B. Mitchell (ed.), *The Philosophy of Religion*.
8 Howard Selsam, *Ethics and Progress*.
9 Newton Garver, 'What violence is', *The Nation*, 209 (June 1968).
10 Plato, *The Republic*, 514 ff.

4 Freedom

O Freedom, what liberties are taken in thy name.
                    Daniel George, *The Perpetual Pessimist*

Discussion concerning matters such as abortion, civil disobedience, private education and censorship often drifts into argument about freedom. Censorship may be decried as an offence against freedom. A right to engage in civil disobedience may be defended as the prerogative of a free man. Abortion may be defended on the grounds that a woman should be free to determine what happens to her body. But such appeals do very little to advance the argument, not least because in many instances one man's freedom is another man's restriction. The object of this chapter is to clear the ground for subsequent chapters by making some general points about freedom. My main contention, following the argument of John Stuart Mill's essay *On Liberty*, will be that, with the exception of free speech and free thought,[1] there is nothing that people ought necessarily always to be free to engage in, no action that might not legitimately be interfered with by the state, and that the test of whether an action should be prohibited is a question of whether the consequences of letting it be freely engaged in would be harmful. If, and only if, it is reasonable to suppose that, if people were free to perform a certain act, the consequences would be more harmful than if they were prohibited from doing it, should there be a restriction on people's liberty to do it. At this juncture, those who do not understand points of principle may say, quite correctly, that it is very debateable what is, and what is not, harmful. Those who do understand points of principle will observe that that is a quite distinct problem, to be reserved for another day (or, more specifically, to be picked up in other chapters, for when one deals with specific issues such as the morality of abortion, part of what one has to consider are the relative degrees of harm involved in the consequences of different courses of action). What is harmful is a distinct question from whether harm should be a criterion for limiting freedom. The latter is the question of immediate concern.

To declare that one was opposed to freedom would be rather curious, somewhat on a par with declaring oneself opposed to love. And yet none of us value freedom without qualification. We do not welcome freedom for anybody to do anything. Not only are there things that we would ideally like to prevent anybody doing, such as torturing innocent people, there are also people whom we would like ideally to restrict considerably, such as homicidal maniacs. There are in addition restraints or constraints such as schooling and traffic laws that we approve for the sake of various goods that they give rise to, directly or indirectly. Not even anarchists (at any rate serious anarchists such as Peter Kropotkin) value the idea of everybody freely doing whatever they like; their belief is that in time, given propitious circumstances, people could come to be self directing, so that *legislation* would not be needed. They do not deny that restraint or restrictions on what people may do are needed.

Everybody, then, whilst acknowledging the value of freedom, also recognises the value of restraint. We do not merely recognise natural and logical restraints of the sort that prevent me from jumping forty feet in the air or being a married bachelor; we also accept, and sometimes welcome, many social and legal restraints on ourselves and others for the sake of our own and others' good or well-being. We are even capable of welcoming restraints, or, at least, seeing sense in restraints, on our primary desires, as when smokers acknowledge the value of prohibitions on smoking. The claim that we value freedom, therefore, is no more true than the claim that we value restraint, and the view that we have a right to freedom scarcely more true than the view that we have a right to restraint.

Some have attempted to avoid facing up to this obvious, and entirely undisturbing, conclusion, by defining freedom as something positive. The truly free man, on such an account, is depicted as some idealised being, let us say as 'master of himself' or 'fully developed morally'. Various restrictions are noted as being contributory to that end, and therefore not antithetical to true freedom. Thus, it is concluded, freedom involves or even means restraint. I cannot see what is gained by such playing about. 'Freedom' is not a complicated word, and it certainly does not mean 'restraint', though some particular restraints may enhance and protect some particular freedoms. There can be no doubt that 'freedom' means 'absence of restraint', and one is the more free insofar as one is the less restrained. The point is that, contrary to conventional rhetoric, which always stresses the value of freedom rather than the value of restraint, that is not to say that one is necessarily better off for having more freedom. That depends upon whom and what we are talking about, and in what circumstances.

Part of the difficulty when discussing freedom arises from our tendency to talk of it as if it were a commodity, an identifiable something, rather than the name for a negative state. 'The inalienable right to freedom' is a fine phrase and, properly understood, a fine ideal. But to some it suggests a something that simply doesn't exist. There no more 'is' freedom than there 'is' health. Things are healthy insofar as they are not sick, and what constitutes sickness varies from thing to thing. When we say, 'this plant is healthy', we are not attributing an observable quality to it, as we are when we say that it is green. Likewise, freedom is not an empirically locatable quality or commodity, akin to greenness, sugar or even air—something that one might in principle measure and want a certain amount of. 'It' isn't anything. The word 'freedom' signifies an abstract ideal that we arrive at by extrapolation from various particular freedoms, or, to be more precise, from various particular situations involving absence of various specifiable restraints. Furthermore, since there are always some restraints upon people, claims to freedom also necessarily involve judgements about the relative importance of restraints. A man with a strong sense of duty might be less free to do certain things than a man in hiding from the police. There are a thousand and one things that I am not free to do at the moment, but because I am free to do much that we consider important, and because I am free from a number of obvious and generally disliked restraints, it makes sense to see me as a free man. (This is the point that is seen but exploited by some dogmatists. Of course it is true that people are still unfree in various ways, despite being free of some of the restraints of the past. And of course it is negotiable up to a point as to which restraints are most objectionable. It is not, however, adequate simply to assert that since restraints can still be pinpointed, freedom has not been won. Complete freedom in the literal sense never could be won.) In political and social contexts, evaluation of freedom has to take the form of objection to particular restraints; and, historically, being an advocate of freedom has in practice usually meant being in favour of more freedoms. It is, however, important to recognise that there is no necessary connection there. It is conceivable that increase in foreseen and valued freedoms should lead to increase in unforeseen restraints, so that the advocate of freedom turns out to have been an advocate of an increased number of restraints, and he might well accept that.

It is clear, then, that, in order to engage in a coherent argument about freedom, one needs to specify either particular freedoms or a criterion, or set of criteria, for determining whether to impose restraints. It is not freedom that is good, but being free to do or free from certain things. The view that freedom is good in itself, but bad when abused or when it leads to bad consequences, is not so much false as incoherent. What is this 'it' that might be abused? If I freely murder people, what is this 'freedom' that is in itself good and that can be distinguished from the deaths and acts of slaughter? There is not freedom and various behaviours. There is only more or less free behaviour. Admittedly, people do say things like 'freedom is good', but that can be adequately explained. One possibility is that given our tendency to value autonomous behaviour, notwithstanding a recognition that the line will have to be drawn somewhere, people *generally* value freedom. Or again people may mean by the unqualified claim that freedom is good to refer to a collection of unspecified, but in principle specifiable, freedoms. Or the context itself may suggest qualifications. But none of these interpretations of the claim that freedom is good can absolve us from the need to consider on what grounds people might value particular freedoms or justify particular restraints.

Why should anyone value being free to do certain particular things? Is there any good reason to care about whether we do anything in particular freely? One affirmative answer suggests that acting freely is a natural state. But that line of argument, besides being rather obscure since it is far from self-evident what constitutes a natural state of affairs, would not in fact give us a reason.[2] For all manner of types of behaviour are natural, in whatever sense free behaviour is, and we do not therefore conclude that they are desirable. Besides, in many obvious respects it is not true that natural life is free; civilisation has brought freedoms as well as restrictions with it.

Surely the origin of our evaluation of freedom is to be found in our wanting to be able to do what we choose to do, combined with the beliefs that others are no less entitled to having that same want satisfied and that the broad question of the ideal form of life is not a cut and dried matter to be settled by experts. That is to suggest that a self-interested feeling, a moral belief and an epistemological belief lie behind our inclination to value a large number of particular freedoms.

Not much needs to be said about the element of self-interest, except to note that it is an explanatory reason or motive rather than a justificatory reason. To some extent we value freedom because we enjoy it. One might argue independently that a little of what you fancy does you good, and many people believe that it is morally desirable that people should gain some enjoyment from life.[3] But in itself the fact that we enjoy having various freedoms does not constitute an argument to show that it is right that we should enjoy them.[4] Note furthermore that the situation in respect of enjoying specific freedoms might well have been different in the past or become different in the future. One of the effects of successful and well-planned encroachment on freedom by the state apparatus may be to diminish people's desire for freedom. And psychologists have long warned us that humankind cannot bear too much freedom, as have poets, even while existentialist philosophers have warned us that in a sense we cannot escape our freedom.[5] So, although on a superficial level it remains true to say that man likes his freedom, that claim should be handled cautiously, and it alone cannot bear the weight of a case for valuing freedom.

But the other two reasons, particularly when combined, perhaps can. The epistemological point is that the question of how a person may best live his life is to be sharply distinguished from technical questions such as how to build a bomb or what the constituent parts of liquid gas may be. All three questions, no doubt, are complex in the sense that they may be broken down into any number of further interrelated, delicate and difficult questions. But at the end of the day there are some who are clearly better equipped than others at answering the various technical questions, and who can satisfactorily demonstrate their expertise. The question about the good life, despite the fact that when broken down it will involve many questions that can be answered authoritatively by those with expertise of particular sorts, will also contain fundamental evaluative questions and crucial empirical, but currently unresolvable, questions. (For instance, one's view of the way one ought to live one's life may depend partially upon unproveable estimates about economic matters, or about the likely responses of others to certain situations.)[6] Any considered view on the good life, in other words, must amount to a doctrine.

This elementary but important point is to be distinguished from the quite different claim that value judgements are merely a matter of opinion. It seems to me quite implausible to suggest that moral judgements can be reduced entirely to matters of opinion. But, even if it were to be agreed that certain basic moral judgements are objective and, in a not unnatural sense of the phrase, matters of fact, it would not follow that there is in principle an appropriate blue-print for the best way for each individual to live his life, as there may be for the best way to construct various types of bomb. One must distinguish between the point that there may be a degree of objectivity in the range of intelligible value judgements, and the point that judgements about the acceptability of a vast range of alternative life-styles must be regarded as open. That gratuitous cruelty to sentient beings is morally wrong seems to me a simple matter of fact. But, whether that would be generally agreed or not, claims such as that keeping promises is always morally required, that people should honour their fathers and mothers, that people should not commit adultery, that people should attend church and that people should live on collectives, quite obviously cannot be taken for granted as established truths. So the point being made here is not tied up with any particular view about the status of moral judgements. It is simply that nobody can unequivocally demonstrate whether it is right or wrong for me to live as I do, rather than as you do, as my grandfather does or as Robert Mugabe does, even if one or two specific criticisms may legitimately be made. Similarly, though isolated points about a way of life, or, conceivably, very extreme societal forms themselves, might be criticised, in general nobody has the expertise to judge societies as having good or bad ways of life. At any rate, nobody can convince us that he has such expertise, as I should perhaps say, for I presume that followers of Milton Friedman, Jesus Christ, Marx, Kropotkin and the like, would claim such expert knowledge for their chosen guru. It is here that the distinction between doctrine and dogma become crucial. Given the state of play, the openness of the situation, who is to say, within broad limits, that one should not advocate or live any way of life? To commit oneself to a way of life is to adopt a doctrine, and most of mankind seem to find it hard to resist the temptation to do that. What is unforgiveable is to surrender to one's doctrine and become a dogmatist. The epistemological point we are considering, particularly when reinforced by the moral point, gives us strong reason to value a great deal of openness in this respect.

Central to any coherent moral theory is the idea of individual persons being deserving of respect simply in virtue of being individuals. As a matter of historical fact, moral codes have always incorporated this idea, taking care to classify those to whom it is desired to deny respect as non-persons, as the Greeks did with slaves, Nazis with Jews, and others with infidels, savages, bourgeois exploiters and so forth. The historical pattern proves nothing, of course, although it is richly suggestive. But arguments for the centrality to morality of respect for persons run through the history of philosophy. Most notable is Kant's formulation of the basic law that one should act only in such ways as to treat others as ends in themselves, and never as a means alone.[7] Regardless of origin, what is clear is that it is an essential part of what we understand by morality that it should involve respect for others as persons. That is not to suggest that morality demands that we necessarily *like* our neighbours, respect the *intelligence* of all and sundry, or want to spend our time in the company of any other being who comes our way, but rather that, like them or not, we recognise others as beings whose interests deserve to be taken into account no less than our own. The simplest way to demonstrate that this is in fact essential to morality is to contemplate any moral situation and recognise that what distinguishes a moral stance from a simple preference, a political stance or a doctrinal stance, is precisely this point that the actual identity of the person is neither here nor there. The wrongness of my stealing your wallet does not depend upon you being who you are, but on you being somebody. By definition, moral behaviour is concerned with conduct without reference to personal whim or favour. It is impersonal, if you like, which is to say that it is owed to any comparable being, no matter what his personal characteristics. That morality presupposes respect for persons, then, is as certain (and to be perceived in the same kind of way) as it is that football presupposes you play with your feet rather than with sub-machine guns.

It is because other people are equally and indistinguishably sources of interest and centres of concern (although some individuals may, by their behaviour, come to forfeit something of their right to equal concern), and because we various centres of concern have different ideas of how life ought to be lived, that, prior to particular arguments in particular situations, people ought to be free. We know that some people will live stupidly, some maliciously and some short-sightedly, but so unclear and uncertain is it whether the hermit's life, the communist's life, the religious life, the socially active life and most other kinds of life are necessarily acceptable or unacceptable, that there is an initial value placed on each of us being free to do as he sees fit. Indeed, frequently, what is objectionable about social and political movements is not what they stand for, but the manner in which they are prepared to stand for it. By the premise, the ideals of many of these competing life-styles cannot be shown to be objectionable. What is objectionable is when the doctrine becomes a dogma, and dissident voices are treated as imbeciles to be pushed aside. But there is a very clear distinction to be drawn between the plausibility of many particular claims, and the plausibility of the claim that any one of them should be imposed upon people. Argument about the moral rightness or wrongness of abortion, for example, is distinct from argument about whether the state should impose a particular view, by law, on people. In the same way, to put up a good case for a certain life-style is not the same thing as putting up a good case for making people live by it.

There can be no question, then, that we owe a *prima facie* allegiance to freedom, but it is nonetheless clear to all of us that, as things are, we are not prepared to let people freely do whatever they like. What is it about such things as stealing, murder and torture that makes us generally agreed that people should never be free to do them? What is it about tax fiddles and dishonest sloping off from work that makes us regard them as things that ideally people should not be free to do, but that somehow are less morally significant? What is it about smoking and drunkenness that makes us uncertain whether people should be free to engage in them, regardless of what we think of the activities themselves? How can we determine the limits on freedom?

A popular view has it that people should be free to do whatever they like, provided that they do not do anything that impinges on the freedom of others. In spirit, despite the fact that it rather ignores the idea that we might have some positive duties to help others, this seems a most plausible view. The problem is that it is not in the end coherent. It works well enough if we take some simple physical examples: I should not be free to lock you up, because that would limit your freedom. But, by this criterion, stealing, torturing and talking to you over the garden fence would scarcely be distinguishable, because all, though in different ways and to different degrees, impinge upon your freedom to do what you want. Besides, on closer examination, the criterion doesn't seem quite to hit the nail on the head. What is wrong with locking you up is more than that it limits your freedom. What is wrong, essentially, is that I am harming you, and that, surely, is a more plausible criterion for limiting freedom than any attempt to limit it by further reference to freedom alone.

According to this criterion, masterfully set forward by Mill, the sole warrant for interfering with people's freedom is consideration of the harmful consequences of not so doing. The fundamental principle is that nothing that affects the agent alone (no self-regarding activity, to use Mill's phrase) is under any circumstances fit for social restriction. People should be free to do anything which concerns themselves alone. (Mill is sometimes wrongly said to have believed in freedom as a good in itself. In fact he believed that happiness alone was good in itself.[8] His not unreasonable assumption is that, since an act that doesn't affect anybody else obviously can't harm anyone else, more happiness will arise from letting people do as they want in such cases, than from restricting them.) Acts that do impinge upon other people, however, may be restricted if they would harm them.[9] The only apparent exception to this overall strategy is that freedom of thought and speech should be absolute. But this is not really an exception, since Mill's argument is that in the long run mankind will gain in terms of happiness by treating these freedoms as absolute, since such freedom is in the best interests of truth, which in turn serves happiness in the long run.

Criticism of Mill's views on freedom has largely revolved around the following questions: can one distinguish a self-regarding from an other-regarding activity? what counts as harming someone? and why should freedom of thought be made absolute? An interesting feature of these questions is that none of them challenges the plausibility of the thesis as such. They all involve raising doubts about the ease and manner of putting it into practice. That is an important difference, being the difference between arguing a point of principle and arguing a point of fact. Whether a particular action could be said to harm another or not is a point of fact, albeit partly conceptual and partly empirical, and not on the face of it much to do with the principled claim that harm is the significant criterion. The question of whether an action does harm others, for instance, is in theory capable of resolution, and, even in particular instances when it cannot be resolved, it does not amount to a question mark against the claim that, if it caused harm, it should be restricted, if not, not. We do not need to be able to determine the precise limits of harm, in order to accept or reject the principle.

It is important not to fall for the slippery slope fallacy here. From the fact that night slips into day, you cannot legitimately conclude that there is no distinction between the two. Even in those cases where two extremes are less directly ascertainable than night and day, one cannot ignore them. Pure happiness may never have been enjoyed by a living man, but one can conceive of it, and one can intellectually distinguish between happiness and misery; consequently, however difficult in practice, one can accept the principle that one should try to promote happiness. Similarly, in this case, we may have to concede that very few actions are literally self-regarding, especially when we take indirect consequences into account. But, if we know what is meant by self-regarding activities, we are in a position to accept the principle, and even to judge certain actions as self-regarding enough to count as such. There will always be genuine borderline cases, but that is not problematic for the principle, any more than genuinely difficult offside decisions in football show that nobody is ever truly offside. So sensible decisions can be taken. The area of sexual activity would clearly count as self-regarding in point of performance, but when it becomes a matter of procreation or public exhibition it becomes other-regarding and as such, if harmful to others, possibly to be restricted. What I and my family eat and drink, or what we do in our own home, is our affair, but if we get drunk on public transport the case is clearly different. It cannot be denied that there is room for argument about what constitutes impinging on others and harming others. My points here are that nonetheless in many cases it is very straightforward and that, anyway, the point of principle is quite distinct, and can be upheld even in those circumstances. It might be suggested, as a last resort, that, though the principle can be upheld, there is not a lot of point in adhering to principles that are not easy to implement in practice. The answer to that, apart from repeating the observation that in many cases it is fairly easy to abide by the principle in practice, is that the point and value of a principle of conduct lie in the fact that it sets an ideal for us to strive towards, rather than a practical guide for daily behaviour. A man who believes in the absolute freedom of self-regarding activities is a very different man from one who does not, even if both are uncertain whether a number of activities should be classified as self-regarding.

Another possible line of criticism of the view set out here is to suggest that freedom of speech should not be regarded as absolute, but should, like any other activity, be curbed when it is evidently causing harm. But that is to be strongly resisted. The argument for absolute freedom of speech is a straightforward instance of rule-utilitarian argument. Nobody disputes that speech is other-regarding nor that it may cause harm, both directly and indirectly. But it may plausibly be maintained that despite the harmful effects of individual acts of speech, mankind gains in terms of well-being in the long run, by allowing all people absolute freedom of speech, and by refusing to leave the question of when to curb speech in the interests of the general happiness to individuals, groups or governments. The argument for absolute free speech is that this is one of those activities (like truth-telling, refraining from killing, refraining from stealing, and keeping promises) the absolute commitment to which by a society produces more good, on balance, than leaving it to individual judgement would do.[10]

If we now apply this principle of leaving people free to do as they please except (a) in those few cases where a rule has been established on utilitarian terms, and (b) where what they would choose to do would cause more harm than would be caused by a restriction on such behaviour, we see that it fits and explains our commonsense everyday assumptions very well. What is wrong with telling lies, stealing and killing is that they cause a great deal of harm—far more than a blanket ban on them does, notwithstanding the fact that circumstances might arise in which in itself an act of killing, stealing or telling a lie would benefit people. The reason that we feel very confident about the wrongness of these acts is that the harm they generally cause is very clear. We readily see the utility of forbidding them absolutely. Our moral sentiments in respect of them are strong. When we are less certain of the likely outcome of prohibiting actions by rule or leaving them to individual judgement, we are less dogmatic about the rights and wrongs of the actions in question. Moon-lighting, sloping off early from work and minor tax fiddles probably are wrong, we say—alright, *are* wrong—but we can't take these wrongs as seriously as killing and stealing. Their consequences are not, or are not thought to be, as drastic. If circumstances were such that we became absolutely convinced that moon-lighting was threatening our society's stability and welfare, it is certain that our sense of moral indignation would increase accordingly. Smoking and drunkenness, however damaging and unpleasant they may be, are seldom regarded as moral wrongs, because they are seldom thought of as strongly detrimental to the general good.

The main purpose of this chapter has been to clear the ground for discussion in subsequent chapters, by dissolving any notions of freedom as something towards which in itself one can have any attitude. When discussing particular freedoms (or restraints) one misses the point, if one seeks to appeal to freedom in the abstract or a right to freedom without qualification. There *is* a presumption in favour of freedom, but that is to say only that we expect reasons to be given in support of any restrictions proposed for particular activities. Such reasons should be related in some way to considerations of harm. (At any rate to forbid or restrict activity which is agreed to be causing no harm, direct or indirect, to anybody, would appear to have no justification.) But although it can be agreed that reference to harm is required in order to make a case for restriction, it must be conceded that the mere reference to harmful consequences may not be enough to settle the issue. Firstly, there is room for further discussion about what constitutes harm. Secondly, there is room for argument about the likely effects of different courses of action in terms of harm. Thirdly, and this takes us back directly to the point made in the first chapter and the burden of the remainder of this book, there will very often be a need for a more precise characterisation of the activity in question. This means that in discussing particular issues, such as sex-role stereotyping, abortion,

Freedom 55

democracy, civil disobedience and the value of art, it is necessary to discriminate as carefully as possible. The broader and more sweeping the claim, the less illuminating and the less plausible it is likely to be: 'dissent against the government is always wrong', 'taking life is never justified' and 'art is a luxury we can't afford', for example, are very unclear, for all their stark simplicity, and very implausible as they stand. In the end questions such as whether people ought to be free to have abortions, free from sex-role stereotyping or free to participate in government, are questions about what exactly constitutes abortion, sex-role stereotyping and free participation in government, respectively, and what exactly the consequences of such specific freedoms are likely to be.

NOTES

1 I distinguish free expression (including freedom of publication) from freedom of thought and speech. See Chapter 10.
2 For further discussion of the problems with 'nature' and 'natural', see John Stuart Mill, *On Nature*, and Robin Barrow, *Radical Education*, chs 1 and 2.
3 Most obviously utilitarians.
4 At least, not unless we assume both the truth of utilitarianism and that enjoying the freedoms in question is on balance more conducive to happiness than any alternative arrangement.
5 See, for example, Erich Fromm, *Fear of Freedom* and T. S. Eliot's *Four Quartets*. The freedom that existentialists such as J. P. Sartre warn us we cannot escape is essentially the freedom of choice or responsibility, and that freedom is seen as bringing with it a great burden of *angst*.
6 These are unproveable in the extended contingent sense explained in Chapter 3.
7 Immanuel Kant, *Groundwork of the Metaphysic of Morals*.
8 See *On Liberty*, Chapter 1.
9 Strictly speaking, as formulated in the text above, acts should be restricted if not to do so would cause more harm on balance than doing so.
10 Then what is the difference between the rule about free speech and the other proposed rules about telling the truth, not stealing, not killing and keeping promises? Firstly, it admits of no qualifications. One might adopt a rule like 'never kill except in self-defence', but not 'never curb speech except in circumstances X'. Secondly, the claim is that the rule must stand, come what may, whereas it is conceivable in the case of the other rules that circumstances might arise in which on utilitarian grounds it seems right to dispense with them.

5 Feminism: Language and Thought

> I have no predilection, sir, for defamation. I make a point of speaking the truth on all occasions; and it seldom happens that the truth can be spoken without some stricken deer pronouncing it a libel.
>
> Thomas Love Peacock, *Headlong Hall*

Despite the title of this chapter, I can see no more point in attempting to discuss feminism in a few pages than there would be in trying to discuss Marxism, fascism, or indeed most other 'isms'. For nearly all such terms are used very broadly (and often vaguely) to cover a multitude of sins. To be a Marxist, a Christian or an evolutionist is to be one of a family, having more in common with other members than with those outside it. But, equally, different members of the same family can have markedly different traits. Lamarck and Darwin, Lenin and Stalin, Protestant and Catholic, Mosley and Hitler—yes, there are significant similarities between the members of each of these pairs that allow us to call them, respectively, evolutionists, communists, Christians and fascists. But there are also differences between the members of each pair, differences for which many have died. To discuss any such 'ism' one either has to remain on the general and unilluminating level of the common denominator, or else disentangle the different species of the genus and examine each one individually. In the case of feminism the variant species are more than usually diffuse, and it is arguable that some of them do not even belong to the same genus, or that there is not even a common denominator. Janet Radcliffe Richards has argued, in *The Sceptical Feminist*, that anyone who accepts that women suffer from systematic social injustice because of their sex is a feminist.[1] But while that seems a sensible enough definition to me, it is extremely broad and has the disadvantage of being plainly insufficient to characterise the position of many prominent feminist groups; and possibly it does not even constitute a necessary element for others. The militant Redstockings, for example, would define their brand of feminism in terms of achieving power for women *qua* women, by more or less any means, and would not include any reference to the question of social justice in delineating their creed (though certainly they would agree that there has been great social injustice done to women).

Without further qualification, the statement 'I am a feminist' tells the audience no more than that the speaker is dissatisfied with some thing, or set of things, about the role of women in society, probably with an implication of male dominance being involved somewhere. Discussing feminism, at any rate in only a few chapters, is therefore simply not feasible. What we can do is discuss some specific issues that are of importance to at least some feminists, as one would more wisely discuss particular problems relating to Christianity than discuss Christianity itself. But because I am a feminist in Janet Radcliffe Richards' sense, and presume that few readers, if any, would dissent from the view that some injustices have taken, and do take, place against women because of their sex, I am less interested in arguing that point than in considering a number of relatively contentious issues. I shall therefore concentrate on the questions of sexist language, sex-role stereotyping, abortion and reverse discrimination. (The last two of these, though they may, and frequently do, arise in a feminist context, also have a wider interest and significance.)

For the time being I accept the premise that in our society males have a superior and advantageous role. It is not perhaps self-evident that this is the case, but, without agreement on some such premise, the first of these issues could scarcely get off the ground. For the claim now to be considered is that our everyday language is sexist, which is to say that its structure both helps to create and consolidates the superior and advantaged status of the male.[2] This particular claim may very well be seen as part of a wider claim about the relationship between language and thought, which owes something to the remark of Wittgenstein in his *Tractatus* that 'the limits of my language mean the limits of my world.'[3] Although this and other similar remarks by Wittgenstein are both equivocal and fairly limited in scope, they have exercised a disproportionate effect on recent philosophy and thinking generally. In particular, such gnomic utterances have led people to claim that the way in which we identify or label something is our conception of it. To take a familiar instance, it is suggested that to refer to an adult Afro-American as 'boy', as was typically the case in the not so distant past in the southern states of America, is to indicate one's paternalistic attitude to such people.[4] But just how plausible is such a claim?

It is obviously true that there is a close relationship of some sort between words and concepts, and that our capacity for thought is closely tied up with our capacity to use language.[5] More specifically, it may very well be the case that words are always, or at any rate generally, first applied in new contexts or to cover new instances, because of connotations that derive from other contexts or previous uses. It is very likely indeed that the word 'boy' was originally used even of adult Afro-Americans, precisely because of the dependent, inferior, quasi-chattel implications of that term. It is also entirely plausible to suggest that, if you bring people up to call others 'boy', you are doing something to encourage them to think of those others as inferior. Similarly, the tendency within our culture to call women by such terms of endearment as 'poppet', 'petal', 'flower' and 'sweetheart' very probably both arises out of a particular conception of femininity, and reinforces it. And while we are making necessary concessions, let us concede the frequent feminist claim that the fact that we typically categorise by reference to gender, rather than say, age or size, tells us something about our interests and priorities (as well as strengthening them).[6] It is generally speaking true that, if you talk to me about your friend Frankie, I will want to know whether Frankie is a boy or a girl, before I will bother myself, if indeed I ever do, about his/her age or size. Similarly, our use of words such as 'mankind', 'chairman' and 'manslaughter' quite possibly arose originally out of the fact that the society in question was male dominated. (Most words have a long and complicated etymological history, and one might have to trace origins way beyond the early days of our own society. But the point remains: if the world had always been predominantly female dominated, it is very likely that we would have inherited terms such as 'womankind'.)

But we must not get carried away or over-intoxicated by the significance of the points conceded. Words and concepts, however closely related in practice, are not the same thing. By the same token, to exhaust all that may be said about particular words, their history, use and implications, is not necessarily to have said everything (or even, in theory, anything) about the ideas of the person who uses the words. It is possible, logically and practically, to have an idea or a concept without knowing the appropriate word for it, or indeed without having any specific word for it. (It is arguable that it is not possible to have a concept without having any language with which to structure one's recognition of it, but that distinct point does not concern us here.) Thus a child may consciously perceive the triangularity that is common to several triangular shapes, without knowing any single word for 'triangularity'. A new opera goer might

Feminism: Language and Thought 59

pick up the phenomenon of leitmotivs without ever having heard about them. And it is possible to have a word in one's vocabulary, but not to use it in relation to the same concept as other people, as, say, Soviet and British ideas of democracy differ, while the choice of word does not.

The consequence of the possibility of divorcing words and concepts is simple, but extremely important. Information about the origins, uses, connotations and implications of *words* in one context, or for one person or set of persons, is not necessarily information about the *thoughts* of another person or set of persons using the same words in another context. Even if it is true that the word 'boy' was originally applied to blacks in a patronising way, deriving from the usual meaning of the word, and even if it is true that, through continued use in a particular context, it has acquired a specifiable set of connotations, it does not follow either that it necessarily must continue to do so, or that anyone who uses the word in reference to blacks necessarily has such attitudes as the word usually suggests. The most obvious case in point is the sort where an individual from one background uses a word familiar to those from a different background: it would be very foolish indeed for anyone to presume that everything that I mean, when I use the word 'black', corresponds to everything that Martin Luther King intends to convey by the word, or that either of us necessarily wishes to suggest anything of what the National Front conveys by use of the word. Not only do different people very possibly have individual conceptions associated with a public word, it is also quite possible that events may radically change attitudes within a group or community, so that a word may acquire new, possibly antithetical, nuances. The word, that is to say, may remain the same and continue to be applied in the same way, but the conception may change. Something like that has clearly happened over the years with words as diverse as 'aristocrat', 'nazi' and 'nigger'.

It follows from the fact that words may be distinguished from concepts and that they do change their meanings according to place, time and person, that you cannot be sure of anybody's attitude to something simply from the word(s) he uses to refer to it. Some people will call homosexuals 'homosexuals'. Some will call them 'queers', some 'pansies', some 'fairies', some 'faggots', some 'gays'. Though one might make assumptions and perhaps be proven correct in the event, notwithstanding what may be known about the origins and usual implications of any one of these terms, you cannot be sure about a particular person's attitude to homosexuality simply by knowing which term he prefers to use to refer to them. One might guess that 'faggot' was abusive and 'gay' neutral, but one could be mistaken. A person may use the particular words he does for so many reasons, of which trading on the normal connotations is but one. He may use the vocabulary of his peer group, of his family or of his particular circle. He may choose his words to please, to offend or to pass unnoticed. He may have been well-informed or misinformed about the implications of terminology. He may size up his audience well or badly. To apply this to the point at issue: the fact that I talk of 'a giant step for mankind' does not necessarily reveal that I think in terms of male dominance, nor that I wish to perpetuate the idea of male dominance in my audience, nor that the idea is in fact being reinforced, though conceivably any or all of these claims might be true.

Something similar must be said of the particular point that our language very naturally lends itself to gender distinctions. We make reference to gender in most sentences, even when it is clearly not the, or even a, point at issue. We include reference to he or she, as we do not casually include reference to fat or thin, dark or fair, old or young. That this fact arises out of a social situation in which gender differences were seen as of relative significance is hardly to be disputed. But then gender distinctions obviously are of considerable significance. To counter that they should not be, besides standing in need of independent argument, implies far more than mere verbal changes: to obliterate consciousness of gender differences will require changing people's sexual drives and changing every social phenomenon that is an expression of the difference. But the immediate point is that once again the inescapable, but superficial, verbal implications are being confused with what particular people actually intend by using the words in question. That I say, 'Here she comes', is not proof that I am making a point of gender distinctions, even though gender is clearly noted. It would generally not even be plausible to suggest that it shows I am conscious of the person as female. Sophisticated language users have long since acquired the capacity to use words out of their most familiar context, without their usual associations. 'God help us' is quite different from 'God exists', and only the simple-minded try to argue that the use of the former phrase is evidence of the speaker's belief in God. 'It's a dog's life' is an expression that has a life of its own that owes very little to the meaning of 'dog' in 'Fido is a dog'. In just the same way 'Here she comes' differs exceedingly from 'she's my type' or 'she's a woman'. Certainly, the latter two remarks use the word 'she' to pinpoint gender that is very much in the forefront of the speaker's mind. But there is no more reason to assume that 'she' in 'Here she comes' indicates even conscious awareness of, let alone concern for, gender, than there is to assume that the occurrence of 'God' in 'Oh, my God' indicates religious commitment.

The above points have been points of logic. To make them is not to dispute that one can make more or less sensible empirical claims about the significance of particular language use. It would seem to me quite likely that somebody who used the word 'boy' of blacks took a patronising attitude towards them, but quite ludicrous to treat the use of the expression 'Oh my God' as evidence of belief in God. Perhaps it involves something nearer to the absurdity of the latter than the plausibility of the former to treat use of the male and female pronouns as evidence of preoccupation with gender. Without doubt, to most people, 'wop' is more abusive than 'Italian'. Possibly, very often, 'chairman' suggests to speaker and/or audience a male person. Conceivably, for some, 'mankind' conjures up the image of a multitude of males. But, true or false, these are empirical generalisations only. Nor can one legitimately argue that, even if they are only true as empirical generalisations, they clearly constitute sufficient reason to alter verbal practice. One cannot convincingly argue, for example, that since, in general, the term 'wop' is used offensively, Italians must always resent its use. For whether they always or increasingly resent its use in future will depend partly on the upshot of this particular kind of argument. If those who over-simplistically argue that, 'wop' being generally a term of abuse, he who uses it must be taken to be being abusive, win the day, then clearly, whenever the word is uttered, offence will be taken. Then we will have to drop it entirely from our vocabulary. If on the other hand the obvious truth of what I am saying can be got across, namely that words acquire their connotations in context, so that 'you old wop' may be a term of endearment between an Italian and non-Italian comparable to 'you old bugger' between what some are pleased to call 'straights', then its use without automatically generating heat and resentment becomes possible. It then ceases to be empirically true that we have to call for a change in language and a ban on certain words. (I have deliberately taken a somewhat extreme example, but that should make it easier to carry the point that with less typically abusive or divisive words there is no obvious need to rule them out of court.)

To summarise the argument so far: the mere fact that some person or persons call Afro-Americans blacks, negroes, or whatever, is not necessarily significant of whatever it may be empirically established the term in question is generally used to imply. What is signified on a particular occasion needs to be worked out on that occasion. The fact tnat in popular usage 'mankind' stands for 'humankind', and 'womankind' does not, whatever its historical origins, tells us now only about the way we typically use the words in question. As such, it is quite on a par with the information that 'Here they come' can be replaced by 'they're here'. There are no *a priori* grounds whatever for holding that the fact that 'mankind' is interchangeable with 'humanity' holds any significance for us today generally, still less that it does for any particular user of the term 'mankind'.

The suggestion, therefore, that in using the word 'mankind', 'I exclude women from humanity',[7] is mischievous nonsense. The suggestion comes from Robert Baker, who also makes the claim that our vocabulary of endearment, the words we use about, or to the face of, our female loved ones, indicates that men think of women as mindless playthings and/or sexual objects. (He concentrates on the way in which males talk and think about women, rather than vice versa. Readers may draw their own conclusions as to the significance of that.) To that he adds that the language of sexual intercourse always takes the forms he X's her, rather than she X's him, whatever the word in question, and that that is further evidence of male dominance and the desire to perpetuate it. The latter claim turns out to be of considerable interest, because, by chance, time has falsified it, and thereby made a nonsense of the whole approach that Baker employs. There was a time when the grammatical fact to which Baker alludes could not be denied, and he is obviously correct in observing that the facts of the matter do not demand that we see the man as always being the active partner. She might as well have been perceived as engulfing him, as he penetrating her. But the point of interest is that since 1972 when Baker wrote his piece, there has been a marked change in usage, particularly amongst the young, so that in many circles all the familiar words are in play, but it now seems natural to talk of her Xing him. This small social fact is of immense significance to the wider argument of this chapter. Of course it does confirm that there is a connection between language and thought. (Speech patterns have changed; attitudes and perceptions have changed.) But that has never been disputed. What it also shows is that attitudes and perceptions may change *prior* to language changing, and therefore *independently* of language change. In this case, a new social sexual climate in which men and women, for whatever reason, just did not see their relationships as simply him penetrating, screwing, fucking or making love to her, has led, not to a new vocabulary of engulfing, taking in or what have you, but to the same old song carrying completely new overtones. 'Fucking' has taken on a whole new meaning. As before, we see that the words used are not a sure index of the thinking going on, and radical realignments of thought can take place without changing the vocabulary we use.

The same crucial points can be made again, by reference to the example of 'chairman'. Even with the point that the origin of the term is to be found in the social conditions of male dominance conceded, and, in addition, with the unproven claim that *most* people, in using the word, think of, suggest and thereby strengthen the hand of males, being allowed to stand, it neither follows that an individual speaker or audience is moved in that way by the term, nor that changing the term is necessary or sufficient to changing people's habits of thought. For many of us, perhaps because for a number of years we have worked with various female chairmen, the word carries precisely the connotations that 'chairperson' is supposed to carry, and no more suggests men than 'manager' does. The plain fact is, as this sort of example amply illustrates, words can grow away from one set of connotations and acquire another, as 'anarchy' has outgrown its associated image of wide-brimmed hats and smoking bombs, and 'happiness' has outgrown its etymological implications of chance or good fortune. The climate of thought can change, without a change in vocabulary, and, having done so, it may change the implications of the familiar language. Not only *is it* possible to come to use the word 'chairman' without reference to gender, but, sadly perhaps, *it is not* possible to legislate by verbal fiat for people's thoughts: those who, for whatever reason, do not think women should be chairmen, will invest the term 'chairperson', if it is forced upon them, with the same masculine odour as 'chairman' previously had for them. Changing a person's words without changing his thoughts merely changes your perception of him; whereas if you change his thoughts, he will either change his own vocabulary or give the old a new meaning.

But still it might be said, although changing people's vocabulary is not logically necessary to reorientating their thought, and certainly not sufficient, it might nonetheless be a reasonable practical expedient. To replace 'he', 'she' and 'it' by some common pronoun ('sher'), to replace 'chairman' by 'chairperson', to refuse to use 'he' generically—these, and other similar steps, may not guarantee anything, but taken together they would create a climate in which it would be harder for people to persist in sexist attitudes. So, at least, it may be said. But why on earth should we think so? To insist on a common pronoun removes one easy way of rendering our remarks more specific, and presumably would serve to intensify our awareness of gender distinctions when they are necessary. ('I'm taking sher to the cinema', when it is of no immediate relevance whether the person is male or female, might become 'then I'm going to see if she'll let me kiss her', because the speaker does not wish to be taken for a homosexual. That sort of thing is not going to help feminism.)

A rather similar point has to be made about the often quoted example of nurses and doctors. A fairly asinine puzzle has been devised wherein one is told that somebody will be operated on by a doctor who is closely related to, but is not the father of, the patient, and asked to guess what the relationship is. Few, apparently, suggest that the doctor is the mother, and this is cited as evidence of how male orientated we are. In fact it seems altogether more reasonable to cite it as evidence of the fact that most of us know that the majority of doctors are male. If people do not specify that they are referring to a female doctor, the reasonable assumption is that it is a male doctor. The same applies, in reverse, to nurses. The same applies in this country, but presumably not so obviously in Israel, to soldiers. Do people have the same assumptions about 'traffic wardens' as they probably do about 'policemen', if those are the terms used? I doubt it. By and large policemen are male and we therefore expect notification of reference to policewomen. Males and females seem about equally distributed in the traffic warden business, so the term serves for either and 'traffic wardress' becomes pedantic. The truth is that our use of 'doctor' to cover male and female, and our assumption that the doctor will be male unless otherwise stated, because they generally are, is evidence of our *lack* of preoccupation with gender. As is the kind of experiment cited. People don't think, 'well, maybe the solution is that it's a female doctor', because they did not, in the first place, think of the doctor as decidedly male. I pass over in silence the lack of fit between complaining that we do pinpoint 'he' as against 'she', and complaining that 'doctor' is neutral.

Whatever some feminists may choose to assert, I persist in my claim that, when I use words like 'chairman' or 'mankind', I might just as well have used '$\alpha\rho\chi\omega\nu$' or 'les gens', for all they reveal about my attitudes, and that, when in a philosophy seminar I say 'suppose a man were to . . .', I am not thinking in terms of a gender distinction. (I am thinking of the problem in hand.) If it be replied, but other people will assume that you mean a male chairman, an exclusively male mankind or that your logic is somehow only applicable to males, the answer has to be twofold. Firstly, whether people assume that chairmen are necessarily male and such like is in the end of very little significance in the context of serious feminist complaints; people's prejudices are not fed by words alone and will survive verbal changes in isolation, while they can render verbal change obsolete, if changed themselves by other means. Secondly, the simplest solution to the particular examples we have dealt with here is to teach people to understand the English language as she is currently, conventionally, deployed. People who think that 'chairman' implies a male person are making a simple mistake.

Language does of course evolve. It changes more or less slowly to meet changing or changed circumstances (including changes in abstract thought). Sometimes the words employed change, sometimes their meanings (in the widest sense) change. But to seek to put the cart before the horse, and to change thought by changing words is, notwithstanding the dire warning of Orwellian Newspeak, in practice puerile. It is comparable to changing the currency and imagining one has solved an economic problem. Even in the idealised setting of 1984 or Brave New World, still more in actual totalitarian states, the changes in language accompany active steps to change thinking. Without those they are ineffective, with them they are an embellishment. Words are symbols. What matters is what they represent for people, and people, by and large, are not long fooled by changes in appearances only.

Before concluding this chapter I should draw attention to a rather different kind of argument against the so-called generic use of the pronoun 'he' put forward by Peter Singer.[8] He opts for the use of 'she' generically, in order to redress the balance of the past. He calls it an instance of reverse discrimination on his part, but, whatever its name, it is rather curious. If 'he', so used, is objectionable, as Singer claims it is, then so must 'she' be. To talk of redressing the balance, though no doubt humane in intent, has very little logic about it, and we seem rather to be faced with a classic instance of two wrongs not making a right. That is on the assumption that we grant, as I do not, that using 'he' is wrong.

Singer himself gives no good reason for seeing the practice of using 'he' as objectionable. He merely observes that 'he' does bring to mind males rather than females, so serving to perpetuate the unconscious idea that most writing is about males.[9] Unconscious ideas are always a little bit suspect, and it looks very much as if Singer would like to raise our consciousness, with all the attendant problems that that implies (see Chapter 2). But my conscious idea is certainly not that most writing is about males (despite the fact that it probably is). My conscious idea, when a philosopher writes 'suppose a man were to . . .', is, as I've revealed, that he means 'suppose a person . . .'. Then, it may be asked, why not change the wording

66   *Injustice, Inequality and Ethics*

to that? Because I have a feeling for the English language, and would rather teach people to use it, than change it to suit their limitations. One wonders, in any case, what would happen if one did change every generic usage to something such as 'person'. It remains, I stress, an empirical question as to whether it would make the slightest difference to people's assumptions about male domination. Personally I doubt that it would. Most of all I wonder what good Singer's use of 'she' is supposed to do.

Finally, let me note that nothing I have written in this chapter should be read as an endorsement for or a denial of either the claim that it is a world where males are superior or advantaged, or the view that it ought to continue to be such a world. I have confined myself to arguing that language changes of the sort considered are not worth instituting.

NOTES

1   Janet Radcliffe Richards, *The Sceptical Feminist*.
2   It might still be regarded as sexist, if it was thought that it helped to create and consolidate merely a *different* role for male and female. But that would presumably generate less specifically feminist heat, and in fact most feminists seem to adopt some such premise as the one I introduce in the text.
3   L. Wittgenstein, *Tractatus logico-philosophicus*.
4   The example is taken from Robert Baker, ' "Pricks" and "Chicks": A Plea for "Persons" ', which also offers an uncompromising, not to say excessive, statement of the view I criticise in the text.
5   Indeed I have argued for the positive implications of this connection in my *Language and Thought*.
6   The meanings of the words 'sex' and 'gender' are not uniform. I shall take sex differences to be, more or less, biological differences, and gender differences to be differences associated with male and female roles, including sex differences.
7   Robert Baker, *op. cit.*
8   Peter Singer, *Practical Ethics*.
9   *Ibid.*

6 Feminism: Sex-Role Stereotyping

> To think is one of the most unpardonable errors a woman can commit in the eyes of society. In our sex a taste for intellectual pleasures is almost equivalent to taking the veil; and though not absolutely a vow of perpetual celibacy, it has almost always the same practical tendency.
>
> Thomas Love Peacock, *Melincourt*

The question to be considered here is the relatively narrow one of whether sex-role stereotyping during childhood is immoral. There are further questions, such as whether it is desirable, avoidable, necessary or attractive, which, though I shall need to refer to and touch upon some of them, I do not intend to try and answer. It is often assumed, without argument, that sex-role stereotyping is inherently objectionable, and it is that assumption that needs to be examined first and foremost. Few, I imagine, would deny that we do, as a society, tend to impose stereotypical roles on both boys and girls. By our own examples, by our expectations, by the images we present and the things we say, we present a more or less consistent picture of a certain range of behaviour and activity being particularly woman's work. Fashions change in respect of both ranges, but, broadly speaking, at the present time, things such as wearing trousers, smoking pipes, mowing lawns, watching football matches, using tools and understanding cars are taken to belong to the male domain, while dresses, cooking, wearing jewelry, housework, shopping and looking after baby are typically seen as part of the female domain. There are also differing mannerisms and attitudes typically expected. Coarse bluff behaviour, dogmatic and loud views pass as manly, while feminine attitudes are demure and shy. Getting drunk is acceptable in men, and not in women. The examples could continue for a long time. Most of us are well aware that there are significant exceptions to these stereotypes, at both the individual and the group level. Nonetheless, as generalisations, these distinctions between our image of male and female roles stand and represent the norm. The question that needs to be asked is not whether it is right that there should be such differences (for the answer to that must depend partly on the answer to other questions such as how they come about), but the prior question of whether it is right that we should actively cultivate such differences. Is there something morally wrong with the way in which, through the environment we control, we bring up boys to be boys, and girls to be girls?

Let us approach this question by considering, in turn, the different arguments there might be for objecting to the practice of sex-role stereotyping amongst children. The first, and probably commonest, line of argument goes as follows. 'The things that parents and teachers say and expect of boys and girls respectively, the images projected by films, television and books, the example set by other boys being boyish and girls being girlish, all add up to suggest one natural role for my son, Tommy, and another distinct natural role for my daughter, Jane. That must be objectionable, because there is no such thing as a natural role for boys or a natural role for girls.' This argument is certainly a welcome advance on the idea that man's natural role is known to be that of a dominating aggressor, while woman's natural role is beyond a doubt to play his meek and submissive helpmate. Few people today would accept Rousseau's confident assertion that 'woman is specially made for man's delight . . . it is the law of nature. . . . To be pleasing in (man's) sight, to win his respect and love, to train him in childhood, to tend him in manhood, to counsel and console, to make his life pleasant and happy, these are the duties of women for all time, and this is what she should be taught while she is young.'[1] That line of argument is vulnerable on three counts. In the first place it is, to say the least, factually debateable whether this or any other is woman's natural role. In the second place, if it were true that woman is 'specially made' to be this, that and the other, then there should be no need for all this fuss and bother about ensuring a certain kind of femininity through upbringing. (Parent fish don't have to take special steps to bring their young up to swim, for they were indeed born to do that.) In the third place, the argument provides a notable example of the obviously fallacious move of switching directly from talking about what is the case, to talking about what ought to be the case. Human beings, perhaps, are naturally aggressive. But even if that is so, there is no warrant for concluding from that fact alone that it is morally good that they are, or that they ought to be. The history of civilisation is almost one and the same thing as the record of mankind's struggle to overcome natural behaviour of various types. Without question, then, the claim that males and females are by nature different, whatever the extent of its truth, would be inadequate to justify the further claim that they ought to be brought up differently. (It is directly comparable to the inadequate attempt to justify apartheid by insisting that black and white just are, by nature, different.)

One of the problems with all such arguments is the equivocal nature of the word 'natural'. It can mean so many different things, ranging from 'spontaneous' to 'innate', and very often has connotations of appropriateness thrown in for good measure. There are senses of 'natural' in which people indubitably have natural roles. For example, there are roles typically or usually associated with particular groups, and, when somebody tells us that 'banking is the natural preserve of middle class whites', probably all he means is that usually it is middle class whites you find in banking. In this sense it would be true to say that in our society a woman's natural role includes bringing up the baby. But then there is nothing sacrosanct about this sense of natural. Yes, in our society woman's natural (= conventional, typical, usual) role includes bringing up baby, but to say as much is no answer to the question of whether this should be woman's role. If, by contrast, 'natural' is to imply something like an innate and inescapable potential, as the acorn, if it survives at all, will naturally turn out to be an oak tree rather than an ash tree, then it is very debateable indeed whether boys and girls respectively do have a natural role. There are obviously some biological and physiological differences between boys and girls that set broad limits on what they could, respectively, do. Women have to bear the children, even if in other respects their lives are indistinguishable from those of men. But despite the impressive efforts of those, such as Stephen Goldberg,[2] who have tried to show that there is an inevitable physiological basis for male dominance, we are still a long long way from drawing conclusions of the type 'girls are born to do the housework, while boys are born to go out and earn money'.

However, although talk of natural roles is usually confused, because of the uncertainty as to the meaning of 'natural', even if we cut clean through it, by conceding that in no important sense is there a natural male role to be distinguished from a natural female role, that admission does not yield the desired conclusion that imposing distinct roles must be morally objectionable. Let us grant that cleaning the car, going out to work, drinking beer, gardening and watching sport on television on Saturday afternoon, are not, in any significant sense, 'by nature' father's work rather than mother's. But that does not lead directly to the conclusion that it would be wrong to bring Tommy up to presume that these are the sorts of things he may be expected to do, while Jane will adopt a different pattern of life. On the contrary, since, on the premise (now that we have conceded that there is no innate, inevitable tendency towards a particular role), any role is the result of environmental factors, no distinction can be drawn between roles in respect of their imposition. If we must be the product of circumstances, one cannot object to the determining of roles through the provision of a particular set of circumstances. One cannot cry, 'what is wrong is that you are forming roles that have no justification in nature'. Nor can one say, simply, that treating Tommy and Jane to different environmental expectations is wrong. For, either it is wrong because all children ought always, in any circumstances, to be brought up to fulfil the same kind of role, which seems a very extreme and implausible position to wish to defend; or it is wrong because Tommy and Jane, while legitimately being treated differently to, say, the late Csar of Russia's children, in deference to the social conditions in which they find themselves, nonetheless have a similarity between them that demands overriding the social conditions in which they find themselves. The point is that one cannot have it both ways. If we are what our environment makes us, then talk of it being wrong for our environment to make us what it demands does not make sense. The objection would have to be directed, not against bringing up boys in the male role and girls in the female role, but against the existence of one or other role as such. If various roles are acceptable in society, and if people adopt the roles they are initiated into, and can do no other, then no criticism of sex-role stereotyping based simply on the observation that it is going on can get off the ground.

What one could say, and here we move on to a second and more sophisticated thesis, is that if, broadly speaking, a child might conceivably adopt any of a range of roles, then he should be free to choose his role autonomously, or, slightly differently, that it is wrong for us to differentiate between children on grounds of sex though it might not be on other grounds (such as, for example, that some are children of the Csar and others are not). An over-simplistic retort to the first of these arguments suggests that, whatever the influence of upbringing, people are free to choose what role they wish to adopt when they grow up. But that is really rather disingenuous, given that most people have by then grown into a particular role. It is true that instances can be cited of people who swap or merge their roles, but some of these may be people who were never effectively initiated into a stereotypical role, and others may have made such shifts only with immense difficulty. They do not really amount to evidence that there is no difficulty and no problem in the idea of making an autonomous choice when adult, nor do they seriously challenge the fact that most of us are prisoners of the role that we have, by whatever means, acquired. That is not to say that we resent those roles (most of us probably do not), but we are no more free to change our roles than we are to become different people. We are permitted to change if we wish to, but, by and large, we are not able to. Though it may be true, therefore, that most men and women would say that they had freely chosen their male and female roles, respectively, and that, if they wanted to change them, they would, there is something in Thomas Hill's contention that 'if socially fostered ignorance of (a woman's) own talents and alternatives is the cause of her submissiveness (i.e. her acceptance of her role) her consent shouldn't count.'[3] At the very least, people's conviction that they have autonomously decided to remain as they are is not conclusive evidence that they really have done so.

Superficially this is a persuasive line of argument, if one values autonomy. It seems to take the heat out of the issue by saying, 'look, let's not fight each other about whether girls should be different to boys, or about what exactly is masculine. Let's let every individual decide for himself.' Unfortunately, on closer consideration, it turns out to be no more effective than the previous line of argument, and for essentially the same reason: it does not face up to the implications of its own observations about choice and autonomy. Certainly it is true, as has just been acknowledged, that most of us are not in any real sense free to be anything, or in a position to choose to be other than what we are. But in such senses of 'freedom', 'choice' and 'autonomy' none of us ever can be. It may be true that 'socially fostered' role-acceptance shouldn't count as truly autonomous acceptance, but given the premise of this argument, to the effect that all adults are more or less successfully socially directed into roles, truly autonomous acceptance must be an impossibility. Once again, one cannot have it both ways. If truly autonomous role selection is straightforwardly possible, who is Thomas Hill, or anyone else, to insist that women who claim they like their stereotypical role, and wouldn't choose to change it (undoubtedly the vast majority of women) are in a state of 'socially fostered ignorance'? If it is not straightforwardly possible, then it means little to insist on it. The truth of the matter is that, wherever one is disposed to place the emphasis, the individual child, brought up in an atmosphere where example, exhortation, books, television and peer group behaviour offer no clear stereotypes, but either uniformly present female and males roles as identical or indiscriminately mix them up, is no more free, autonomous or able to choose his role than the stereotypically brought up boy or girl. He will be, to exactly the same extent, whatever that extent may be, the product and the prisoner of his upbringing. To bring up children as we tend to do now is to foster the assumption that girls are of such and such a sort; it involves directing girls towards a particular kind of role. But to change the mix, in howsoever many ways, does nothing to put an end to the fostering of assumptions, or to lessen the degree of the direction. It does nothing for autonomy, so, if autonomy is what is required, we need to look elsewhere than at the tendency towards sex-role stereotyping.

Admittedly, with the sort of changes envisaged in the previous paragraph, the outcome would be different, and one might start from there, and try to mount an argument in favour of the difference of outcome. But that would not be a principled difference. Instead, we would be being presented with an argument to the effect that it is better to initiate all children into this stereotype, or some into this and some into that, rather than an argument against stereotyping as such, or in favour of autonomy. We would not have an end to stereotyping, but a different set of parameters within which stereotyping took place and a different set of roles. So, if the argument put forward is that children should grow up with their options absolutely open, the answer is that in realistic terms, cultural and social influence being what it is in relation to human beings, they cannot. If the argument is that there should be no rules against rejecting one's allotted role, if one can escape it, the answer is that there are none (though see below). The sort of change envisaged here (making Tommy and Jane indistinguishable in books, treating them identically in practice) would make it harder to predict what either of them will turn out to be like as adults, but that is an altogether different matter from giving them more freedom to choose what they will be like.

It is at this point that the third thesis, the variant on the second referred to above, comes into play, for it may be said that what is at issue is not people's freedom to choose, but partial treatment or unjust discrimination. It may be reasonable to bring up the Csar's children differently from a smallhold farmer's children, because they are presumed to be destined for very different kinds of life-style. Impartial treatment demands making no distinctions except on relevant grounds, and it might be conceded that being a future Csar is a relevant difference from the rest of us. But what we are faced with is differentiation between children simply on the grounds of their sex. Since there appears to be no link between femininity and domesticity, demureness and submissiveness, except arbitrary social convention, and, likewise, only an accidental link between masculinity and conventional male behaviour, to treat children differently on the grounds of a difference in sex, is surely comparable to treating blacks and whites differently on the grounds of their colour.

Since we must concede the point that most, if not all, of the differences we associate with male and female roles are indeed matters of convention, and might conceivably have been, or be in the future, otherwise, this is by far the most powerful of the three arguments for objecting to bringing up boys to be our idea of men, and girls to fulfil our idea of women. It does not seem to me, however, that it succeeds in delivering a knock-out blow and in establishing the moral wrongness of traditional practice; although, by forcing a more fully articulated explanation of the reasons supporting traditional practice out of us, it must destroy any complacent assumption that the traditional way is the only morally acceptable way.

It appears at first blush as if conventional sex-role stereotyping must be an instance of partial discrimination, because it seems as if we are saying purely and simply, 'the mere fact that a human being is male is sufficient reason for initiating him into such and such a role, and similarly, *mutatis mutandis*, in the case of females'. That certainly would be inadequate reasoning, just as, it may now be pointed out, to say that 'the mere fact that a human being is the Csar's son is sufficient reason for initiating him into such and such a role' would be inadequate. What has to be added in either case, and in any case where the relevance of reasons is not a matter of logical connection, is some kind of a setting, some kind of a context, that explains why this factor or that is taken as relevant. There may then be objection to the story we tell, the context we outline, or to some part of it, but that will take us on to a new and different debate. What makes the fact of being the Csar's son relevant is a context in which we take it for granted that the Csar's son will rule all Russia. Somebody might obviously enough take exception to their being a Csar of Russia at all, but in that case he would be well advised to argue about that, rather than the alleged impropriety of stereotyping the Csar's son. The parallel should be immediately obvious. There is a widespread belief in our society that it is expedient and pleasing for men and women to pursue broadly differing but complementary roles, and that given certain limited but more or less uncontentious physical differences, such as the capacity to bear children in women and relative physical strength in men, some features of either role are intuitively quite reasonable. Given that belief, the fact of being male is self-evidently a good and sufficient reason for bringing a child up in a different way from that of a female child. There is, in short, nothing wrong with sex-role stereotyping in upbringing, though the stage is now clear for those who want to argue that there is something wrong with our female and/or male roles, or with the idea of having distinct roles at all, or with the idea of having distinct roles for different sexes, rather than, for example, different ages or different colours. But any of these views would necessitate quite different kinds of argument. It does seem to me, for instance, that there is a much more plausible and much more straightforward line of objection, to the effect that in our society, at this time, the roles of men and women have acquired unbalanced value. This is to refer again to the premise, accepted in the previous chapter, that a woman's lot is less desirable and subordinated to the man's role. A parent might quite well argue 'the female role is less desirable for a human being, so I don't want to condemn any of my children, male or female, to that role.' Such a position is plainly coherent, and quite distinct from those we have considered, being not an objection to the principle of stereotyping nor to the criterion of sex being used, but to the actual content of current roles. Without going into details (for they are a matter for those whose prime interest is in changing patterns of behaviour, while mine is in arriving at coherent arguments for particular claims), it seems plain to me that there are certain respects in which women get a raw deal as compared with men. There are individual points on which they are systematically discriminated against. But that, I repeat, has nothing to do with the propriety of sex-role stereotyping as such.

I am not, incidentally, as those who read with care will have appreciated, arguing that we necessarily ought to engage in sex-role stereotyping, whether according to current stereotypes or any other, or that it is morally required. I have argued merely that it is in principle morally legitimate. It may well be added here, however, that any serious attempt to avoid it (and sex-role stereotyping, as opposed to stereotyping of some sort, could of course be avoided) would run into one particular practical difficulty that also raises a moral problem. The difficulty is that, whilst one might legislate against traditional roles being depicted for males and females in books and on television, one would still be faced with the influential factor of males and females at large (including parents themselves, teachers and peer group). The parents who, for whatever reason, do not want their child growing up into the conventional role for his or her sex, have an uphill struggle on their hands, for they must remember not only to censor the books read, but also to avoid displaying a consistently male or female pattern of behaviour themselves, and they must somehow seek to minimise or thwart the consistent pattern projected, in all likelihood, by friends and neighbours. The child is likely to have a hard time of it, and it might well, in all conscience, be kinder to work on society at large first, bearing in mind that what needs to be shown is that there are various things wrong with the roles themselves, or the idea of differing roles being useful. There simply isn't a case for saying that there is something inherently morally objectionable about women tending to take on a distinct role from that of men.

The way forward on this issue seems clear enough. We should cease to imagine that influencing children towards stereotypes is wrong, and we should cease to imagine that sex differences cannot serve as a good criterion for different treatment. We should cease to prate of nature or principle. Instead, we should consider the behaviour and activities we typically expect of men and women, and ask whether, on balance, we do gain from having different styles of life for males and females respectively; we should also ask what aspects of either style of life might be regarded as undesirable and either eliminated or evenly shared. Far more important than fretting about the phenomenon of sex-role stereotyping is to understand it, and consequently refrain from investing either stereotype with any particular sanctity. In turn that, most importantly, helps us to resist the temptation to judge people in terms of the stereotypes. It is not the stereotypes, so much as our attitudes to them, that need to be revolutionised. A true liberation would be achieved if we stopped assuming that every male will be, and ought to be, manly in the conventional sense, or that every female will be, and ought to be, feminine in the conventional sense. But with those important provisos, the argument suggests that it is not unreasonable, partial or unfairly discriminatory, to accept two complementary, broadly distinct, styles of life for men and women and to steer boys and girls towards either one. It is not inevitable that we should proceed in this way, and there may be better ways to proceed, but it is certainly not morally objectionable.

NOTES

1 Jean Jacques Rousseau, *Emile*.
2 Stephen Goldberg, *Male Dominance*.
3 Thomas E. Hill, 'Servility and Self-Respect'.

7 Reverse Discrimination

> All philosophers, who find
> Some favourite system to their mind
> In every point to make it fit,
> Will force all nature to submit.
>
> Jonathan Swift, *Cadenus and Vanessa*

I have already made reference to reverse discrimination, in the context of the suggestion that 'she' should be used to replace the generic use of 'he'.[1] But the notion of reverse discrimination in general now requires closer attention, for, muddled and resistable as I shall argue it is, it is frequently appealed to, particularly in relation to treatment of women, treatment of ethnic minorities and provision of schooling. The essential idea is that people who have hitherto been discomfited and disadvantaged in some way should now, in justice, be correspondingly advantaged. Extra state funds should go into depressed industrial areas, extra money should be allocated to schools in underprivileged areas, special consideration should be given to ethnic minorities hitherto discriminated against, women should get preferential treatment today, to offset the poor deal they received yesterday. The phrase used may vary —'reverse discrimination', 'affirmative action', 'positive discrimination'—but the idea remains the same. It is an idea that seems directly to challenge the classic view on the distribution of goods, introduced in Chapter 1, according to which everybody should be treated the same, except where relevant differences can be shown to exist between them. According to that view, other things being equal, blacks, whites, women, men, citizens of flourishing South or depressed North, should all be treated the same, whereas, according to the doctrine of positive discrimination, some of them should receive better treatment than others. Positive discrimination introduces the idea that what in itself might be agreed to be partial or preferential treatment (a better deal for blacks than whites, for instance) can be justified by reference to past sufferings, socially fostered inequalities, or, possibly, simply gross current disadvantage. (It may well be felt that each of these represents a distinct thesis, and that one or other may be more convincing than the rest. One of the problems with appeals to 'reverse discrimination' is that the exact thesis being promulgated is seldom clear. In what follows I hope to disengage the plausible from the unacceptable, although in any event I would be in favour of dropping such terms as 'reverse discrimination'.)

It is reference to the past that no doubt explains the choice of the word 'reverse', for the intention is to reverse rather than halt the pattern of the past, while the use of words like 'positive' and 'affirmative' draws attention to the militant tendency implicit in the principle: not only are disparities being redressed, they are being revenged. Thus, although there are no obviously relevant differences between you, a coal-miner's son, and Lord Fauntleroy, which entitle either one of you to more than the other, a simple example of reverse discrimination would arise if someone were to argue that you should be provided with better medical treatment than he, in view of the difficulties and disadvantages you have in general faced. Specific examples of proposals for reverse discrimination include the substitution of 'she' for 'he' already mentioned, the provision of extra resources for schools in poor areas, and a celebrated legal case involving the admission of black students to the University of California Medical School. These and other proposals will be examined below. But it is my broad contention that the notion of reverse discrimination, unless it is paired down, is incoherent, so that, while some of the particular practices that people have sought to justify by reference to this principle may in fact be justified, that is not because the principle is a good one. I shall also argue that some of the particular practices recommended, such as, most notably, the reserving of places in academic institutions for members of groups previously discriminated against, are certainly not justified.

There are three preliminary points to be made. The first is that whenever one considers questions of redistribution of goods (and, although ideal talk may imagine no prior arrangements, in reality all distribution involves redistribution), there is the quite unanswerable question facing one of where to start or how far back to go. We may agree that a world in which Lord Fauntleroy has everything and the coal-miner nothing is intolerable to our ethical sense. We want, let us suppose, equality of medical and educational provision for both. But in planning to provide that, do we start from the assumption that Lord Fauntleroy has enough in the way of resources to provide his own educational and medical services, or do we start from the assumption that both are individuals deserving equal benefit from the state? If we wish to argue (as is commonly done) that the coal-miner should have more spent on his schooling, because he lacks for more in his local environment, why stop there? Why not say that he should have a better environment, that he should have Lord Fauntleroy's castle? I raise this point neither as an argument for absolute sameness, nor as an argument to reduce demands for much greater equality to absurdity, but as something frankly perplexing. If one is not convinced that all should live their lives with more or less identical material wealth, but yet feels that vast variations in wealth cannot be morally tolerable, what kind of criteria does one look for, to decide where to draw the line? Because I do not believe that there is a straightforward answer to that question, I am naturally disinclined to accept arguments for particular instances of reverse discrimination which are based on no more than a general claim that thus the balance will be redressed. What balance?

The second point to be noted is that there is an ambiguity in the word 'fairness', for we may mean by 'fair' something very general such as 'honourable' or 'morally acceptable', or we may mean, far more specifically, 'impartial'. The difference often depends upon whether we are referring to the process or the end result: we talk about fair treatment, meaning impartial treatment, but a fair result or distribution, meaning a morally justified one. The two are certainly closely connected, but they are different and can be separated from each other. A man might conceivably get a fair trial (impartial) but nonetheless not in the end be fairly (justly) treated. Similarly, it is arguable that it would be fair, in the sense of impartial, to take all of the coal-miner's and Lord Fauntleroy's goods and split them evenly between them, but that that would not be a fair thing to do in the sense of morally correct.

Thirdly, we need to be able to distinguish between the question of what is impartial treatment within a group, and the question of what justifies inclusion within a group. Clearly slaves were discriminated against in classical Athens, if they are regarded as part of the social group. Equally clearly animals are discriminated against today, if they are regarded as part of the social group. Conversely, one could deny that young children are discriminated against, by claiming that they do not count as full members of the body politic. Arguments about partial and impartial treatment presuppose that we are referring to people who belong to a common group. I may have been discriminated against by my football team, but you, not being a member of it, cannot have been, even if, by some freak of circumstance, they do to you what they do to me. Very often past injustice arises out of unwarranted exclusion from a group, rather than from any partial treatment. In that case one's immediate response is surely to feel that the excluded member(s) should be accepted, and treated impartially along with everyone else. The case is certainly different from that of the member(s) of a group who, while being acknowledged as such, have been systematically discriminated against.

In a typical case of reverse discrimination (if such there can be, given what has already been said), an identifiable group of persons are agreed to have been discriminated against in the past, in consequence of which they are now to be given extra advantage. Such a line of argument has specifically been used more than once with reference to the employment of blacks and the treatment of women. There are evidently two important questions to be asked here: what, if anything, justifies this procedure? and why call it 'reverse discrimination', if it is justified, rather than simply morally justifiable? A very common view is that such redressing of balance is justified as compensation. We generally accept the principle whereby, if I damage your car, I pay you a certain amount as compensation for the damage; likewise, though the assessment may be harder to make, if a man's character is publicly defamed, he may seek damages by way of compensation. As far as it goes this would be fine. If we discover that an individual has been discriminated against by the water board and made to pay proportionately more than anyone else, we expect him to be compensated (but then we don't need to introduce a phrase like 'reverse discrimination'). But this compensatory argument seldom applies, for in most cases that excite attention (blacks, women, schooling) we are not compensating those who might be said to deserve it. If the idea is to compensate for centuries of racial injustice, then what is owed is owed to those who have long since suffered and died. Compensation, by definition, has to go to the victim. So this argument could only apply in particular cases, as if a particular woman were to be compensated for having been discriminated against all her life. But then the question arises of who should do the compensating. We, who have never met her, may choose to befriend her, but we cannot conceivably compensate her. Only those who did the initial damage can do that. Particular individuals could argue that various state provisions have discriminated against them, and that therefore the state owes them compensation. But now we encounter the crucial hurdle: why in such a case should extravagant treatment by the state be thought necessary to compensate for prior mean treatment? It could just as well be characterised as going from one unjustifiable extreme to another. In other words, granted that discrimination against blacks, women or any other groups or individuals should be halted, why is it suggested that preferential treatment should replace it? Excessive love does not compensate for excessive cruelty.

What is required in such cases, one would have thought, is not further discrimination (whether called 'positive', 'reverse' or anything else), but sorting out and removing the initial injustice. If we not only have to stop discriminating against women, but also have to make up for past discrimination, where will it end? In thirty years' time, will we have to make up to men for the discrimination they suffer while we provide so-called compensatory advantage to women? If women have been discriminated against in previous centuries, that is too bad. If women are being discriminated against now, that is bad. It should be stopped. But to discriminate against men (which is what giving women 'extra advantage' and what the phrase 'reverse discrimination' must mean) is not, and cannot be, any more fair. If that is reverse discrimination, then reverse discrimination, like any other discrimination in this sense of the word, is bad.

But, it may be said, is it not a good thing to give those who have been previously disadvantaged the thick end of the stick for a bit, at least until people generally wake up to the injustice that has been done, and in order to hasten that waking up. This view is suggested by both Singer and Richards.[2] They do not mention atonement, but it is difficult to avoid the feeling that that too is part of their thinking on the matter. It is as if they are saying: 'Blacks have been shockingly treated. By whom? By the likes of us. Let us abase ourselves, as well as put things right. Let us atone for the wrong we have collectively done.' This line of thought may be endearing, and it may actually be demanded by some particular religious or ethical positions, but it certainly should not be allowed to confuse the issue yet further. If we ought to be penitent and show outward signs of penitence, that is strictly our problem. Atonement is not owed to victims, but to one's God. What is owed to victims is rectification of wrongs. So why, if it cannot be a matter of atonement or assuaging guilt feelings, do some suggest that we hand the advantage over to the erstwhile victims (needless to say, for an unspecified period)? I can only make sense of Richards' general claim that they are 'owed an improvement of position until society is fair to them',[3] by distinguishing between *calling* for reverse discrimination and practising it. One may concede that, as a tactic, demanding extra advantage in place of extra disadvantage has all the hallmarks of the classic opening bargaining gambit. The general public may sit up and take notice of extravagant demands, and finally settle for simple justice. But to suggest 'an improvement of position until society is fair to them' as a practice doesn't even make sense. Society *is* being fair to them once the improvement is made from discrimination to lack of discrimination, so on what grounds can one justify a further 'improvement' towards discrimination against the previous exploiters? Singer's proposal to use 'she' until it seems as natural as the use of 'he', at which point we can all do what we like, is manifestly a tactical exercise, and as such might be justified.[4] If we agreed that using 'he' generically was wrong, we might accept that a policy of using the equally wrong 'she' would pay off in time, and we might further concede that in an imperfect world it is sometimes justifiable to do things that are wrong in themselves. But it is imperative that we resist the temptation to pretend that using 'she' generically is fair, in the sense of impartial, which it certainly is not. Nor in calling it 'positive discrimination' should we blind ourselves to the fact that (given the premise about the unacceptability of the generic use of 'he') it is, straightforwardly, discrimination, in the sense of preferential treatment on no relevant grounds. Similarly, it may be argued that in various respects both blacks and women have been badly treated, and should now be properly treated. It may further be argued that merely saying this isn't going to make any practical difference, and that therefore, as a tactic, we should start talking of, and practising, discrimination in their favour, in order to shock people into conceding the main point (proper treatment) more quickly. I am not convinced that such tactics are justified in the particular case of blacks and women, and certainly they are not generally justified, being no more than the deployment of a new wrong to end an old wrong. But the main point is that such a tactic, even when it is justified, remains a case of straightforward discrimination. It involves differential treatment on irrelevant grounds. It may be fair in the sense of morally justifiable, but it is not fair in the sense of impartial.

There are at least some cases where it is clearly justifiable to treat different people differently; the question is whether there is any reason to label such cases examples of discrimination (whether positive or otherwise). The rich are generally required to pay more tax than the poor, and most of us think that justified. But why should we call the imposition of a higher rate of tax on the rich affirmative discrimination? It isn't discrimination at all, because it is differential treatment based on relevant reasons. Why, therefore, should we not likewise say (if this is our belief) that schools in economically depressed areas should be provided with more resources because they are in such areas, rather than suggest that we are discriminating in their favour for good reason? Precisely because there is good reason, we are not discriminating! Here, of course, I am only arguing about what we call it, but it does seem important to resist the introduction of new jargon, such as 'reverse discrimination', unless it pinpoints something that really is new. In the first place there is something to be said for calling a spade a spade, so that everyone knows exactly what we are talking about. In the second place, refusing to call the tax and schooling examples cases of reverse discrimination allows us to distinguish between them and the cases of blacks and women. And they are quite distinct. Devoting extra attention or resources to those who have less in order to bring them to the same level as others is decidedly different from giving more to those who have hitherto had a worse time of it.

One of the most famous cases of reverse discrimination involved a white American named Allan Bakke.[5] In 1973, and then again in 1974, he failed to gain admission to the University of California Medical School, despite being better qualified than a number of black students who were admitted. The reason for this was quite clear and straightforward. By deliberate policy the University reserved sixteen out of every hundred places for members of minority groups such as Blacks and American Indians. These special admissions were not themselves indiscriminately made. Candidates had to be assessed in a similar way to that in which regular candidates were assessed, and they had to be judged to be generally competent. But the fact remains that a better qualified white might lose his place to a black. And that is just what happened to Bakke, whereupon he sued the University, and in 1978 was adjudged by the United States Supreme Court to have been unfairly discriminated against (by a vote of five to four. Nothing comes easy).

As far as the principle of impartiality goes, there can be no doubt that the majority decision was correct. Bakke was the recipient of differential treatment simply on the grounds that he was white, and that is not impartial. What would be rather different would be for someone to argue that it is not fair, in the more general sense of honourable or right, that blacks, having been systematically disadvantaged in terms of housing, local environment and education, should now be told that opportunities to enter medical school are equally open to them. But that line of argument would need to be assessed individually in each case (was this particular black the victim of a poor environment?), would apply no less to individual whites (did anyone check Bakke's background?), is not self-evidently convincing, and, above all, need not be called 'reverse discrimination', since, insofar as it is convincing, it has nothing to do with discrimination. There may, in other words, sometimes conceivably be a case for giving certain individuals special advantages, perhaps because it is in society's long-term interest that we should do so, or to compensate for specific disadvantages that society feels responsible for. But it would be far less confused and confusing to see such cases as a particular, perhaps rare, kind of straightforward impartiality, involving different treatment for good reasons. In this respect, allocating extra resources to particular disadvantaged people, whether it finally seems a sensible policy or not, is no different in principle to allocating extra resources to the physically handicapped. In that case nobody sees fit to talk of positive discrimination. After all, if extra resources are felt to be justified for handicapped children, that is to say that their handicaps are felt to constitute a good reason for giving them special treatment. In which case it is not partial, but impartial, so to proceed. To justify it as 'reverse discrimination' is extremely misleading, both in that the phrase suggests something inherently incoherent, and in that it suggests that a principle of special treatment for disadvantaged groups has been established. But such a general principle has not been established, nor is it obvious that it should be.

Clearly, to return to the Bakke case, the argument that all social groups ought to be represented in academic institutions, or anywhere else, in proportion to their size in the community at large is absurd. The fact that there are, let us say, 55 per cent of females and 10 per cent of Asians in a society does not warrant the conclusion that the police force ought to have 55 per cent females and 10 per cent Asians in its composition. There is no *a priori* figure that represents the proper number of female or Asian doctors, dustbinmen or anything else there should be, even when it is clear that such groups are less well represented in a job than the qualifications they have might qualify them for. The groups in question might be very good at some things and very bad at others, and consequently over-represented in some areas and under-represented in others. There might be extraneous reasons for wanting to change this state of affairs, as one might plausibly argue that it would be in society's interest if more coloured people would join the police force, but there is nothing intrinsically unfair or wrong about it. Again, particular groups may have no interest in particular types of job or, just as there may be extraneous reasons for wishing a particular group was better represented at something, so there may be extraneous reasons for not wanting them represented at something.

Not only is it not the case that a certain group ought to have a particular share of any specific role or job, in direct proportion to and just because of its size, but it is also unacceptable, when jobs are in question, that past disadvantage should be brought into the reckoning. When we appoint doctors, we want to appoint good doctors, and if that were by chance to mean an absence from the medical profession of members of any particular group, that's just too bad. (But it should be noted that the Bakke case drew attention to a situation where worse qualified, rather than unqualified, people were being accepted.) When we accept people for courses, we want competent students. It is of course possible to judge that one candidate, though less well qualified at the point of entry (for job or course of instruction), will make more of the course or job, and should therefore be taken on in preference to a currently better qualified candidate. But that, like so many other justified instances of differential treatment, would have to be argued in each instance. It might have been acceptable to reject well qualified Bakke in favour of less well qualified X (of whatever colour), on the grounds that, given X's particular disadvantaged background, we have reason to think he has done very well to qualify as well as he has, so much so that we suspect he will profit more from medical school than Bakke would. But that is not what happened.

Peter Singer, in reference to this same case, has tried to argue, on slightly different grounds, that it is justifiable to award a job or an academic place to someone whom we acknowledge to be less well equipped for it than someone we reject, simply because that less qualified person is a member of a disadvantaged group.[6] This of course reintroduces some of the points I have already argued against. But the form of his argument is paralleled by the form of the argument of some feminists and some educationalists, and it therefore deserves independent attention.

Singer argues that universities are places that normally accept and reject candidates in relation to their intelligence. Leaving aside the separate problems involved in trying to assess intelligence, the general idea is that those of the highest intelligence should get places. But that is not because people of high intelligence are thought to be more deserving than others. University places are not to be seen as prizes for desert. Rather the allocation of places is made on these grounds because higher intelligence is relevant to the business of pursuing a university course; it is an appropriate qualification for the goal of academic success.

Up to this point, Singer's line of argument seems to me entirely correct. Universities aim at academic quality, and they select people with regard to their bent in that direction, which, broadly speaking, means their intelligence. But Singer's next and final point is that it follows that, if one changes the goal of universities from being that of academic success, then necessarily one changes the criteria of success or qualification as well. Thus, if the university were to adopt the new goal of contributing to social equality, or of ensuring greater minority representation in academic life, or of achieving a better social mix, it would follow that it might very reasonably reserve places for people who would not have been entitled to university places by the old criteria, associated with the original goal. (In exactly the same way, some feminists argue for giving extra places to women in particular professions, simply in order to change the face and nature of the profession. One might demand a large number of women doctors in order to bring some kind of feminine touch to medicine, and thereby change it in various ways. Obviously this particular argument is not open to those feminists who are concerned to play down the notion of male/female difference.)

This final element in Singer's argument is, in itself, no less true than the preceding steps, but it is nonetheless exceedingly curious as an argument. It is certainly the case that, if you change your objectives, you thereby change your criteria for selection. (This comes precious close to saying that using blackness of skin as a criterion to deny Bakke a place was alright, because the objective of the university in question was to do something like that.) What is not clear at all is where the argument for suddenly changing the objectives of a university (or anything else) is supposed to be. Naturally, if it were agreed that universities should be places to encourage social mix between different groups, if it were agreed that the main requirement within the medical profession was the feminine touch, or if it were agreed that the legal profession should have a 50 per cent intake of people of working class background, it would follow that there would be good reasons for bringing more blacks (and others), more women, and more working class people into these respective areas. But, as things are, universities are not created as centres of social mix and no reason has been given for assuming that they should be, that the feminine touch should be a priority in medicine, or that the working class touch should be a priority in the legal profession. One must, therefore, understand a line of argument such as Singer's as being an indication that its author thinks something is more important than, and should replace, the current notion of what a university is for. It certainly does not establish that such is the case.

It remains undeniable that certain identifiable groups have been badly treated and unfairly discriminated against in the past. But, as to the fact that blacks and women have suffered unjustly in the historical past, I can see no more reason why that should affect our current treatment of them than the fact that ancestors of mine were beheaded, and otherwise maltreated and defrauded by the then reigning monarchs, entitles me and my family to any special treatment. As to the quite different point that adult blacks and adult females of any colour may themselves have suffered unjustly in their youth, through such factors as inferior housing and schooling, I still cannot see either in principle why this should entitle them to preferential treatment now, or in practice how one could determine who deserved it by this criterion. Regrettably, the only legitimate response to such deprivation is to get rid of it, as from now.

George Sher, however, has specifically argued against this view.[7] Concentrating on the issue of employment, he argues that those who have suffered, in the sense of being deprived by circumstance or society of certain advantages that would have affected their ability to compete for employment, such as housing and education, ought to be compensated as a matter of desert and fairness. It is fair to compensate individuals 'for lost ability to compete on equal terms'.[8] The reason he offers for thinking it fair to thus advantage such people over the more able is, at any rate, ingenious. It is that it is the more able who would benefit disproportionately, if such were not done. 'Thus it is only because they stand to *gain* the most from the relevant effects of the original discrimination, that the bypassed individuals stand to *lose* the most from reverse discrimination.'[9] But, thought-provoking as this line of reasoning may be, it is surely not persuasive. Indeed it seems almost to amount to saying that, if somebody like Bakke, with a decent upbringing, then loses out, and cannot get a university place, or a job, as a result of a deliberate policy to exclude him in favour of a less qualified candidate, he should not complain; because what he would have gained would have been more than he deserved. Once again we seem to be faced with a claim to the effect that a second wrong is justified by the first.

Admittedly Sher is careful and cautious in mounting his argument. He appreciates that the immediate cause of the loss of an individual's competitive edge may vary from case to case. Some persons may begin adult life in a weak position as a result of poor education, others may have had difficulties at home, others may have made a calculated decision not to take advantage of school, others may have had personality defects of one sort or another. One might feel differently about the idea of compensating the deprived, the wastrel and the no-hoper, respectively. Sher is also careful to point out (and thereby lends support to the argument above) that his argument, even if sound, would not justify preferential treatment for groups as such, because whatever is said about the past treatment of groups such as blacks or women, it is not necessarily true that each individual member of such a group has suffered the experience in question. Since the argument is supposed to be that he who has had disadvantage heretofore now deserves compensation, it must be applied individually, if at all.

But, despite such careful qualification and moderation on Sher's part, it is difficult to be impressed by his argument. What he has done in effect is replace the idea of *A* being disadvantaged with stress on the idea of *B* being advantaged. This certainly makes it easier to accept psychologically that what *B* complains he is being done out of by preferential compensatory treatment for *A* is not necessarily what he deserves. But that does not alter the fact that the proposal now involves treating *B* worse, simply because at some past stage (and through no fault of *B*) *A* had a raw deal. That may make some kind of pragmatic sense when dealing with children, for example, but it does not approximate to an acceptable principle of fairness in any sense. What Sher ends up effectively saying is, 'If you end up less qualified than other people to take a job, and social factors can be pinpointed as explanatory in this, you are entitled to special treatment, insofar as it is not your own fault that the social factors in question overcame you.' This would be quite unworkable in practice, for at what point do we decide the 'end' has come, who determines whether social factors were responsible and, above all, how do we distinguish between those who 'allowed' social factors to overcome them and those who were truly victims of circumstance? And in any case, as a principle, this is quite unacceptable, at least in respect of jobs or roles. (It is conceivable that the type of argument here employed might be used to justify flat equality of material reward, but that is a rather different matter to be discussed below).[10] Granted that I may end up as a doctor, having had every advantage along the way, while you, having had every disadvantage, end up unqualified to be a doctor. One may object to such a social situation and one may want it altered. One may concede Sher's point that this system has given me advantages at the end of the day which are gained at your expense. The fact remains that we neither see the desirability of accepting you, unqualified, as a doctor in preference to me, nor see anything just or fair in differentiating to my disadvantage against me on the extraordinary grounds that you, for whatever reason, have proved relatively unsuccessful along the line leading to this particular form of employment. (Incidentally, it is very unclear to me why anybody should be fool enough to try and provide advantageous homes and schooling for their children in a world in which advantageous compensation was offered to those least benefited by them.)

What is fundamentally tricky about Sher's approach, and many other arguments in favour of programmes of reverse discrimination, is that he alights arbitrarily on some point in life, such as finding employment, and decides to make that the moment to wipe out the sins of the past. But why start compensating A at B's expense at that point rather than when he first goes to school, when he goes to secondary school or when he retires? Suppose I were to point out that though I had an advantaged childhood and schooling, things have gone badly for me as an adult. Would that entitle me to preferential treatment now, at the expense of those who have been doing well (perhaps as a result of a preferential send off into adult life at my expense, following a disadvantaged upbringing)? To suggest is to reduce to absurdity. If there are particular unfair differences between people when it comes to upbringing, as without doubt there are, argument needs to be centred on eradicating those unfairnesses at source. Arguments for reverse discrimination tend to confuse the claim that some people never had a real chance in life (or by extension that some talented people never had the chance they deserved or needed for their talent) with the faintly ridiculous claim that those who have proven, for whatever reason, less able, should be given a compensatory advantage. It is an attempt to make all entrants in the race win. But that is the one obviously absurd line to take. Either we race or we do not. One can see a case for a competitive society (involving a race), and one can see a case for a non-competitive society, in which we merely run alongside each other. But there is no case at all for a race without winners, competitive situations in which qualifications are ignored. Furthermore, even if we choose not to compete, we cannot afford to ignore specialist qualifications completely. Even if we are not racing, we need to send faster people to carry urgent messages, whether we choose to reward them for it or not.

In conclusion, we should note the importance of drawing a clear line between allocating rewards and deploying persons (as the race/running example suggests). When it comes to appointing people to courses, jobs, or places, what is relevant to what they should be accepted to do are their qualifications or talents. So-called 'reverse discrimination' here would be straightforward discrimination, in the sense of differential treatment on irrelevant grounds. It is therefore in itself obnoxious, although the ultra-imaginative may be able to conceive of social situations in which such a particular injustice might be accepted as justifiable for extraneous long-term reasons, rather as giving in to high-jackers might conceivably be justified on occasion. When it comes to allocating material goods, good reason for giving more to some individuals may sometimes be found in past disadvantages they have experienced. But this, though it might require explaining, does not require any special label, being straightforward impartial treatment (differentiation on good grounds).

NOTES

1 See above Chapter 6.
2 Peter Singer, *Practical Ethics*; Janet Radcliffe Richards, *The Sceptical Feminist*.
3 Janet Radcliffe Richards, *ibid*.
4 Peter Singer, *op. cit.*
5 See University of California vs Bakke (1978).
6 Peter Singer, *op. cit.*
7 George Sher, 'Justifying Reverse Discrimination in Employment', *Philosophy and Public Affairs*, 4, No. 2 (Winter 1975).
8 *Ibid*.
9 *Ibid*.
10 See Chapter 9.

8 Abortion

> Organic life, we are told, has developed gradually from the protozoon to the philosopher, and this development, we are assured, is indubitably an advance. Unfortunately it is the philosopher, not the protozoon, who gives us this assurance.
>
> Bertrand Russell, *Mysticism and Logic*

A miscarriage involves the premature birth of a foetus which dies. An abortion, at the level of a dictionary definition, is the wilful causing of a miscarriage. Behind that seemingly simple definition, however, lies a host of fascinating questions. At what point does the foetus become a person? Can killing a person be justified? Can killing things other than persons be justified? Does killing need justifying? There is the question of whether the mother-to-be has any obligations or duties to others, including not only the foetus, but also her other children and the father and/or husband. There is the question of whether she does not have certain rights herself, to use her body as she will, perhaps, or, more generally, to do as she chooses. That may give rise to more general questions about who should make decisions about a matter such as abortion. Is it for the state to legislate, the doctor to decree, or the individual to follow his conscience? In a clash between claims of mother and child, or wishes of mother and doctor, who is to decide? There are also a number of complicated practical questions, which, though in principle empirical, may not be readily resolvable by empirical enquiry: what psychological effects will follow from having or not having an abortion for the mother, the foetus, other children, the husband? What physical consequences will there be, and what other material effects? Can the parents, for example, afford to bring up another child? What might the general effects of accepting the practice of abortion be? Might we become more brutalised, less concerned about the value of life in general? Might acceptance of the practice contribute to an increase of casual encounters and heedless sex? Would it matter, if it did? There are also questions to be asked about foetal research that are inextricably bound up with some of our answers to those other questions. At the present time foetal research *ex utero*, which is to say research on aborted foetuses (including, it should be said, some unintentionally aborted) is widespread, and by all accounts most useful in terms of what we learn from it. Is that a factor to be weighed with all the others when considering whether abortion may be justified? Would we regard such research as justified automatically, if abortion is shown to be justified, and, conversely, as discredited, if abortion is discredited? Or might we agree that, although deliberate abortion is morally wrong, foetal research on accidentally aborted foetuses is legitimate? Is an aborted foetus comparable to an adult being, to a piece of tissue (like a removed appendix), to an animal, or does it, as Wasserstrom has tried to argue, have a unique status close to, but distinguishable from, one of the adult human?[1] I shall only make passing reference to the particular problems of foetal research, but it is worth remembering that it too requires thought, and that some of what is said about abortion may have a direct bearing on this further question.

There are two preliminary points to be made in relation to this issue. Firstly, we are unlikely to arrive at a definitive answer to the question of whether abortion is morally acceptable. As in the case of most significant questions concerning human conduct, what ought to be done depends upon a complex interplay of empirical, conceptual and evaluative questions, and, regardless of the logic of the matter, it is in practice beyond human ingenuity to solve all of them clearly and unequivocally. What we can do is attempt to organise our thoughts, in service to reason, so as to arrive at a rationally coherent and defensible position. This applies to most of the problems discussed in this book, and is part of the reason why dogmatists are so suspect, but there is particular point in drawing attention to the fact here because of the second initial point I want to make, which has to do with talk of 'rights'.

Discussion of abortion is more than usually hedged about with talk of rights. Proponents of the various possible viewpoints are all liable to resort to a position that consists in asserting some right as self-evident. A mother has a right to do as she will with her body. The foetus has a right to life. We have no right to take life. This kind of talk, I maintain, is unproductive, and should not be engaged in during the course of discussion on the matter. But in objecting to such talk I do not wish to be taken to be saying that nobody can have any moral rights. No more should Jeremy Bentham be thought to have been unconcerned to accord people moral rights when he referred to the idea of the existence of certain natural rights as 'nonsense on stilts'.[2] What Bentham was concerned to oppose, as I am, was the tactic of appealing to some alleged right as a step in the argument. The objection is to throwing the assertion 'there is a natural right to X' into a discussion about whether there are grounds for recognising a moral right to X. To assert that it is natural is just another way of asserting that it does obtain, which is what is at issue. When we are discussing the morality of abortion, it may be said that what we are considering is what moral rights there are in this domain, what rights should be recognised or accorded to what people. In a sense therefore we all care about rights. What must be ruled out is the tactic of introducing as part of the argument a claim such as that the foetus has a natural right to life, for that is to beg something of the question at issue. We know that from some viewpoints the foetus does have a right to life, and from that viewpoint it may be seen as a natural or inevitable right. But we know also that different viewpoints deny that that right exists, and some would substitute rival claims to rights. Our task is precisely to challenge and critically consider all and any such viewpoints, considering what, if anything, might support and justify them. To merely assert a particular right (very often in the name of some doctrine) is indeed 'nonsense walking on stilts', in the context of an attempt to substantiate rather than assert a position. It is worth adding, as R. M. Hare has pointed out, that such appeals to 'rights', besides begging the question, are very often ill thought out and ambiguous.[3] How many of those who 'feel' that the mother has a right to do as she will with her body, for instance, have paused to consider whether distinctions should be drawn between deducing that she has a right to terminate a pregnancy, deducing that we are wrong to prevent her doing so, and deducing that we ought actually to assist her? But the more immediately important point remains that our concern is to work out what seems morally acceptable here, and to do that is to arrive at a view of what our various rights may be. To assert some right is to short-circuit the discussion, not resolve it.

A primary question must be 'can killing ever be justified?', for, whatever the exact status of the foetus, it seems certain that destroying it or removing it from the womb amounts to killing it. If killing is never justified, then abortion must be wrong. But, clearly, killing, though for some of us it may always be morally regrettable and in itself unwelcome, can be justified on occasion, if only because it may prove the lesser of two evils. Most readers will, perhaps, all too readily and unreflectively accept that killing may be justified in respect of other species. Many will also accept, however ruefully, that killing other human beings may sometimes be justified. It is true that some people believe that life is absolutely sacrosanct, just as it is true that some people believe that the world is flat. But very few of us believe either, and there is no good reason why we should. For, consider: if I encounter a maniac about to shoot my family, and the circumstances are such that it is a question of my shooting him or they being shot by him, then surely I am justified in shooting him. Note that all that is required here is one example that we can agree involves justified killing. (We don't even have to agree on an example, provided that we agree some example may be found.) I am not making the elementary mistake of presuming that, if people think that killing can be justified, then it follows that it can be, nor, at the other extreme, am I trying to establish that killing is positively desirable. I am merely concerned to point out that a situation is conceivable in which it would be justifiable to kill another human being, and that is enough to show that to say simply that it involves the taking of human life cannot be sufficient to condemn abortion. (By the same token, neither euthanasia nor capital punishment can be rejected on that ground alone.) We have to show why this particular type of killing can never be justified, or else concede that on occasion it may be. Many people would argue that, deplorable as it may be, in and of itself, killing may be quite often justified: in time of war, for example, to save one's life, to remove a sadistic torturer, in the case of suicide, or to save the lives of many others. But, paradoxical as it may seem, to multiply such instances, even if they carry conviction, does not strengthen the point, which is simply that, as any one example serves to show, killing can be justified. We therefore have to consider what kind of thing may justify it, and whether abortion may fit the case.

Our *prima facie* objection to killing presumably arises out of recognising others as centres of consciousness like ourselves, who enjoy living (or at any rate would not choose to stop living). Whether or not there is an inescapable moral sanctity about life, or human life in particular, it is evident that we as individuals, for all our complaints, want to go on living. On what conceivable grounds may I reasonably treat others as I would hate and fear to be treated? In general terms, though it is easy to point to differences between people (such as physical strength) which justify different treatment in particular respects (such as climbing mountains), it is impossible to establish differences that constitute good grounds for ignoring completely the interests of certain people. We, as individuals, do not want to be killed, and consequently, if we are going to assert that we ought not to be, we must concede that other people should not be either (whatever we may privately think of them). However, from time to time some individuals do things that do seem to constitute good reasons for treating them differently. They put themselves beyond the pale, as we say, or they forfeit the presumption that they too have a right to life. It is here that the examples come in, for it is because torturing people, or indeed killing them in most cases, does seem to mark a man off morally from others, that we can legitimately consider treating the torturer differently, even in respect of something so fundamental as life. In fact we can surely go further and, tentatively at least, formulate some general account of what may justify killing, producing some rule or set of rules that would explain the factors common to such instances of justified killing as we cite. That formula, as far as most of us are concerned, will be that killing may be justified, if, and only if, it is the only means of preventing further killing or otherwise unavoidable suffering of great magnitude. If it is suggested that such a formula is vague and impractical, the response may be that that is because moral dilemmas in life are hard to resolve, and not because the formula is inadequate. But as a matter of fact the formula is not vague, but general, and it is at a high level of generality because that is the nature of basic principles. Any impracticality arises not from the formula itself, but from the difficulty of determining questions such as what the consequences of actions may be, and how great a degree of suffering is insupportable. The point being made is that, while it may be agreed that in itself killing is bad, we would accept a defence that convinced us that a particular killing had taken place to prevent further killing or intolerable suffering.

At this juncture we must raise the question of the status of the foetus, for many people would agree with Roger Wertheimer that whether an embryo constitutes a form of human life is crucial to determining the rights and wrongs of abortion.[4] Actually, it is not necessarily so. Since the taking of human life can be justified, establishing that the embryo counts as human does not establish that abortion is necessarily unjustifiable. If it were to be established, on the other hand, that the embryo is not human, it would not automatically follow that we can kill it, if we feel like it, since we have so far merely *assumed* that it is morally acceptable to treat non-human life as we see fit (and in a subsequent chapter I shall explicitly argue against that view).[5] Nonetheless, we do need to be clear about this question of the status of the foetus, for we need to have some understanding of what it is we are talking about, whether or not that understanding resolves the central issue.

This is a difficult as well as interesting question, and it is important to have a thorough grasp of its nature at the outset. An embryo is obviously different from a young child in various ways; far more different than a child, or even in some respects an animal, is from an adult. The question of whether it counts as a person is, therefore, a question about what a person as such is. It is a conceptual question rather than an empirical question. I, we presumably would agree, am a person. I have, amongst other things, a peculiar sense of humour, a certain nervous system, a capacity to experience pain, two ears, a liking for the novelist George Gissing, a pot belly, a certain kind of heart, and eight pints of blood in me. The question is which of these and all my other features and characteristics are necessary and sufficient to make me a person. To put the same question another way: are such differences as may be cited between me and the embryo relevant differences so far as being a person goes? It must also be recognised that 'person' here is being used in a sense that includes reference to moral claims. It is the moral sense of personhood, rather than the purely physiological, that must interest us in the context of this discussion. For, if 'person' were given a purely biological definition, then establishing that something was a person would not necessarily count for anything. What is being asked is whether embryos are persons in the moral sense, and therefore we need to establish a moral sense of personhood. So it will readily be seen that the medical stages of early human growth, that have been clearly distinguished and defined, do not help us very much. The ovum, the zygote, the conceptus, the embryo, the foetus and the infant are all carefully discriminated in medical science. The ovum is the female egg, the zygote is the fertilised egg. Once the zygote moves through the fallopian tube into the uterus it is known as the conceptus. Once embedded in the uterus it is called the embryo, until about the eighth week following conception, at which point it is possible to monitor brain waves, when it is called a foetus. It is not our business to dispute these distinctions, but to ask whether they are in each or any case morally relevant differences or differences that make or deny personhood.

It has been said that the problem we face is where to draw the line. An ovum, it may be felt, is evidently not a person, and it makes little sense to think of moral obligation to it. A grandparent, on the other hand, is a handy enough instance of a venerable person, fully deserving of moral consideration. Yet there is a continuous line of development through from ovum to Grandad. Where to draw the line? That lines can be drawn is not in dispute. One can say that one doesn't have the beginnings of personhood until the egg is fertilised, one can say that the person begins when the zygote acquires recognisable human features, one can say that the significant point is when viability is reached (when, that is to say, the foetus could survive independently of the mother), or one could say that the crucial moment is that of quickening (which is to say when there is recognisable physical movement). But none of those seems obviously morally significant. To be sure, a zygote is less developed than a foetus, but does a foetus have something that it takes to mark out morally significant personhood from morally insignificant matter? It is important when faced with such a question to bear in mind possible implications of one's answer. For example, if one were to argue that personhood begins once the foetus has recognisably human shape, one commits oneself to denying moral personhood to physically maimed or badly disfigured adults, such as the so-called Elephant Man. The moment of quickening, though taken by some as the morally significant moment, seems one of the least plausible suggestions, if one dwells upon it, even as a criterion of the start of recognisable human life in the non-moral sense, still more so as a criterion of moral worth beginning. It should also be remarked that, though the moment of birth makes the most dramatically obvious turning point, it actually marks a very insignificant change in physiological or biological terms, so that settling on this as the beginning of personhood would be, on the face of it, strange. A premature baby might be in all ways less developed than an unborn foetus, so this criterion amounts to saying that what matters as far as moral concern goes is whether one is inside or outside the womb.

Viability perhaps appears to make more sense *a priori*. Before the moment of viability, to abort the foetus would amount to removing support necessary to sustain life. After that moment, to abort the foetus would be to fail to assist the foetus to live. Singer has objected to making viability the significant factor on the grounds that the stage at which the foetus can survive outside the body varies with technological know-how and, therefore, with time and place.[6] The point is valid, but it does not seem a strong objection. Clearly, circumstances in which people, of whatever age, can survive do change, and that makes a legitimate variable in what it is acceptable to do to them: it is morally acceptable to leave old people outside in warm climates, and morally reprehensible to do so in sub-arctic temperatures, perhaps. In the same way, on this view, it might be morally acceptable to abort after a certain period in some conditions, but not in others. But that does not represent an objection to the view of any consequence. On the other hand, viability seems no more convincing as a criterion of moral personhood than any of the other suggestions. Why should a minimal degree of self-sufficiency (for it is not as if the viable foetus can, Lazarus-like, take up its bed and fend for itself) mark out personhood? (And note again, if it did, the consequences for our moral responsibility to the elderly and infirm, or at least the helplessly handicapped.)

It has been argued by Wertheimer that the question of whether the embryo counts as human life is unanswerable, since both parties to the dispute are using an inverted form of the same argument.[7] The liberal who wants to argue that abortion is at least sometimes permissible, asks what the zygote has got that is of any particular value or significance. The conservative in effect replies, 'Nothing, but it is a human being.' That is scarcely convincing as an argument, one might feel. But, if the boot is put on the other foot, we find the conservative asking the liberal what a foetus lacks that is of such value and significance in the infant. 'Nothing', the liberal replies, 'but a foetus is not a human being.' There may be some truth in Wertheimer's contention that argument about the status of the embryo takes that form, but I am far from convinced that it has to. Certainly, argument of this type, sometimes labelled the slippery slope argument, which consists of concluding from the difficulty of drawing a line at any particular point that no line can be drawn anywhere, is counter-intuitive. It is true that baldness is a fuzzy concept, inasmuch as nobody quite knows where the boundaries are, and it would be arbitrary to assert that a maximum of X hairs was allowable for a head to count as bald, but it does not follow from that that a hairy man and a bald man are the same thing. Likewise, 30 k.p.h. is an arbitrary speed limit in the sense that no good reason can be given for choosing precisely that figure, but it does not follow that it is idle to distinguish between safe and dangerous speeds. In the same way, while it must be conceded that the line from ovum to old man is direct, and that at various given points it is impossible to see any noteworthy difference between the state of affairs before and after, it does not follow that we have to regard the ovum as being as fully a person as an old man, or indeed as a person at all. What Wertheimer's observations should perhaps suggest is that looking for the point at which the embryo becomes a person is a mistaken tactic, and that it would be more sensible to consider what the defining characteristics of personhood may be in the abstract. That would allow us to make positive statements to the effect that 'such and such certainly doesn't count as a person', while conceding that we cannot accurately tell in certain borderline cases.

Mary Anne Warren has argued that moral personhood is dependent on five criteria.[8] These are, consciousness (including the capacity to feel pain), reasoning ability (involving a developed capacity to handle relatively complex problems), self-motivated activity, the capacity to communicate and the presence of a concep of self. I cite this particular view because it is far from implausible or unpersuasive, and yet it is an extremely stringent conception of personhood that would involve classifying a number of severely handicapped people, some very sick people, and young infants (not to mention the embryos we are primarily concerned with here) as not being persons. (Warren is aware of this, and explicitly recognises that on her view of moral personhood infanticide no less than abortion might conceivably be justified.) But, even if we wish to resist her suggestion that a being who met the other criteria, but happened to lack any developed reasoning ability, does not count as a person in the moral sense, Warren's criteria surely are of the right kind. It is in the broad domain of autonomy, self-awareness, rationality and consciousness that we have to look for the factors that go to make up our ideas of moral personhood. It is necessary at this point to recall that what lies behind our need to define moral personhood is the assumption that obligations and duties are owed to others who like ourselves are centres of consciousness and interests. Following on from that, I should be inclined to say that what makes a being *prima facie* deserving of moral respect is that it should be capable of autonomous thought and action, even to a low degree, and be susceptible to the conscious experience of feelings such as pain, pleasure and fear. But one thing that becomes quite plain, when we approach the issue in this way, is that it is very difficult indeed (I would say impossible) to come up with a convincing account of what constitutes moral personhood that could be applied to the foetus at any stage. One may make the point that we don't know where to draw the line and cannot pinpoint any morally relevant difference between, say, premature baby and foetus unborn, one may feel that the embryo should be treated as if it were a person (one may in any case feel that it is not only the life of persons that should be respected), but one cannot adequately define moral personhood in such a way that it would include the foetus.

This, or something like it, has led some people to argue that the important thing is that the foetus is a potential person. Just as the acorn will become an oak tree, or as the tadpole will become a frog, so the embryo will become a person. Such observations have, perhaps, a certain pertinence when we are considering treatment. It makes sense to say, 'don't plant the acorn there, because it will grow into an oak tree and knock that fence over.' But something that is necessary for, or owed to, something in its final state is not thereby shown to be necessary for it, or owed to it, in its previous state. Tadpoles, for instance, do not require space to jump about in. If a stone were to be changed into a person by a magician, it would then by dint of being a person deserve moral respect, but prior to that time it does not, and, in exactly the same way, while there are some ways of treating the foetus that are necessary to allow it to become a person, it does not deserve moral respect until it becomes a person in the moral sense. Hare has suggested that, as potential persons, foetuses deserve respect just as we do, on the grounds that, were we foetuses still, we should not wish to have been aborted, and there are no relevant reasons for treating other potential persons differently from the way in which we would wish to have been treated.[9] But this line of argument, quite apart from raising questions about whether it would lead to the conclusion that we have a positive duty to procreate (which Hare acknowledges), is absurd, for it is not simply an instance of applying the acceptable rule 'treat others as you would desire to be treated yourself'; it also involves a projection about what we would have thought had we been in a position to think as embryos, when we never have been and never could be. By this reasoning it would be equally wrong to kill a rat, for, were we rats, we would not want to be killed. We are not rats and we are not embryos, albeit we were once the latter and never the former.

It may be as well to summarise the points made so far. It is not established that the fact that a foetus will, other things being equal, become a person deserving of moral respect means that it deserves that respect now as a potential person. Moral personhood goes with having conscious interests. Embryos do not have such interests. There is a direct line of development from ovum to elderly person, and it is in practice impossible to draw a clear distinction between non-personhood and personhood on it. Some of the more obvious steps along the way, such as the moment of birth, clearly involve no morally significant change, though some of the less momentous steps might. But the fact that we cannot draw a line does not involve the conclusion that we cannot deny personhood to some early stages of development. My own view is that the foetus, and even the small infant, do not count as persons in the moral sense, but in any case the status of the foetus cannot in itself determine the issue of abortion. Killing, even of a person, may sometimes be justified, and killing of beings that are not persons in the moral sense is not necessarily justified. Therefore, whatever our views of the foetus, we still have to face the question, can it ever be morally justifiable to cause the death of a foetus?

One of the most famous attempts to answer that question affirmatively is that of Judith Jarvis Thomson.[10] For the sake of the argument, she concedes the status of personhood to the foetus. But she points out that the legitimate interests of the foetus may conflict with those of another, most obviously the mother, especially if she is very ill, has been raped or is very young. It is precisely in cases of this sort that many feel that abortion, even if generally undesirable, may be justifiable, and Thomson's argument is designed to establish that there is nothing logically problematic about acknowledging that the foetus deserves to be treated as an end in itself, and yet concluding that in the mother's interest there should be an abortion. Our obligation to the foetus (or indeed any person) cannot lay on the mother (or, again, anyone else) an unqualified obligation to preserve its life. Thomson invites us to imagine that a woman wakes to consciousness one day to discover that a famous violinist has been plugged into her, in order that he may partake of such organs as her liver and heart, and that he needs to remain attached to her for nine months, if he is to survive. Surely, she suggests, though we might think that the woman would be heartless to refuse, despite the manifest inconvenience to herself, or even that on balance she ought not to refuse, it can hardly be felt that she is obliged not to refuse. In the same way, even granting that the foetus and the mother are two persons, the former cannot be thought to lay an unequivocal obligation on the latter, and having an abortion would no more be a case of murder than would unplugging the violinist. Thomson's thesis is thus that, though persons, here including foetuses, have the right not to be killed unjustly, there may nonetheless be cases of justified abortion.

It has been maintained by Singer that this thesis is unacceptable to the utilitarian at least (and possibly to others), because it is based upon a theory of rights which the utilitarian does not accept.[11] But that is a confused response. It is true, as we have seen, that utilitarians do not believe that there are natural rights in the sense of *a priori*, inevitable, absolute rights, intuitively recognisable. But certain particular rights may be arrived at by utilitarian calculations, and hence justified. It is true therefore that the claim that the foetus has a natural right to life which is self evident, means little to the utilitarian. But a utilitarian, at any rate a rule-utilitarian, can quite coherently argue that, in general, life ought to be preserved, and thereby come to think and talk in terms of a right to life. He may also then, quite consistently, argue that, though in general one ought not to take a life, it may be reasonable to allow the killing of foetuses in particular circumstances, such as rape. He may do this either by qualifying the rule (if a rule-utilitarian) or by judging the individual act, or, as may happen with any moral system, by seeing the situation as a clash of two equally binding moral demands, so that one has to be denied. Certainly, Thomson's thesis seems to me quite unassailable. Apart from the merit of being unaffected by the status of the foetus, it has the great attraction of preserving our sense that abortion is not the sort of thing that involves no moral considerations, and can therefore be indulged in at whim, while allowing that it may nonetheless be morally justifiable. It amounts to the view that: the form of killing that involves refusing to sustain a life which cannot in practice survive without assistance is justified in circumstances where the individual who refuses to give sustenance would himself suffer severely were he to provide it. It is therefore a particular instance of the justified killing to protect oneself or family *genus*, and, as such, already acknowledged to be justifiable, although of course we may still argue about whether particular cases meet the criterion.

I regard that as the weak thesis, and would like to turn now to sketching a strong thesis, to the effect that abortion is not a moral issue at all. This thesis, unless it were to be based upon establishing that a foetus is not a person and that only persons have moral significance, depends upon the premise, which here I merely wish to suggest, that fundamentally what is wrong is suffering, and that what essentially makes for moral personhood is the capacity to suffer (so that, incidentally, animals may have moral personhood). The crucial reason why I am not morally permitted to ride roughshod over others, as I may over sticks and stones and possibly some forms of animate life, the reason why I should treat others as ends in themselves, as I would treat myself, is that we are all sentient beings. On this view, killing is wrong because people don't like being killed. It may nonetheless be justified sometimes in the interests of less overall suffering. And, to the immediate point, it may be justified in the case of foetuses, because they do not suffer and are not sentient in the requisite sense.

It may well be responded that, by this argument, we would be justified in killing adults in their sleep, and in practising euthanasia, since in such cases adults would know no more than foetuses do. But, although it is possible that the argument does justify certain forms of euthanasia, it is a mistake to see it as justifying indiscriminate killing of adults when they are unaware of what is going on. With the degree of self-consciousness and self-awareness that we have, we gain incalculably but immensely from the knowledge that we live in a world so ordered that we will not be quietly killed in our sleep. That knowledge is a vital part of our peace of mind, our allayed anxieties. To accept that humans may be got rid of when they are felt to be a nuisance, would itself create great suffering. But that argument does not apply to the foetus, who does not have the relevant awareness. In essence the argument here is that any being might in principle be justifiably killed, given certain conditions and calculations as to the utility of both killing and not killing, but that an enormously powerful utilitarian argument can be mounted for the adoption of, and adherence to, a rule against killing other self-conscious beings. Such a rule however, loses its force, as does the argument for it, in the case of non-self-conscious beings.

Germain Grisez has mounted an objection to this utilitarian position, but in doing so she makes certain common mistakes of misunderstanding.[12] She asserts that, 'our belief in equality in the right to life is incompatible with utilitarianism', but that claim is ambiguous. If it means that utilitarians do not believe that there is some heaven-sent right to life for every living thing, come what may, it is true, but no less true of most non-utilitarians. If it means that utilitarians do not believe that all beings, *qua* beings, are *prima facie* equally entitled to life, it is false. Nor is her claim that, 'if a utilitarian theory is accepted, not only the personhood of the unborn, but the personhood of us all is put in jeopardy' acceptable or devastating. It is true, as we have said, that from the utilitarian perspective nobody has a right to life come what may, but that is true from many other perspectives too, and, as the argument has shown, the possibility that abortion may be justified does not in itself carry over to justify the taking of adult life. Conversely, Grisez's own position amounts to no more than an assertion to the effect that human life is sacrosanct and that the only thing that might conceivably justify taking it is the saving of another life (and it is dependent on establishing that the foetus is a person in the moral sense, since Grisez does not extend her concern beyond human beings). Rape, chronic ill-health, patent unsuitability for motherhood and such like could not be relevant reasons for abortion in her view, for she holds that even a severely defective life is better than no life at all. To that position, I respond, as a utilitarian, by urging the reader to consider whether this is always and necessarily so, for that is what is really at issue. It is misleading to suggest that utilitarians are in favour of killing defectives, or want abortion on demand, or hold human life cheaply. None of these claims is necessarily or indeed likely to be true, but the utilitarian does believe that, conceivably, it may one day be right to take a life to minimise great suffering. On the face of it, a rule-utilitarian might even accept an absolute rule against killing. What divides him from Grisez is her assumption that the particular values she holds are unassailable under any conceivable circumstances, in particular under circumstances involving great suffering.

But, it may be more plausibly suggested, as it has been in the context of foetal research, that though foetuses do not have the kind of self-awareness that enables them to suffer directly, there are nonetheless 'suffering' considerations to be borne in mind, if one practises an abortion. There is the element of grief amongst friends and relatives (and indeed strangers of a strongly anti-abortion temperament) to be considered; there is the possibility that those involved with abortions become brutalised, and less respectful to life in general; there is the possibility, more generally, that a society that accepts abortion thereby begins to brutalise itself. Perhaps, as Bok believes, these considerations are less telling in the context of abortion than, say, euthanasia, since whatever the logic of the matter, people don't feel that foetuses are human beings in the way that old folk transparently are, but they nonetheless deserve to be considered and taken into account.[13]

And there, perhaps, is the rub. For we cannot do more than think carefully about all the factors mentioned, and 'take them into account'. I do not believe that it is possible to demonstrate whether, or when, abortion is justified; nor is it easy to be confident about whether particular abortions are or are not justified. But it is possible to form one's own opinion in the light of careful elucidation of what is at issue, and this chapter has been designed to contribute to such elucidation. I shall conclude by drawing attention to the common presumption that the onus is on those who would justify abortion in some circumstances to make their case. That presumably arises out of the widespread and traditional acceptance of the thesis that life is sacred. However, it seems to me that the onus should be on those who oppose abortion to explain why, since it is generally agreed that killing can sometimes be justified and that suffering is a bad thing, it is presumed that it must always be wrong to kill a non-self-conscious being whose continued existence will cause great suffering. It is difficult to avoid the speculation (though it is only that), especially since most anti-abortionists show no concern about animal life or suffering in general, that we are sometimes dealing with rampant speciesism. That is to say that what really lies behind objection to abortion is the conviction that merely being a member of the species *homo sapiens* is sufficient reason for preferential treatment. But why on earth should a zygote be regarded as being as significant as a gorilla, let alone more so? Only emotion could account for the feeling that it is so.

I am not advocating light-hearted and widespread practice of abortion. On the weak thesis, to which I am strongly committed, we are only saying that abortion should be regarded as morally justi-

Abortion 105

fiable, and permitted in certain fairly limited circumstances. But even the strong thesis does not maintain that whether or not an abortion is performed is a matter of moral insignificance. There may be something in the suggestion that to accept abortions begins to brutalise us; one may be moved, as a utilitarian, by the thought that the more human beings there are the greater the sum of happiness. But even if one were not moved by these or any other considerations, accepting abortions no more commits one to the view that it is a good thing to have them, than accepting the need to kill certain animals establishes that it is a good thing in itself to do so. The point is that abortion may be justified, not that it should be widely practised. As to that, how widely it should be practised is dependent on what kind of a mess we are in.

One implication of the foregoing argument, at least, can hardly be ignored. Given the complexity and uncertainty surrounding this issue, it must be for the individual to determine his or her attitude to the matter and consequent behaviour, rather than for the state to legislate.

NOTES

1 Richard Wasserstrom, 'The status of the foetus', *Hastings Magazine*, June 1975.
2 Jeremy Bentham, *Anarchical Fallacies; Being an Examination of the Declaration of Rights Issued during the French Revolution*.
3 R. M. Hare, 'Abortion and the Golden Rule', *Philosophy and Public Affairs*, 4, No. 3, Spring 1975.
4 Roger Wertheimer, 'Understanding the abortion argument', *Philosophy and Public Affairs*, Vol. 1, No. 1, 1971.
5 See below Chapter 12.
6 Peter Singer, *Practical Ethics*.
7 Roger Wertheimer, *op. cit.*
8 Mary Anne Warren, 'On the Moral and Legal Status of Abortion', *The Monist*, Vol. 57, No. 1, January 1973.
9 R. M. Hare, *op. cit.*
10 Judith Jarvis Thomson, 'A defence of abortion', *Philosophy and Public Affairs*, Vol. 1, No. 1, 1971.
11 Peter Singer, *op. cit.*
12 Germain Grisez, Abortion: The Myths, the Realities and the Arguments.
13 Sissella Bok, cited by Maggie Scarf, 'The Foetus as Guinea Pig', *New York Times Magazine*, 19 October 1975.

9 Equality and Wealth

> Good and evil fortune depend so much on the combinations of external circumstances that the utmost skill and industry cannot command success; neither is the result of the most imprudent actions always fatal.
>
> Thomas Love Peacock, *Melincourt*

In many obvious ways most contemporary societies involve considerable inequality. Whether we think in terms of material goods, psychological and cultural advantages, treatment at the hands of others or opportunities of various sorts, different people get a different deal. It is possible to argue that this is as it should be. It is as unjust to treat unequals equally as it is to treat equals unequally, and there may be good grounds for treating people differently in various particular respects. Besides, usually, the inequalities go only so far, and 'it is fairly generally agreed', according to Benn and Peters, 'that, property incomes apart, our system of distribution by desert, supplemented by redistribution according to need is right in principle.'[1] That is to say, a system that allows considerable difference, but ensures a certain minimum for all. On the other hand, though such a system may be generally accepted, there are certainly some who regard it as indefensible and our society as unacceptably inegalitarian.

There are three factors that vitiate most discussion about equality. The first, which I shall return to below, is the failure to distinguish between wealth, or the medium of exchange, on the one hand, and all other particular goods on the other, despite the obvious facts that wealth is *sui generis* and that, whereas one may have varying talent for doing particular things, there is no such thing as a talent for making money. The claim that somebody does have such a talent needs to be construed to mean something like 'he does succeed in making money', or 'he has talents that he can market', or, very specifically, 'he is talented at playing the stock market.' The second, which I shall handle in a separate chapter, is the vexatious problem of schooling, which is both to some extent a product of existing social arrangements and a determinant of future arrangements.² The third, which I shall explain here, is the equivocal nature of terms such as 'egalitarian' and 'equality'.

There are three trouble spots at which it may be unclear what the call for equality involves. Firstly, when someone asserts that he favours equality, it may be unclear whether by 'equal treatment' he means identical treatment or fair treatment. 'Equal rights for women', for instance, could be construed as a slogan demanding that women and men have exactly the same rights, or as one demanding rights, possibly different in content, but of the same worth. Secondly, we need to distinguish between calls for equality that are directed at redressing particular inequalities (of pay, housing, holidays, etc.), and those that are directed at redressing some general unspecified inequality (of treatment, provision, rights, etc.). It is not that these different demands cannot be very closely associated, but that they are nonetheless different in kind. 'Equal pay for men and women' is a much more straightforward demand than 'equal rights for men and women', because the latter does inevitably raise the first ambiguity we noted. Thirdly, even when it is clear that we are dealing with a call for equality in the sense of the same amount of something specific for various people, it may still be unclear whether we are faced with a call for equal opportunity to attain or acquire that something, equal provision of it, or arrangements to ensure an ultimate equal outcome. An equal housing policy might be taken to mean equal opportunity of access to accommodation, provision of similar housing to all in the first place (which might rapidly become dissimilar, as a result of different actions by the homeowners), or a perpetual watchdog policy to ensure that we all continue to occupy similar housing space.

It seems evident that no one interpretation of 'equality' or 'egalitarianism' will necessarily serve every occasion. When people say they are in favour of equality, without further qualification, it is unlikely that they mean that in all matters they are consistently in favour of the same end result or the same distribution. Rather, they are likely to be found to favour, say, the same medical treatment being constantly available, the same initial provision of schooling, the same basic securities at the end of the day, equal opportunity to gain state accommodation, and different rights of similar value for various different groups. Obviously, there is little or no ambiguity when the claims made are relatively specific. 'Treat people of different colours as equals' presumably means do not differentiate between people simply on grounds of colour. 'Give them equal shares of X' presumably means give each of them the same size share of X. But generalised pronouncements about equality might mean that we should treat people impartially, that we should give everybody the same opportunities, that we should give everybody the same shares, or that we should ensure that everybody ends up with identical shares, and each of those four suggestions is quite distinct.

Many have felt that 'equality of opportunity' is the answer to both the ambiguity of egalitarian demands and the problem of what we should do in the name of equality. Let the state ensure equality of opportunity for all, and then it is up to the individuals to achieve what they can. If some do better than others, that's only fair. If some fall by the wayside, they have only themselves to blame. So, in crude outline, the argument runs. But there are grave problems in it and serious objections to be levelled against it. One of the more obvious criticisms is that the comfortable assumption that, once we have started everybody off with an equal opportunity, anything that subsequently happens is their own responsibility, just isn't true. People who have indeed had opportunities may fail to take advantage of them through no fault of their own (such as ill-health). Behind this point lie two rather more complex and serious ones: how are we to determine where the equal provision of opportunity should begin and end, and how are we to determine what is somebody's own fault or responsibility, and what is not? We may say, as it commonly is said today, that it was not fair to talk of equal opportunity in the past, when only a few had access to education, and that we must therefore ensure that all have access to schooling. But why stop there? Since we have strong evidence to suggest that home background is an important factor in shaping the child, does not the desire for equal opportunity require that we equalise home environment in the same way? Then, consider the situation fifteen years on: when the children were five, we said, in the name of equal opportunity, that all should go to school. Now they are twenty, and their opportunities are manifestly unequal. Should we not equalise them again, by sending them all to university? If this individual has gained less from school than that, because of the problems he faces at home, shall we nonetheless say that it is his fault that he has not taken advantage of his opportunity? What, furthermore, is this opportunity supposed to be for? To succeed in life? Then evidently we do not provide it. To realise the individual personality? Is that, however desirable, remotely adequate to meet the claims of equality? It is very difficult to resist the conclusion that the equal opportunity to be provided is that of starting a competitive struggle for life's advantages from the same somewhat arbitrary line. The catch is that, while it may be reasonable to offer people an equal opportunity to attain certain particular things, either because they are available in limited quantity or because they are not of crucial importance to all, the matter becomes quite different when we are talking of a generalised opportunity to gain life's goods.

The fundamental implausibility of the crude thesis of equality of opportunity is, in fact, implicitly conceded by most people, for it is very common to couple it with some further provision designed to affect its more blatantly unjust effects. Some of these further provisions might also be proposed independently as alternatives to the equality of opportunity thesis, and I shall accordingly consider each one in its own right.

A widespread view is that whatever else we do we must ensure that certain minimum needs are satisfactorily met for all persons. This is an important aspect of the communist formula 'from each according to his ability, to each according to his needs', no less than Benn and Peters' liberal-democratic perspective. The problem here is to determine what people can be said to need (or, if one is only concerned with basic needs or minimum needs, what needs can be said to be basic and minimally necessary). As far as words go, we would probably all agree that ideally people's needs should be met; the problem is that a defender of our current equal opportunity system would say that our state schooling, medical and social services, social security payments and so forth do ensure 'a redistribution according to need', while a critic would deny that they meet the needs of the relatively disadvantaged. Needs, unfortunately, are not properties, qualities or characteristics that a person either has or has not, as he either has or has not two legs, a deep voice or a sense of humour. What a person needs is a product partly of what he lacks, but also of specifying some objectives. I lack an expensive car, but it would not normally be felt that I need one, since I can well do without it, and it would not generally be accepted that objectives such as my showing it off around town, for which I do indeed need it, should be taken seriously. On the other hand, we do accept that I need food, because the objective of staying alive is widely recognised. It is possible that a person may need something without recognising that he does, as a sick man may need penicillin to stay alive, while not appreciating the fact, or as a person may need to read literature to develop critical powers (for which he would be grateful once developed), but be unaware of the fact. Conversely, a person may be mistaken in his views of his own needs, either because he does not recognise his true objectives, or because he does not know that something is the appropriate means to his chosen ends. For these conceptual reasons determining needs is never simply a matter of looking at what a person lacks. The practical problem resides in the fact that agreement on what people need depends upon prior agreement about what objectives should be met, and that is often precisely what is lacking.

Some have taken this point further, arguing that concepts are socially determined and structured, and consequently always in transition. Take, for example, Marx's prediction that the working class would experience 'increasing misery'. On the face of it, the reverse has happened in the advanced industrial societies where working class poverty, alienation and misery were most confidently expected. One does not have to be a capitalist lackey to recognise that, by and large, people, including the working class, suffer less today than in Marx's day. But what one does have to do, to make such a judgement, is accept some set of measures. I may support that judgement by pointing out that sanitary conditions are better, that diet is better and that social services are more copious and efficient. But some would respond by asserting that those measures are irrelevant, and that poverty today means something different from what it used to mean, because circumstances have changed.

It may be said that in any society there will be a standard view of what constitutes a minimally decent life, and one view would define this as 'a life which persons with average income can afford' so that 'anyone is poor whose income is substantially below the appropriately designated income'.[3] However, this particular definition is clearly unsatisfactory, unless one is explicitly arguing for flat equality of income (in which case, one does not require, or gain from, this roundabout exercise of redefinition). It is unsatisfactory because, since it defines poverty as less than average, wherever there are differences of wealth, no matter how slight, no matter for what reason, no matter how rich people actually are, there must be poverty. Using today's common ideas of valued possessions and pursuits, even presuming that the least well off had two cars, a yacht, time to enjoy them, excellent food and pleasing accommodation, they would still be classified as poor. But there are surely many good and obvious reasons for wanting to distinguish between those who earn slightly less than average in Sweden and those who earn much less than average in India. What is gained by lumping them both together in a vast general category of 'poor'? What is gained by defining 'poverty' in such a way that no practical steps to alleviate misery can make any difference, since it logically cannot be reduced, except by redistribution of wealth in terms of flat equality? Besides having no obvious point, poverty, defined in this way, is not what is generally meant by 'poverty', and is not what Marx meant by 'poverty'. To define 'increased misery' into existence in this way is not to show that Marx's prediction has come true. Indeed, it has not come true.

Bernard Gendron, while rejecting this 'variable relative income approach' to the question of poverty, because he senses the counter-intuitive consequences outlined above, offers in its place a variant, which he terms the 'variable absolute income approach'.[4] This is based upon the observation that, even if we accept some broad notion of poverty defined in terms of subsistence needs (and therefore relatively stable, and certainly independent of the immediate economic base), the cost of producing, and hence satisfying, those needs, does vary with the economic climate. Advanced capitalist societies, he points out, far more than rural communities or planned economies 'tend continuously to raise the cost of avoiding poverty as they grow economically'.[5] Looking at the matter in this way, he suggests that we can now reduce argument about poverty to a matter of fact, rather than a matter of conceptual differences or evaluative differences, and see that it may indeed be true that a wealthier society does not necessarily reduce poverty.

So far this argument is plainly correct. The mere fact that people earn more than they did proves nothing. We have to consider whether increases in transport costs and production costs, or the consequences of some monopoly organisation, have put certain people into the category of poor who were not there before. We must, more imaginatively, take into account factors such as health hazards too, and we must concede that control of market forces, and possibly control of social pressure, by means of advertising and the like may affect the issue. What constitutes poverty is partially bound up with our expectations. In a situation where beef is the only nutrient food available or where social pressures suggest you must eat beef or hang your head in shame, poverty will be associated to some extent with the inability to buy beef.

But it is possible to go absurdly far with this initially sensible thesis, as Gendron does when he suggests that, in a relatively prosperous society, television sets, washing machines, cars and holidays abroad become subsistence needs, such that their absence betokens poverty. The point is not that by an extension of the argument they could not be seen as such, for they obviously could: the social climate could suggest one should have at least two cars, as easily as it might suggest that a self-respecting family should eat meat. Nor is it that a dramatic change in circumstances could not make such things necessities, for conceivably it could. Still less am I suggesting that people should not expect that all should have these things as a matter of course. But nonetheless the argument is phoney. Say what you will, these are not *subsistence* needs. Gendron has confused the point that the social climate may give us a new view of what we do need for healthy subsistence (beef) with the point that it may give us a new view of what we should take for granted (yachts). All the pressure in the world to have two cars does not make it a matter of fact that one does need two cars at the level of subsistence, although of course it does affect the extent to which you will be satisfied with less. In other words we still need to discriminate between what is truly a need (for survival, for comfort, or for luxury) and what is not, or, alternatively, between poverty in the sense of inability adequately to sustain human life, to sustain human dignity and to sustain human satisfaction; and here we are back with evaluation. Gendron's modification, handled sensibly, does keep the question factual, but it then fails to establish that poverty has not diminished. To establish the latter he has to make evaluative claims to the effect that in our society absence of various goods is insupportable.

It must be conceded, then, that what will be accounted poverty will vary as a result of varying expectations, and that what wealth is necessary to avoid poverty will change as costs and expectations change. But this does not, unfortunately, mean that determining who is poor is a simple matter of fact. It is undeniably the case that, bearing in mind these points, many more people should be accounted poor than are officially recognised as such by conventional government indices. But the thesis almost certainly goes too far, if it is claimed that there is as much or more poverty and misery today as there was one hundred years ago, and such a claim would in any case be partly dependent on a judgement as to what should count as the necessities of life, and not simply a matter of fact. On the other hand the basic, Platonic, insight that poverty is relative is importantly correct, and explains why talk of satisfying basic needs, minimum needs or avoiding poverty can never be entirely satisfactory. Even if satisfaction of minimum needs were all that we owed each other in the name of equality (and I shall argue below that it is not), 'to each according to his needs' would remain a well-intentioned but unuseful formula, since it is open for some to claim that we need a diet of beef, some that we need a car, some that we need a television set, some that we need a private aeroplane and so on. For this reason both the communist formula, despite its attraction and the plausibility of its first clause ('from each according to his ability'), and attempts to prop up equality of opportunity by safeguarding minimum needs, have to be rejected as ineffective.

At the time of writing, the economic theory of Milton Friedman has gained a certain amount of popularity. Does he provide a solution to the problem of just economic distribution? One thing that he does do well is to distinguish clearly between four questions which sooner or later have to be distinguished. What is fair, in the sense of impartial? What is morally justifiable, even if imperfect and a little unfair? What is an effective strategy for producing more wealth? and to what extent do we want to enforce what we think is fair, justifiable or productive, by legislation?[6] If we take a very simple example, such as the biblical story of the distribution of talents to his sons by a father, it is obvious that these different questions may lead to quite different practices. On the face of it, it is fair, in the sense of impartial, for a father to give each of his children the same amount of money, on the grounds that, whatever the differences between them may be, they are not relevant differences to this distribution. But it is not difficult to conceive of situations where one might feel that a slightly unfair distribution would be justifiable. (Suppose, for instance, that one son has married a rich wife.) But then again the father might consider that one of his sons, perhaps the richest, would make the most of his money. He might want to give to him that hath, for that reason alone; but the case could be made even stronger, if we presume that the father has reason to believe that out of the increased prosperity the rich son will look after the rest of the family better than they could have managed for themselves on an equal share of the original sum. Finally, all of those options leave unanswered the question of what conditions the father should lay down in his will. Suppose that he believes the second option is the one to go for (unequal shares, justified by some extrinsic factor); should he nonetheless try to bind the son who receives the largest sum to secure the basic interests of the others should the situation change?

It is the third option to which Friedmanite theory tends. At the heart of his view there are two distinct principles, one empirical, the other moral. (He himself sees his economic principle as non-moral, but thinks that the justification of capitalism lies in the principle of freedom, which is scarcely adequate.) His main point is that a free and competitive situation produces the most wealth, or makes available more of what we want. It is arguable that this is true, but that, even if it is, it leaves at least one crucial question unanswered, for without some reference to a principle of distribution it remains an incomplete theory, and on the face of it an unacceptable one, since nobody thinks that the mere fact that a system produces wealth makes it a morally good one. As we have noted, it will not suffice to add a qualification about satisfying basic needs, since what these may be is negotiable and to some extent fluctuating. The moral principle that Friedman chooses to introduce is the Rawlsian principle of justice,[7] coupled with a subsidiary principle to the effect that he who risks all deserves all. The subsidiary principle, based on the analogy of a lottery, is surely suspect and can be ignored. If we were all free agents with similar resources, it might be argued that the brave deserve the rewards, the cautious not. But we are really arguing about the prior question of whether and to what extent we should be free agents, and whether we should have equal chips or not. The important question is whether Friedmanism can be justified by something like Rawls' view of justice, and, if so, whether that view is persuasive.

Basically the view in question has it that a distribution may be unequal provided that the outcome of such an unequal distribution is better for the worst off than alternative, more equal, distributions might have been. The fact that in practice it would be difficult to know in advance whether a particular unequal distribution would have this effect should not be counted an objection. It is not directly comparable to the point made about needs, for there the point was that to accept a formula about needs would be empty since we can legitimately have different views of what people do need, rather than that it would be a matter of practical difficulty to assess them. Here, as very often, we are faced with practical difficulties in working in accordance with a principle, but no difficulty about its meaning. Rawls himself argues that there should be equality in basic rights and duties, but that inequalities of social and economic circumstance are just, if they result in compensating benefits for all. 'It may be expedient, but it is not just that some should have less in order that others may prosper. But there is no injustice in the greater benefits earned by a few provided that the situation of persons not so fortunate is thereby improved.'[8]

Rawls' own argument for accepting this principle is indirect. It takes the form of saying that a view as to what is just should be assessed by reference to what we imagine rational, self-interested men who nonetheless have no way of foretelling the future, and who are therefore ignorant of what their individual lot might be in the future, would think of as just. But it is far from clear why we should accept that as a test of what is morally just, and why we should presume that people so placed would in the event adopt Rawls' principle. On the face of it, though obviously a system involving differences of wealth that raises all our standards of living is preferable to one involving differences that does not, it would be at least as reasonable, some would say more so, to opt for a system involving less inequality, even if this meant a generally lower standard of living—particularly when we bear in mind the truth that to some extent acceptable standards of living are assessed in the light of expectations. A society where all have butter for tea and do not bother much about jam or honey might be regarded as preferable to one in which some have jam and wish they had the honey enjoyed by a few. And it might even more plausibly be regarded as *morally* preferable. Admittedly, to suggest as much invites the charge that one is a dog in the manger, prompted by simple envy. But what are we trying to discuss? Men's psychological drives and reactions or what constitutes ideal fairness? There seems to me no doubt at all that, while one might well accept a Rawlsian or Friedmanite society as on balance preferable to some others, indeed while in particular circumstances one might reasonably argue it is morally justifiable to have such a society, the basic assumption that generating more wealth (for everybody) is more important than a morally fair distribution is very curious indeed, and quite unargued for. In other words, though one can readily see why people might opt for such a society, it remains to show what on earth *justifies* some in having much larger slices of a cake than others. To answer that by saying that the cake would have been smaller but for the few seems to misunderstand the nature of justice in the moral sense.

Another way to try and soften the blow of equality of opportunity, and to make it clear that it is not a matter of equal opportunity to be unequal, is to define it more precisely, so that it is not simply a formula for starting us all off together, but more specifically geared to some end state. John Plamenatz argues for equality of opportunity in the sense of people having 'as much chance as any other of living the kind of life that seems good' to them.[9] The point about a formula like this, unlike the simple call for equal opportunity, is that it suggests that it may be legitimate for society to provide a constant set of controls, checks and balances, to allow each individual to live his life. Indeed it might be rephrased in something like the words of the Alva Myrdal report to the Swedish social democratic party as the claim that 'all men have the same right to live a full and satisfying life', which is to say that each should have equal freedom of choice, so far as possible, to shape his own future.[10]

The objection to this sort of approach is that it takes us away from any clear directive. 'A full and satisfying life' is a fairly nebulous phrase, and stressing the desirability of equal freedom of choice in respect of one's life-style is no substitute for settling questions about the distribution of roles, power, status and material goods in society. Plamenatz, for example, not unnaturally, moves rapidly into talking about a society which has wealth-producing capacity combined with a minimal set of restrictions.[11] He argues that restrictions can only be justified in order to safeguard citizens, get service from citizens, or ensure an adequate upbringing for future citizens. He ends up talking about a society that provides equal opportunity to formulate one's own purposes, except insofar as one's own defects of nature or moral turpitude hinder one. That is all very well as an account of current equal opportunity orthodoxy, but it bypasses altogether the question of whether that is good enough. What about material equality, both as a claim in itself and as a factor that to some extent influences one's freedom to formulate one's own purposes? The Myrdal report is less disingenuous, explicitly recognising that, since one's social and economic situation has a bearing on one's chances of living the kind of life that seems good to one, a more equal distribution (presumably meaning more nearly the same amount) of resources, influence and opportunities for choice is required. Even so, at the end of the report there is something of a cop-out in the reference to the need for society to 'restore balance',[12] when people suffer from natural disadvantages. We could spend the rest of our days agreeing on the need to 'ensure fairness', 'protect minimum needs', 'restore balance caused by natural disadvantage' and 'give all an equal opportunity for a satisfying life', while arguing about what to do. What a theory of equality needs to do is explain and spell out what counts as a 'natural disadvantage', what 'restoring the balance' involves, and how one defines 'a satisfying life'. It needs to give us explicit criteria for determining a fair distribution.

And so we come to the most popular defence of a degree of inequality, namely the view that merit is what entitles us to rewards. Though most meritocrats will add the usual saving clauses about 'basic needs' and 'redressing the balance', the essence of meritocracy is the belief that you should get what you earn. Of course, the argument goes, an individual should not have more than another just because he has blue blood in his veins, because he has red hair, because he has white skin, because he is male, because he is intellectual or because he is the child of wealthy parents. But that is because those are irrelevant reasons for differential treatment, and not because it is necessarily unjustifiable for some people to have more than others. What does justify a greater slice of the cake is merit.

As well as being most popular, this is perhaps the most confused and morally pernicious distributive theory of all. The problem starts (and possibly ends) with the question of what constitutes merit. Is it to be identified or associated with talent, with hard work, with brains, with performing a socially important job, or what? Whichever way we turn, the road is rough.

There is a trivial sense in which we are all meritocrats. If 'merit' is defined formally as 'deserving' (that is, without any reference to what does deserve what) then we agree that everybody should get what, and only what, they deserve. But that merely postpones the questions of how one measures merit or desert, and in the light of what purposes. A trap that must be avoided is that of identifying merit with success, which would result in the paradoxical conclusion that all inequalities are justified. There may be respects in which particular successful men, or even successful men generally, are more meritorious than failures, but to identify success and merit would be to ignore the palpable fact that people may be more or less successful for a wide variety of reasons. Besides, there is nothing logically peculiar about the idea of someone being meritorious, but not getting his due reward. We still need to pursue the question of what it is that we are maintaining when we assess somebody as meritorious.

We might be saying that he has talents or skills. Undoubtedly people do vary both in the range of talents and skills they possess, and in the degree to which they are skilled, and it can scarcely be disputed that talents and skills are to be prized and made use of where possible, both individually and collectively. Ability to do a job well is a good reason for being entrusted with the job, and, given certain forms of institutional arrangement, certain talents may justify placing a person in a place of authority. One might say, therefore, that a person merits his place in an organisation because of his skills. But why should it be thought that he merits a differential extrinsic reward because of his skills? There are in any case two well-known but intractable problems here. Firstly, if one does want to offer extrinsic rewards for skills, there is the problem of how one determines whether one piano player is more skilled or is not more skilled than another, and likewise with all other skills. Consideration of that point raises the simple, but potentially devastating, question of whether, when we claim to be rewarding merit in the sense of rewarding the most skilled in various fields, we in fact do so or could hope to do so. Secondly, it is even harder to see how we are going to arrive at a coherent way of estimating the relative value of different skills. If merit means talent and merit should be rewarded, then we need to find a way of estimating the relative merit or talent of good footballers, good pianists, good coal-miners, good surgeons and so on.

But the fundamental objection remains that not a shred of argument is forthcoming to support the idea that particular talents deserve special material rewards, and consequently, if merit is identified with skills and talents, we have no good reason for approving of meritocracy. Much the same may be said of the attempt to identify merit with the possession of certain virtues. To be sure, virtuous persons are meritorious in the sense of deserving of our respect, but why should they necessarily be deserving of special extrinsic rewards. Why should either the fact of being rather kinder than some people, or the fact of being rather a better carpenter than some people, be supposed to entitle one to a differentially large slice of cake?

An attempt to answer that question would lead many to push the argument one step backward and say that what matters is supply and demand. Rewards go, not simply to those with talents, skills or virtues, but to those with marketable talents, skills and virtues. One could hardly dispute that that is what in fact goes on much of the time in our society. But, again, not a word has ever been offered, to my knowledge, to explain why it should be thought that this is an equitable state of affairs. (It might conceivably be a necessary state of affairs, if we want to achieve maximum economic growth, but that is a different question.) It is quite unclear why being blessed with a talent that various people should happen to want or need to avail themselves of should justify one, still less entitle one, to a disproportionate reward, any more than being blessed with blue blood should. The fact that I am a good left-arm spinner is a good reason for choosing me to play cricket, but why should it be a good reason for giving me special rewards? Arguments to the effect that special rewards are necessary as inducements are very unconvincing, since, in the first place, generally unpopular jobs are seldom the best rewarded, and, in the second place, such strength as that argument has derives partly from a situation in which there are wealth differentials. When it is possible for me to earn more or less, that certainly may become a motivating factor in what job I try to do. But were it not possible, people would be motivated only by all the other motivating factors with which we are familiar. It simply isn't true that nobody would be willing to take on the managing-directorship of a firm unless he were paid more than everybody else. There may be good reason for the market to control what jobs people do, but there is no morally adequate reason for allowing it to determine people's rewards in life. (This is a point that even the most hard-hearted market-economists recognise when they concede that nobody should be swept aside. Why not? If it is supposed to be morally justifiable for me to have an easier life than you, because people happen to like my singing voice, why is it not morally justifiable that you should go altogether to the wall, since nobody wants any of your talents?)

But perhaps identifying merit with talent is too crude. Does the merit that supposedly entitles a man to preferential reward perhaps arise out of the social importance of his job or the responsibility it involves? The same objections apply. Firstly, how one determines social importance is far from obvious, and on any view it is easy to show that in this sense of the term our society is not meritocratic. Is the policeman more or less important than the entertainer, the garage mechanic more or less important than the dustbinman, the business man more or less important than the builder? By what criteria could one justify the presumption that the accountant is more important than the teacher (than whom he earns a great deal more)? Are they the same criteria that explain why the advertising executive is rewarded so much more lavishly than members of parliament? Secondly, ignoring the point that merit in this sense is not a workable criterion, and is consequently not in fact the basis of our alleged meritocracy, why should social importance in any specifiable sense be rewarded? Of course, if 'social importance' is treated as a very general term that covers the kind of importance the policeman has, the kind the entertainer has, the kind the industrialist has, and the kind the labourer has, then it becomes plausible to say that the socially important should be better rewarded than the socially unimportant. But if 'socially important' is more narrowly defined, so as to enable us to differentiate between such categories, then it becomes highly questionable whether 'social importance' should be preferentially rewarded.

But suppose an individual has acquired his reward as a result of his achievement. Surely then he deserves something more than the man who did not similarly achieve? 'Achievement', like 'merit' itself, is an equivocal term. What one achieves in the sense of attains to as a matter of fact may be a matter of luck, birth, family connections, hard work or a number of other things. There is obviously no reason why achieving the position of managing director of a firm as a result of being the son of the owner should be rewarded in some special way. There is also the point that, if achievement is supposed to merit reward, then all who achieve in their chosen walk of life should presumably be equally rewarded. But it is never suggested by those who refer to achievement deserving reward that he who achieves a great deal by becoming a bank clerk, against all the odds, should be rewarded more extensively than he who finds the way to being a barrister paved for him. A more plausible view might be that achievement in the relatively specific sense of in-put should be rewarded. But, although it may seem reasonable to penalise those who, through some choice of their own, do not work as hard or put as much into work as others, in practical terms this criterion will not allow of much discrimination, and certainly would not justify the kind of differences that our supposed meritocracy takes for granted. One needs to allow for in-put taking the form of labour, capital, inventiveness, investment or indeed a chance idea, and, as with other attempts to interpret merit, determining that people have put something in does not settle the problem, since one still has to decide whether it matters into what the effort has been put. Even if we reduce merit to little more than effort, which certainly more nearly approaches something morally acceptable, there is still a problem, since some people 'inherit or acquire certain kinds of handicap', not so much that prevent them doing things directly, but that give them 'little opportunity to acquire the motivation even to do their best'.[13]

Such factors as scarcity, demand, popularity, social importance, economic importance, responsibility, security, talent, hard work and important contributions of other sorts, may well be relevant when it comes to distributing and providing jobs, in a way that blood, possessions, accent, power and looks are not. But they are for the most part as hard to interpret in practice as needs or talent, and they have never been shown to be good reasons for special reward. (There is one plausible argument, to the effect that some should be paid more later in life, because they spent many years being trained, as in the case of doctors. But that is very straightforward. The present argument is about grounds for evaluating different people doing different jobs differently, and not about whether the same end result should necessarily be arrived at in the same way.)

What bedevils every argument about equality is the failure to draw a clear demarcation line between external reward (generally speaking, but not exclusively, financial) and job or role distribution. For instance, John Schaar, arguing for an egalitarian position, and correctly noting that equality of opportunity 'is really a demand for an equal right and opportunity to become unequal', derides the claim that 'those on top are automatically justified because they owe their position to their natural superiority or merit'.[14] It may well be true that none of our 'top people' is meritorious in any of the possible senses of the term. They might owe their positions entirely to grace, favour and luck. But Schaar is quite wrong to suggest that merit (in various senses) would not justify pushing particular people into particular positions (which might be defined as 'top'). Nor would there be anything undemocratic about that, as he suggests. Certain people may very well merit certain positions (despite the difficulties in assessing such merit, noted above). What they cannot merit are special accompanying rewards.

Schaar illustrates how very difficult it is for those of us brought up in a Western tradition to get away from its presuppositions. For his criticism of the current inequality cannot move beyond the assertion that the people who are getting more are not the people who deserve more. He cannot bring himself to recognise that there are no people who deserve more. His egalitarianism therefore amounts to little more than 'more of the same, spread more thinly'. He says that we 'need a social order that permits a much greater variety of games' (that is, greater scope for a wider range of talents), and concedes that 'some vocations and talents are more valuable than others, and more to be rewarded.'[15] But, if we exclude vocations and talents that are presumed to be positively undesirable, that has never been shown to be so, and is actually most unconvincing. If one has a society that is based upon witch-doctors, corn-planters, warriors and child-bearers, then each of those roles is equally crucial to that society. In the same way, if we want teachers, policemen, accountants, greengrocers, sportsmen and publicans in our society, then we cannot claim that any of them are unimportant to our society. In a time of crisis one may be forced to adopt priorities. But when the issue is not whether we can afford to have accountants, but how much they should be paid, given that they are a part of our society, then the question of whether they are more or less deserving than hot-dog salesmen is meaningless. Granted that it may be argued that various particular talents are more or less valuable in specific respects (*A* is more entertaining, *B* is more geared to our security, *C* is more in demand), it does not follow that anything is more deserving of external reward than anything else.

With rather more reason, exactly the same questionable, but unquestioned, premise is accepted by a meritocrat such as Daniel Bell. While Schaar argues that the problem is that too few people are getting too much, Bell asserts that we must recognise a social need for 'those who have earned their authority. . . . There cannot be complete democratisation in the entire range of human activities.'[16] That in itself may very well be true, but, though both Schaar and Bell stress the importance of ability (and misleadingly suggest that democracy as such is somehow necessarily about levelling off talents), they obscure the point that what is of concern is the question of reward. It need not be denied that some 'have earned their authority'; the question is whether they have thereby earned a better material life. Bell does recognise that these are distinct questions, just as he correctly observes that in society today status, power and wealth have become to a large extent separated, thus invalidating all sorts of traditional ideas about how to classify people. He notes that, 'the question of justice arises when those at the top convert their authority positions into large, discrepant social and material advantage over others', which is true as far as it goes, but he should have added, 'or when anyone else converts his particular social role into a means for acquiring large, discrepant social and material advantage.' And Bell's solution to the limited problem he discerns (the aggrandisement of 'top people', as opposed to aggrandisement generally) is the familiar half-hearted reference to a need for 'basic social equality' and to 'reduce invidious distinction', while asserting that 'each person is entitled to a basic set of services.'[17] What these may variously amount to is not revealed, and so we find ourselves once again in the unhelpful position discussed above. Everybody, from communist to capitalist, is agreed that people should ideally have what they need, and that they should do what they are well able to do. The argument starts when we attempt to give substance to the notion of need. Meritocrats, if they wish to argue both for greater reward for some socially necessary roles than for others, and for the equal satisfaction of basic needs, have a double problem on their hands.

So far I have tried to point out that all familiar arguments for unequal wealth seem to take it for granted that some of various qualities such as rarity, importance for security, or social power, would, if they could be satisfactorily estimated, entitle the performer of a job possessing them to extra reward. That quite unsubstantiated view is to be distinguished sharply from the quite legitimate point that there may be differences of talent, and that these may justify differences in role and responsibility. Let us therefore now consider strict economic egalitarianism itself, which is the view that ideally everybody ought to have the same amount of private wealth all the time. (The phrase 'all the time' makes it quite clear that we are not referring to a view that proposes an equal distribution initially, following which some may make more than others, and it avoids the problems of interpretation inherent in a phrase such as 'in the end'.) One quite common response to this is that made by Feinberg: this 'is a perfectly plausible material principle of distributive justice when confined to affluent societies and basic biological needs',[18] but it loses that plausibility when applied to any surplus after whatever are agreed to be basic needs have been satisfied. That there may be societies so poor that circumstances dictate unequal distribution (for example, there may not be enough to go round, or it may be imperative to feed soldiers rather than civilians, or to invest capital in producers), may be agreed. But why should it be agreed that in normally affluent societies such as our own this 'plausible material principle' should only apply at the level of basic biological needs? Why is it assumed that, while it is obvious that you and I are equally entitled to the same amount of food, more or less whatever the differences between us, I am nonetheless entitled to a much larger house than you, or to two private cars, when you have none? Feinberg merely offers the Friedmanite view that 'it is evident that justice does *not* require strict equality wherever there is reason to think that unequal distribution causally determines greater production and is therefore in the interests' of everybody. 'No one', he asserts, 'would insist upon equal distribution' on such conditions. 'That would be opposed to reason.'[19] But this is really a quite extraordinary claim. For, even forgetting the point that this discussion takes place in a context where it makes sense to think of the value that accrues to all from the private investor of capital (whereas under alternative systems it would not necessarily be the case that giving more to the few would be likely to increase wealth overall), many people do insist upon just the claim that Feinberg treats as self-evidently untenable. Many of us think that, in a society as affluent as ours, a fair distribution is morally far more important than increasing our wealth. It is therefore certainly not 'opposed to reason' to resist the Friedmanite position and, still, all that has been proffered in its favour is its alleged self-evidence, despite the fact that the very discussion in progress shows that it is not self-evident.

The first and one of the strongest points in favour of economic egalitarianism therefore remains the point from which we set out. If you want to start giving different people different qualities of life by means of different amounts of material wealth, you need a good reason to do so. No such reason has yet been produced. Secondly, there is the not insignificant practical consideration that none of the reasons that some people assume to be good ones actually operates consistently and successfully. It is not true, on any definition, that the most able, or the most hard working, or the most responsible, or what have you, do regularly gain the most reward. What we actually have is a random hotch-potch of differentials, generally dominated by industrial muscle. Friedman has suggested that much observed inequality of reward is offset by other differences in occupation, such as easier work, shorter hours, more autonomy or greater security.[20] But, by and large, this is nonsense. Who earns a lot of money? Well, directors of large firms, film stars and print compositors, for instance. Who does not have to have an arduous training or to be particularly intellectually gifted? Well, directors of large firms, film stars and print compositors, for instance. Who has relatively good security? Well, directors of large firms, film stars (arguable and dependent on how they invest their money while successful, admittedly) and print compositors. There are examples of jobs where one seeming disadvantage is offset by another advantage, as, for example, university academics sacrifice pay for security. But generally speaking it has never been the case that jobs are balanced out in this way, and it is anyway quite inconsistent of Friedman to appeal to the point. It is no accident that academics have now had their compensating security threatened by a Friedmanite economic policy, for true Friedmanite economics demands that each job gets the market rate. But as Proudhon, for one, saw, what might work in a small unit such as the family or a rural community, where there are other social links and feelings to ensure certain things that will not be protected by a market economy, will not work in a modern industrial state.[21] If the market economy is to rule, then it may lead to an end to cultural concerns, an end to minority interests, an end to people's security and so forth. If we do not wish to embrace such conclusions, then we are not really embracing the Friedmanite market principle, and the sooner we stop saying we are, the better.

It is valuable also to consider some of the likely advantages and possible disadvantages of adopting strict economic egalitarianism, since, notwithstanding the fact that it is more securely based morally than any differential view, or the fact that differential views do not work out in practice as they are supposed to, a common objection is that 'it wouldn't work'. At the moment we live in a society in which, in the name of an incoherent and unjustified creed, what rewards people actually get are determined by a mixture of initial advantage, luck and effort. Basic needs of some sort are generally guaranteed satisfaction, but over a small area and at a low level; for the rest the going rate for the job (to be distinguished from the matter of who gets what job) is determined by a mixture of industrial muscle, business dealing and views as to the social worth of a job. On balance, therefore (and there is quite strong evidence for this),[22] the economic success that an individual will attain is largely a matter of luck, with his family background being likely to play a significant, though by no means conclusive, part. By and large, people can only be said to have earned or deserved their large bank balances in very extended senses of these words. Clearly, where the meritocrats are correct is in sensing that it is absurd to conclude that, since it is not really my fault that I am no good at tennis and nobody's choice of managing director, I should be invited to play at Wimbledon and placed on the Board of Marks and Spencers. We certainly do not want a society that fails to discriminate where there are differences. On the contrary, ideally we want more recognition of actual differences between people. But why reward people more for being in the right place at the right time?

It may be said that egalitarianism is simply the last refuge of the envious and resentful. It is possible that in individual cases it is, just as it is possible that in individual cases vast inequalities of wealth are defended because people either gain from them or think that they may. (When a film star leaves Britain to set up his home in California saying, 'I believe in equality of opportunity and this is dying in Britain', it is not quite clear what he means. Does he mean he believes that it is morally well-founded, in which case we would like to hear his justification, or does he mean he believes it is more pleasant for him to live in a society that enables him to amass a vast amount of wealth?) But people's motives for holding views have nothing to do with the quality of those views. Economic egalitarianism cannot be discounted on the grounds that it is the product of envy, any more than capitalism can be discounted on the grounds that the rich defend it in their own interests. It is obviously true, as Marxists and meritocrats such as Bell will agree, that 'as disparities have decreased . . . expectations of equality have increased even faster',[23] but that too is neither here nor there. In order to show that economic egalitarianism is not acceptable, it is necessary to furnish a good reason for giving some people more than other people.

Sooner or later opponents of egalitarianism will raise the question of motivation, arguing that equal wealth may be a wonderful idea, but it cannot succeed, because, if there is to be no special reward, nobody will work hard. But why is it assumed that people will only work for dollars? Given the indubitable fact that, as things are, most of us work quite hard for relatively little material reward, it is a wildly implausible thesis. Even if it were not, there are plenty of ways in which one could ensure that people do pull their weight. And there are many other actual and potential sources of motivation. It is sometimes argued that the fact of, say, Soviet Russia shows that other methods of motivation cannot work, but, leaving aside the question of how successful the Soviet system is in this respect, that argument is misleading. I am not talking about Soviet Russia, which has many elements such as great centralisation, collectivism and stifling ideology, that are more than sufficient to account for such labour problems as she may have. The argument here is purely and simply about whether people would only choose to be doctors so long as doctors were paid more, and whether the doctor would only do his job to the best of his ability, if thereby he might earn more than another doctor. There seems, yet again, no reason whatsoever to accept that strange claim.

But what happens, it has been asked, 'to the nurse, if you can get a physician for the same price, and to the student dentist, if you can get a qualified one?'[24] This is a curious and revealing question. After all, what happens now? If the implied reasoning were impeccable, the answer to that should be 'the poor', and once again we have to ask insistently why anyone should suppose that that is satisfactory. What have the poor done to be granted (allegedly) inferior health treatment? In fact, of course, it neither need be nor is as outrageous as that. Student doctors, like student teachers, barristers or anything else can be initiated into their profession in such a way that any of us may face them some of the time. In a society that is fundamentally egalitarian, the idea of somebody paying to have a physician, when a nurse would do, will scarcely make sense. Since what goes on will have nothing to do with differing ability to pay, what determines whether you get a nurse or a physician is the precise nature of the job in question.

What may arise in an egalitarian society, however, is a situation in which one person cannot afford to do X because he has deployed his resources on Y. That in itself does not seem to me problematic (although a society might feel the need to safeguard the interests of dependent persons). But many people have argued the inevitability of some people using their money to make more money, so that an equal distribution today results in unequal wealth tomorrow. No doubt that would be so in any society still geared to capital investment as a means of making money, but it would obviously cease to be so in a society reorganised in such a way as to make private investment illegal.

The standard objections to economic egalitarianism, then, can readily be dealt with. All that remain to be pointed out are four very substantial gains to be had from adopting this palpably fair principle. Firstly, such a policy would immediately remove an irrational but powerful inhibition on our schooling practices. So long as schools remain potent sources of determining life chances, or are thought to do so, they will be fought over by those who wish to use them as means to advancement or social change. Only when it is accepted that schooling has nothing to do with what one will ultimately earn will it be possible to ensure a programme of schooling that is concerned with education and socialisation, rather than technical training. Secondly, more generally, the assurance that jobs are equally rewarded will make it possible for people to develop and pursue their real talents and interests to a greater extent, and, insofar as that is allowed to happen, there should in time be a gain in job efficiency. Thirdly, and most obviously, such a policy would bring to an end the time-consuming and hate-engendering ritual of strikes, with all the bitterness, threatening, envy and divisiveness they entail; fourthly, an end to sterile debate about the relative importance of equally crucial elements in the body politic.

I conclude by returning to the basic point: there are differences between people which make it sensible and justifiable for them to live different kinds of life, including taking different jobs, living in different houses, having different hobbies and so forth. It is very important to stress again that I am not arguing for state-control of life in general. What there does not appear to be is a single reason that would justify one person in having more of the means for acquiring the benefits of his choice than another.

NOTES

1 S. I. Benn and R. S. Peters, *Social Principles and the Democratic State*.
2 See below Chapter 14.
3 See Bernard Gendron, 'Capitalism and poverty', *Radical Philosophers' News Journal*, 4 January 1975.
4 *Ibid.*
5 *Ibid.*
6 Milton Friedman, *Capitalism and Freedom*.
7 See John Rawls, *A Theory of Justice*.
8 *Ibid.*
9 John Plamenatz, 'Equality of Opportunity', in Lyman Bryson (ed.), *Aspects of Human Equality*.
10 Alva Myrdal, 'The Need for Equality', in *Towards Equality*.
11 John Plamenat 3, *op. cit.*
12 Alva Myrdal, *op. cit.*
13 Joel Feinberg, *Social Philosophy*.
14 John H. Schaar, 'The case for egalitarianism', in J. Roland Pennock and John W. Chapman (eds), *Equality*, Nomos, IX, Yearbook of the American Society for Political and Legal Philosophy.

15 *Ibid.*
16 Daniel Bell, *Coming of Post-Industrial Society.*
17 *Ibid.*
18 Joel Feinberg, *op. cit.*
19 *Ibid.*
20 Milton Friedman, *op. cit.*
21 Pierre Proudhon, *What Is Property?*
22 See, for example, Samuel Bowles, 'Unequal education', in P. and K. Struhl (eds), *Philosophy Now*, and Christopher Jencks *et al.*, *Inequality*.
23 Daniel Bell, *op. cit.*
24 *Ibid.*

10 Democracy

> Two cheers for democracy: one because it admits variety and two because it permits criticism.
>
> E. M. Forster

Perhaps because our society is thought to be democratic and also, generally, thought to be a relatively desirable form of society, there is a tendency for us to fail to distinguish between the question of what democracy is or involves, and the question of what justifies it as a form of government.[1] I shall attempt to avoid that error. I shall first outline a conception of democracy, then make reference to some alternative conceptions, including those of Dewey and Lenin, and finally elaborate on my chosen conception, and seek to justify it as a form of government.

Although the etymology of a word in itself proves nothing—not even guaranteeing something of the meaning of the word today, let alone anything of people's conceptions—I shall start by reference to the origins of the word 'democracy', since I intend to argue ultimately for the value of democracy conceived of in something closely resembling the original sense of the word. The word comes from two Greek words ($\delta\tilde{\eta}\mu o_{S}$ = demos and $\kappa\rho\acute{\alpha}\tau\epsilon\iota$ = kratei) which mean 'the people rule'. What that meant, at any rate at the time of Athens' democratic glory, may be reasonably clearly explained (as it in fact was in various contemporary texts).[2] Firstly, 'people' referred to the citizen body, which consisted of adult free males of indigenous status. Foreign residents, women, children and slaves were excluded, so that in numerical terms the 'people' was a minority of the persons resident in the state. Secondly, the manner of ruling was direct: legislative decisions were taken by the people at mass meetings, as were the rare elective decisions (though it seems likely that few citizens bothered to attend meetings regularly); the majority of executive offices were filled by lot, in such a way that any citizen would expect to serve in some way or other, two or three times during his life. Thirdly, the Athenians themselves regarded equality before the law and a considerable degree of freedom as part of the meaning of 'democracy'. In democratic Athens one man might be richer and more prestigious than another, but that gave him no special rights nor any special treatment should he find himself in court. (There matters would be decided by a jury consisting of some hundreds of his fellow citizens, again chosen by lot and paid a fee to enable them to attend without financial hardship.) The essence of Athenian democracy, then, which has carried over into our popular use of the term, was that the people (as defined) make their own decisions in matters of government, as opposed to being bound by precedent or priest, or having them made for them by some minority group or individual. (I have ignored reference to the important, but unusual, elected office of general.)

There are two important things to note about democracy thus conceived. Firstly, precisely because it is a direct, participatory, form of government by the people, it is only practicable on a small scale. (Athens had something like 50,000 adult male citizens during the second half of the fifth century B.C.) This was a point appreciated by Rousseau, who argued for something like this kind of democratic arrangement and saw that communities would have to be the size of Swiss cantons.[3] Government by referenda, now a possibility thanks to technological advances, though it would have something in common with direct participation, should not be seen as the modern equivalent. At the very least, government by referenda does not allow for the effect on voting of the mass meeting itself, nor for the community of understanding possible in the Athenian example; it also ignores the factor of participation in the executive branch of government. Secondly, although we glibly talk of the people ruling, that rather ignores the fundamental question of who these people who do the ruling are. Certainly, except in rare instances, they are not 'the people' as defined, for, when there is not unanimity, what is done is not precisely what the people (meaning all adult male citizens) want done. In the case of Athens, a more precise account would be that the people (that is, all adult male citizens) were free to participate in government, in the ways explained, and that the decisions were those of the majority of those present on any occasion. More generally, it has to be recognised that in any actual democracy to say that the people rule, or that the will of the majority rules 'is only another way of describing election or referendum procedures'.[4] Thus, in Britain, to say that the will of the majority rules can mean no more than that we have the electoral and parliamentary system we do have (that is, crudely, all adults may vote for representatives, and what emerges from the thereby elected government, and can be carried through the two houses of parliament, is law). For, in any other sense it is not true that the majority rules. (Most of the time the majority don't even get the political party of their choice in government.)

John Dewey's conception of democracy tries to preserve the idea of direct participation, but to place emphasis on the spirit rather than the mechanics of the thing (partly for the practical reason just noted). For him, 'the key-note of democracy as a way of life may be expressed . . . as the necessity for the participation of every mature human being in formation of the values that regulate the living of men together.'[5] He sees democracy as embodying the antithesis of the view that some are fitted to dictate to others through superior wisdom, though he concedes that some may be less fit than others to contribute to the decision-making process, through lack of practice or experience. But the people at large know best 'where the shoe pinches, the troubles they suffer from'.[6] This is especially so, according to Dewey, if through appropriate schooling they can get democratic practice and experience, for 'the best way to produce initiative and constructive power is to exercise it'.[7] So his conception of democracy is centred on active participation, and his defence of, or argument for the value of, that conception is that people know best what is good for themselves, they get better at contributing to the democratic process with practice, and, besides, 'each one is equally an individual and entitled to equal opportunity of development of his own capacities'.[8]

It will be noted that, however appealing, this is not a very well-marshalled case. Two distinct types of justification are being proferred, one an instrumental one ('this produces the goods'), the other an appeal to moral principle. But the latter does not necessarily yield the desired conclusion, and the former involves poor argument. One may grant that everybody is equally entitled to the opportunity to develop his own capacities, without conceding that that entails a participatory democracy. The claim that people get better at making decisions with practice is unproven, however the terms are defined. While the idea that people are necessarily the best judge of their own interests is simply false, still more obviously so when we bear in mind that, presumably, ideally democracy should make wise decisions in respect of people's interests generally.

A third conception of democracy is that of Lenin. This is markedly different from the two previously outlined and is arrived at by making two important moves: firstly, freedom has to be emphasised as the essential characteristic of democracy (rather than, say, participation), and, secondly, freedom has to be defined in a particular way. Lenin characterises 'bourgeois democracy' as merely 'freedom for the slave owners' or capitalist class, as opposed to the workers. 'Freedom', he asserts, in a manner that has subsequently become familiar, 'in capitalist society always remains just about the same as it was in the Ancient Greek republics: freedom for the slave-owners.'[9] Taken literally, that was palpable nonsense when Lenin wrote it, and thankfully, even more so today. For whatever the indignities and outrages involved in economic poverty, whatever the restrictions it in practice places upon one, there were various ways in which Greek slaves were unfree that have no parallel in contemporary society. (This is not an attempt to whitewash contemporary society. It might be conceded that the poor are worse off on balance today than Greek slaves were, but 'worse off' is a very general term. What is being denied is the more specific claim that this state of freedom is 'just about the same'.) On the other hand, the point that a person's freedom may be limited through economic lack is clearly sound, so, if the point is that while there is poverty there is a diminution of freedom, and if democracy is further defined as a state of freedom, it follows that we are not democratic (or not fully democratic). Lenin's claim was that following a period during which the exploiters would be crushed ('this is the modification of democracy during the transition from capitalism to communism'), 'when the capitalists have disappeared', 'the state ceases to exist' and 'it becomes possible to speak of freedom' and, hence, true democracy.[10]

Theoretically the question of establishing the value of democracy in Lenin's sense does not arise, because it is part of Lenin's theory that democracy in this sense will inevitably come about. But an obvious appeal is made to our desire for order, security and peace, and to the idea of getting what one wants, rather than what we are told we want, in order to render the image of revolutionary democracy attractive. However, that appeal is nurtured entirely by redefinitions coupled with the physical elimination of dissent: we will get a classless, peaceful, free, society, because significantly large elements of opposition will be destroyed, small elements will be classified as 'individuals' and discounted, and freedom is defined in terms of the absence of capitalism. It is not, to put it mildly, a very convincing argument, but, as I have said, it doesn't need to be, since the main thrust is the claim that this is how things are necessarily going to be. There is little point in discussing the moral value of the inevitable.

A fourth type of democracy is representative democracy, which might itself take many forms. The most important distinction is probably that between a system of elected spokesmen and a system of elected representatives in the full sense. In both cases the central idea is that individuals, at periodic intervals, elect for themselves persons to participate in the decision-making or legislative, and to some extent executive, branches of government; but the elected spokesman acts as a well-briefed agent of his electorate, seeking to present their view, while the representative acts autonomously.

The conception of democracy that I wish to defend is a particular type of representative democracy. It is that form in which all adult persons have equal right, both nominally and practically, to vote regularly for any representative they choose, and to stand as candidate for representation themselves, for a parliament that alone has the power to legislate; and in which, additionally, absolute freedom of expression is guaranteed to all, except insofar as the parliament overwhelmingly sees fit to curtail that freedom for a short period in the national interest.

The question of where we draw the line to distinguish between adult and non-adult is a fair one, but not immediately germane, for uncertainty on that score does not render the definition given hard to understand, and, as we have seen many times in this book already, difficulty in drawing a line does not invalidate a distinction.[11] The assumption behind restricting the category of voters to adults is that not every human being is equally capable of holding a coherent view on whom he wants to be his representative. This is not a point relating to wisdom or knowledge, but to the sort of understanding that generally develops with maturity. Typically, even a relatively stupid adult knows what he is doing and why (however bad the reason may seem to others), when he votes for A rather than B; typically, a child does not. Similarly, the question of how often and how regularly voting should take place is ultimately an important one, but it need not stand in the way of our understanding this conception of democracy in contrast to others.

Even before we turn to the question of what is to be said in favour of having a democracy in this sense, it may be wondered why anyone should opt for representation in this kind of way, rather than more direct participation through referenda, especially now that such a procedure could be relatively easily administered. Since I do not define democracy in terms of straight majority decisions, it would not be very meaningful to me to suggest that a system of referenda is any more democratic than a system of representation, but it might nonetheless be argued that it would be preferable. My view is that it would not be, partly because I believe that people generally are more adept at discerning whom they want to act for them, than at discerning what they want done on a wide range of particular issues, and partly because my defence of representative democracy will not be couched in terms of the right of every individual to decide matters for himself. A system of referenda, I suspect (though this is clearly no more than surmise), would in general be clumsy, unwise and intolerant. But the immediate point is that the assumption that it is self-evidently more democratic, or morally preferable, is based upon the view that the justification of democracy resides in the moral desirability of each man being allowed to make a direct contribution to the making of each social decision. I shall argue against that view.

It is a vital element in my conception of democracy that people should be free to vote for whom they wish, and to stand as a representative candidate; to that end, there must be machinery to ensure that nominal freedom can become freedom in actuality, and that people are not effectively disbarred by poverty or commitments of one sort or another. For of course it is true that formal freedom can be circumscribed by circumstance. Again the details need not concern us here, provided it is appreciated that some such machinery to safeguard actual freedom is envisaged. The point of the qualification to the clause concerning freedom of expression (in which I include freedom of publication, though not all rights of dissemination), is to allow for the surely justifiable curtailment of such freedom in time of war or conceivably other periods of internal upheaval. Even then the curtailment must be a matter for near-unanimity amongst representatives, and it must be constitutionally impossible for it to be more than a temporary measure. For, generally speaking, the requirement of freedom of expression is an important and necesary feature of this conception of democracy. It is not just a contingent extra: without it, we do not have a democracy as I understand it. However, it should be noted that I do not include freedom of association within the definition of democracy, as many would do and have done in the past. The reason for that is the belief that, should the right to associate be used in such a way as to cause harassment or menace to others, it is in principle quite right that it should be disallowed in that instance (though the right to express the views in question, by means that do not involve menacing association or pressing them unsolicited on those who do not wish to hear them, should be preserved). In practical terms this conceivably might mean that a man would be allowed to speak but denied any significant audience; but in such a case he would still be free to produce recordings or transcripts of his speech, provided that he did not force them upon people.

For the remainder of this chapter it will be democracy in this sense, this conception of representative democracy, that I refer to when I use the word without qualification; and it will be democracy in this sense (as opposed to the quite different kinds of democratic organisation involved in the TUC, ancient Athens or Soviet Russia), that I shall defend. But before considering the specific question of whether such a democratic form of government is desirable and can be justified, it is worth raising the wider question of whether *any* form of government is necessary or justifiable, by means of reference to the anarchist view put forward by Peter Kropotkin.

Kropotkin claims that his view is based on 'the philosophy of evolution' or, as we should put it, a theory of the evolution of societies or states parallel to, but distinct from, other evolutionary theories such as that of Marx.[12] Like Marxists, Kropotkin therefore thinks that what is at issue is 'a scientific discussion' about what is going to happen, rather than a discussion about what ought to happen. Whether one can have a scientific discussion on this issue, and, still more, whether there is some unalterable pattern of development waiting to be discovered, are, to say the least, extremely contentious questions. And there are surely very few people today who, with full understanding of what they are committing themselves to, can sincerely say that they believe the future shape of society will in all important particulars be shaped by unalterable forces, and still fewer believe, what is different, that it will be shaped by predetermined forces. There are thus three problems with Kropotkin's basic assertion that through history there has been 'a tendency towards integrating labour for the production of all riches in common . . . [and] a tendency towards the fullest freedom of the individual.'[13] Is it true? If so, will it necessarily continue to be so? Even if so, ought it to be so? And the answer to all three questions is almost certainly, no.

It is simply not true that there has been a uniform and steady evolutionary tendency of such a sort (although one might try to argue that, contrary to appearances, the significant underlying tendency is in that direction). There is no reason whatsoever *a priori* to assume that, whether there has been such a tendency in the past or not, it will persist in the future. As to the third point, I must stress that what I am denying is that it would follow from the observance of such a tendency that it was a good or desirable thing that matters are tending thus, just as it would not follow from the correctness of the Marxist view of what will happen, that it is desirable that it should happen so. That is not to say that there is necessarily anything wrong with either presumed end-state as an ideal. Certainly, when it comes to Kropotkin, with his ideal of a society in which people willingly cooperate without need of any government, it is hard not to share it. It is difficult too to dissent from his desire for establishing 'the best conditions for realising the greatest happiness for humanity'.[14] Furthermore, he is certainly correct to say of the parliament of his own time and place, and, one would guess, of our own and foreseeable future times, that it has 'proved to be unable to attend to all the numberless affairs of the community and to conciliate the varied and often opposite interests of the separate parts . . . [and] to find out the men who might represent a nation . . . otherwise than in a party spirit.'[15]

But what is nowhere apparent is how or why Kropotkin supposes that a nation without a system of government would manage to 'conciliate the varied and often opposite interests' of different people. As far as Kropotkin is concerned, of course, as with Lenin, there is no need to consider that problem, since he claims to be revealing how it will be: there just is a tendency towards some such golden age. One can only repeat that it is not self-evident that there has been such a tendency heretofore, it is not strikingly obvious that there will be such a tendency in the future, and, even if there will be, it does not follow that it will necessarily continue towards perfection or that the tendency could not be reversed by man or some non-human force.

The state may in some sense, as some would claim, be unnatural, but it is surely necessary. Even if Kropotkin were correct in claiming that the day is coming for anarchy, that day is not here yet, and we have therefore to consider what form of government is most desirable for at any rate a passing period of time. For the time being, at least, we need some system of government to try to protect and forward our various competing interests. If Thomas Hobbes possibly overstated the case when he said that life in a natural state would be nasty, brutish and short, he at least understood that political states are human contrivances, designed theoretically to guard against man's self-destructive urges to selfishness, dishonesty, momentary gratification, ignorance and so forth.[16]

But why should we opt for democracy? Isn't there something in the charges that Plato puts into the mouths of characters such as Callicles and Thrasymachus to the effect that in a democracy decisions are taken irresponsibly and in ignorance, on the whim of the moment?[17] Didn't Mencken have a point, however embarrassed we may be to admit it, when he attacked democracy more or less on the grounds that the populace at large is an ignorant mob and representative politicians are consequently time-serving rogues?[18] Possibly. But even should some people, allowing for overstatement, be tempted to share Mencken's view, that consideration would not upset the argument that I wish to put forward for democracy.

What kinds of defence of democracy might one offer? Some would argue that no person or group of people is blessed with superior wisdom sufficient to guide the state well or better than other people. By and large, people are equally wise and best know their own interests, and consequently a democratic form of government is required for wise government. This appealing argument is in fact most implausible. On virtually any definition of 'wise', there is no reason to accept that people are generally equally wise; people are not necessarily the best judges of their own interests or needs (as we have seen),[19] and democratic procedures in any case do not by any means guarantee a consensus. Ways of giving people an equal say are not necessarily ways of giving everybody what he wants. There can be no doubt that, if we were looking for the form of government that would produce the wisest decisions, the Mencken type of criticism would be valid, and democracy a poor candidate.

A quite different line of argument suggests that people do not deserve a democracy because they are all equally wise, but because they all have a natural right to self-determination. Democracy is here seen as an institutional means of allowing for self-government. But this argument cuts no ice, since it begs the very question at issue. To say that everybody has a natural right to the vote (or to some mechanism leading to democracy) is to assert, in different words, that it is morally proper that they should be entitled to vote. But the question we are raising is precisely whether and why one should believe that to be the case.

More plausibly, it is quite often argued that the defence of democracy lies in the fact that one cannot discriminate between persons in any respects that are relevant to the question of determining state policy. This line of argument is considerably weaker than is generally admitted, since the usually accepted decision to exclude children and mentally sick people to some extent belies it. The truth is that one can in principle distinguish between those fit and those unfit to make the sorts of decisions required of government, and our practice suggests that, by and large, we concede the point. Even granting, as I do, that there is nobody who can claim to know what is truly right and good for us all, under all circumstances, there are clearly some who have a requisite understanding of the nature of such questions, and some who fail to understand it at all.

When we add, at one extreme, that good government also necessitates a number of technical and empirical judgements, and at the other, that some people are not even always the best judge of their own wants, it becomes clear that we do vary in our capacity to contribute to or make political decisions. Of course, determining who has such capacity to a greater extent than others in practice may prove very difficult, but that is a different point.'In fact it leads us into what is surely the only cogent form of defence for democracy.

For the justification of democracy is to be found in a combination of the fact that certainty as to what a government ought to do, either in terms of overall strategy or more particular tactics, cannot be expected, and the assumption that a democratic form of government is, in the long run, more likely to deliver the goods in the sense of a stable, prosperous, culturally and intellectually productive, happy, fair community. It is, in other words, at bottom, a prudential case. It is not my purpose to make that case here; indeed since it involves speculation, evaluation, and prediction, it is not the kind of case that can be established or refuted with any certainty. But it can be elaborated slightly in order to emphasise its plausibility.

The point that has to be conceded is the point that the dogmatist will not concede, namely that there is very little that we have reason to believe confidently to be the truth, and there is nothing that we know to be the truth. It is absurdly difficult to be justified in being certain about what, overall, should be done by the state. This difficulty is usually attributed simply to the unknowability of in what the Good Life consists, and it is the case that that is a logically crucial factor: the question of how men ought to live their lives is not one that we can legitimately claim to have uncontentious ways of answering. But in practice, such is the increase in, and complexity of, our knowledge today, and the wider range of our experience, it is becoming increasingly difficult to judge people's wisdom generally and to predict the consequences of courses of action. We lack clear conceptions at vital points in empirical fields as well as in the evaluative domain, and economic and social theory are hardly more reliable than moral theory. This means that, although it remains true in principle that some may be wiser than others and better suited to lead or govern, and, in extreme cases, may even still be discernible in fact, in general no one individual can be *shown* to be superior.

Now this in itself would not be sufficient reason to embrace democracy. For it might be said that, since we do not know what we ought to do, there is no more reason to support a consensus or a majority vote than the lead of a minority. It might further be argued that some kind of minority system would lead to greater clarity and certainty of purpose, which might in itself prove beneficial. Certainly that might be so, but the argument for democracy is that given our state of ignorance, given the unpredictable changes that nature or others may inflict on us, even if we hold ourselves rigidly in check, democracy is our best bet. Obviously the argument is not that a majority vote or the view of elected representatives will necessarily be the wisest view. Rather it is that democracy is a system designed to take advantage of diversity and uncertainty, and to allow of flexibility, in order to give control over change, tolerance to cope with divergence, and openness to nurture truth. Since we are faced with so many different possibilities and so many different views, we need to adopt a system that is maximally tolerant and sensitive. Democracy is a system designed to be sensitive to competing interests, to compromise and adjustment. Its justification lies in the fact that in recognising that nobody knows what is best, it recognises each individual as a legitimate source of claims and arguments, while the long-term chances of people in general feeling that life is worth living are enhanced by a society that gives people a relatively high degree of freedom to do and say what they want.[20]

It should be clear that the above case for democracy, besides only being applicable to democracy in the particular sense outlined, is speculative as well as prudential. The argument is not that there is something inherently morally superior about democracy, and it does not definitely establish that democracy is the best system to adopt. The argument is, in essence, that commitment to democracy will lead to less error and less misery for mankind in the long term. I believe that to be true, but in the nature of things it can only be set forth as a suggestion, in the way it has been here, and left for the consideration of individual readers.

NOTES

1 A recent book that avoids this error is William N. Nelson, *On Justifying Democracy*.
2 For a more detailed account of the matter, see my *Athenian Democracy*.
3 See J. J. Rousseau, *The Social Contract*.
4 S. I. Benn and R. S. Peters, *Social Principles and the Democratic State*.
5 John Dewey, 'Democracy and Educational Administration', in *School and Society*, Vol. 45, No. 1162, 3 April 1937.
6 *Ibid*.
7 *Ibid*.
8 *Ibid*.

9 V. I. Lenin, *State and Revolution*.
10 *Ibid*.
11 See in particular the discussion on whether the foetus is a person in Chapter 8.
12 Peter Kropotkin, 'Anarchist Communism: Its Basis and Principles', in Roger N. Baldwin (ed.), *Kropotkin's Revolutionary Pamphlets*.
13 *Ibid*.
14 *Ibid*.
15 *Ibid*.
16 See Thomas Hobbes, *Leviathan*.
17 See Plato, *Gorgias* and *Republic*.
18 See H. L. Mencken, *Notes on Democracy*.
19 See above Chapter 9.
20 Sidney Hook has tried to enumerate the key practical advantages of adopting a democratic system of government in *Political Power and Personal Freedom*.

11 Civil Disobedience

'Dying for an idea', again, sounds well enough, but why not let the idea die instead of you?
                                      Wyndham Lewis, *The Art of Being Ruled*

Two thousand four hundred years ago, Socrates refused to save his life when he might have done, on the grounds that one should always obey the laws of one's land.[1] More recently President Kennedy echoed that view when he said, 'Americans are free, in short, to disagree with the law, but not to disobey it.'[2] Socrates, having been tried and condemned to death by the Athenians, was afforded the chance to escape into exile. He refused, arguing that, as he had lived his life by advantage of the laws, it would ill become him to flout or ignore them now that they happened to be to his personal inconvenience and discomfort. Admittedly there were features of Socrates' case that make it inappropriate to treat it as a norm (the fact that escaping into exile was an established custom, the fact that he probably wasn't guilty of what was anyway a mischievous charge, the fact that, now an elderly man, he may well have welcomed death and martyrdom). But it may nonetheless serve to introduce the question of where our obligations to obey the law of the land begin and end. Can it really be, as Socrates suggests, that we have no right to disobey, come what may, so that allegiance is owed as a moral duty even to the legislation of a barbarous tyranny? That seems incredible. On the other hand it seems absurd that people should be entitled to obey or disobey laws as suits themselves. But then, is it possible to devise some general formula that avoids the apparent unacceptability of either extreme?
   It will be appreciated that an answer to this question of obedience to the state's laws could be tied up with the wider question of whether any form of government can be justified, and if so which. Some might wish to argue that you may legitimately oppose the laws only of certain kinds of state; some that, since no state apparatus can be justified, one has no obligations to any state; some that absolute allegiance is at any rate owed to morally justified forms of govern-

ment. Since I have argued for a democratic form of government in the previous chapter, suggesting that it can be justified on prudential grounds, given certain epistemological and moral facts, and since, even in its simplest form, this issue of the limits of obedience is extremely complicated, I shall limit the discussion in what follows by assuming that we are talking in the context of a democratic form of government (as defined above).

One of the initial problems in this matter, as in so many, is the need to discriminate between various similar but distinct types of behaviour, and to establish precisely which we are talking about. We need, in the first place, to distinguish carefully between revolution, violence, and civil disobedience, and to make it clear what each involves; for it may well prove that one is justified where another is not, and that people confuse each other by meaning one thing while apparently saying another. A good example of the mischief that can be done by playing with words in this way (whether deliberately or not) is provided by Kai Nielsen. His main theme is that 'socialists' should only engage in 'revolutionary violence . . . in response to counter-revolutionary violence'.[3] If one is aware that in much neo-Marxist theory 'revolutionary' means 'in tune with Marxist ideology' and 'counter-revolutionary' 'in tune with non-Marxist ideology', one should perhaps be forewarned against taking such a remark too literally. Nonetheless, the phrase 'in response to' suggests, as presumably it is supposed to suggest, that 'socialists' are only justified in using violence in retaliation for violence used against them. The use of the same word each time may lull the reader into assuming that what is being said is that specific action (for the sake of example, shooting and bombing) may only be engaged in as a response to such action on the part of others. But what Nielsen means by 'in response to counter-revolutionary violence' is 'when the time is ripe', for he goes on to argue that, despite what the bourgeois press would say, a pre-emptive strike against a 'non-socialist' state does not count as initiating violence. Thus, words that are designed to suggest that we will not cast the first stone actually convey quite the opposite message.

What, one might be forgiven for wondering, is going on here? Two quite familiar and central tactics of dogmatism are being deployed. Firstly, there is the assumption (not by any means confined to any one group of dogmatists), that right and wrong are to be assessed in terms of the received dogma (and consequently the dogma itself is never challenged); and then there is an attempt to redefine key words, so as to harmonise the dogma with popular sentiment at a superficial level. As to the first point, that is unaccept-

Civil Disobedience 143

able only in a debate where it begs the questions at issue. Naturally Nielsen thinks his views are broadly correct and justify him in doing certain things that other views might not. Naturally, too, he lives his life for the most part interpreting events in the light of his views, rather than critically examining the views. The objection is to entering a discussion about something such as the justification of violence, on the assumption that a particular viewpoint has already arrived at the answer. It goes without saying that Nielsen believes that it may be legitimate to instigate revolutionary violence at any time *pour épater le bourgeois*, but one does not contribute to establishing the soundness of that belief by taking it as one's premise.

The second point is of more immediate concern. Either 'violence' is being redefined to convey something other than its everyday sense of physical assault, or the word is being used in such a broad way as to ignore actual distinctions in experience. It can only be true that 'socialists' are not *initiating* violence when they engage in pre-emptive strikes against others, if one counts as alike things that are entirely distinct. To be fair, that is precisely what Nielsen wants to do. One of the essential points in his doctrine is that the capitalist system itself should be classified as an instance of violence. And, it may be asked, is that not quite reasonable? Why should we pre-occupy ourselves only with violence in the sense of crude physical blows, when other things can be so much more insidious and damaging? But to ask that question is rather like asking why one shouldn't call a shirt 'a pair of trousers', since they are both articles of clothing. And it quite misses the point. Just as it is quite true that both the shirt and the pair of trousers are articles of clothing, so that, if we were having a talk about clothes, it would be right to insist that I don't confine it to trousers, so, if we were having a talk about what is damaging, I should not confine it to physical violence. But that, to use a suitably violent phrase, is to jump the gun. We are not having a discussion about what is damaging, as yet. (And there are cogent reasons why we should not, relating to the scope of the topic and the need to recognise differences before one classifies in categories.) Whether equally damaging or not, the way in which the American political system does violence to citizens is decidedly different to the way in which muggers on the streets of New York do violence to people. 'Violent', used as a description of capitalism, is not the same thing as 'violent' used as a description of physical conflict. (Unless, as I say, you broaden the scope of the term, so that it is used as a synonym for something like harmful, in which case you say very little of specific interest and beg too many questions to handle at once.) They may turn out to be equally objectionable, but we merely beg the question of whether they are, if we call them (two different things) by the same pejorative name.

(Incidentally, Nielsen makes the same error of confusing words with ideas, when he says that whether revolution will cause more suffering than it is worth, or more than it removes, 'is a question open to empirical assessment which cannot be settled in a philosopher's study',[4] seeking to suggest that defining terms is an idle exercise. Not only is it not idle, but more to the point it is not in itself philosophy. It is true that ultimately whether a particular revolution was worth the candle is an empirical matter. But it is not true that in the real world the question of whether a particular revolution *will* cause more or less suffering than it removes is 'open to empirical assessment', since one cannot 'empirically assess' what has not happened. Rather it is an empirical question concerning which we have to make a speculative assessment. Secondly, it is not true that one could engage meaningfully in such speculation without recourse to 'the philosopher's study', for how could one possibly form one's assessment (or indeed subsequently test the consequences empirically), without a clear conception—not, please note, merely a positively enunciated definition—of suffering?)

The elements of truth that lie behind Nielsen's ultimately inadequate argument to justify initiating violence against states based upon different ideologies to one's own, are the point that things may sometimes be classified as violent, while not being physical, and the point that things may be similar to violent acts in some respects, and equally objectionable, while not being violent in the normal sense of the word. What we therefore need to do here is draw some broad distinctions, so that we can face openly the question of whether we want to observe them or ignore them, in the context of opposition to state policy. As we have already noted, ordinarily the word 'violence' suggests physical harm. If we hear that the police have used violent means with a suspect, we assume that they have physically beaten him up. (Is that not so?) We do not assume (in line with a famous Monty Python sketch) that they have used 'sarcasm' and 'wit' on him. It has to be admitted that occasionally people do refer to psychological violence without specifically saying as much, but the fact remains that physical and psychological violence may be distinguished, and usually people will assume that the word 'violence', used without qualification, refers to physical assault of some kind. It may also be observed that psychological violence may itself cover a very wide area, so that for some purposes it might be profitable to make further sub-distinctions. One perhaps thinks of mental cruelty between two people in close association as a typical example of psychological violence, but ugliness might just as easily do psychological violence to some, and blasphemy to others.

Newton Garver has suggested that we should also note a distinction between overt and covert violence, since he sees violence as having essentially to do with violation of the person in any respect, rather than to do with force.[5] But little seems to be gained by this particular distinction. It is true that, if you talk of violence and exclude reference to things such as blackmail, parents driving their children to suicide through priggish lack of understanding, and inciting to racial hatred, you exclude a nice set of possibly equally unpleasant activities. But for all that, they are very different. There is more of a case for classifying an intense programme of deliberate humiliation as a special kind of violence (psychological), which distinguishes it from the usual type of violence (physical), than there is for classifying such examples as those just mentioned as violent. For the unintentional driving to suicide of their children by foolish parents is so different from the intentional shooting of people, as to make it a mere hindrance to clear thinking to classify them together. I hope, incidentally, that there is no need for me to stress that I am not trying to justify any of the activities that I suggest should not be classed as acts of violence. I am not, at this juncture, trying to justify anything, and I would have thought that in some circumstances some of these insidious forms of behaviour might be more morally objectionable than acts of violence. My point is simply that they are very different, and we may therefore want to say different things about them. That being the case, it seems unwise to blur the difference by classifying them as violent, albeit covert rather than overt.

If we restrict the use of the unqualified word 'violence' to cases involving physical assault, require psychological violence to be explicitly qualified as such, and reject the idea that acts that unintentionally violate a person's selfhood in some way should be classified as violent, there is only gain. There is no loss, because, when it is deemed advisable to lump all these different kinds of action together, we have perfectly good generic terms in 'harmful' or 'causing suffering'.

With the same desire to use words as nearly as possible in the way that people generally do use them and that dictionaries usually define them, I would suggest that we should think of revolution as amounting to the forcible overthrow of a political system by those, or some part of those, nominally subject to it. It follows that we will need to be explicit, if we wish to refer to peaceful or non-violent revolution, since ordinarily revolutions encompass violence. If we stand by this ordinary usage of the word, we shall also divorce it from the connotations imposed by those dogmatists who, as we noted above, wish to associate it exclusively with their own cause. That is to be welcomed for it is ridiculously (or maliciously) confusing to take a perfectly straightforward word in everyday use, and to seek to appropriate it for one's own exclusive doctrinaire use—just another obfuscating failure to discriminate and to communicate.

Now, no doubt 'civil disobedience', which is not a frequent phrase in common parlance, and is therefore to some extent a matter for stipulative definition, could be used to cover any type of disobedience, minimal or revolutionary, peaceful or violent, provided that it was directed against the state, for certainly 'disobedience' is a general term that admits of many varying forms. However, I shall follow Hugo Bedau in saying that 'anyone commits an act of civil disobedience, if and only if, he acts illegally, publicly, non-violently and conscientiously with the intent to frustrate (one of) the laws, policies or decisions of his government'.[6] This allows us to distinguish between civil disobedience and acts of violence, even when they are engaged in for the same purposes, as most of us wish to do, in case we may decide that one may be justified where the other is not. It also distinguishes the nuisance from the principled nuisance, as again most of us imagine may sometimes be necessary, since what may have to be conceded as your right, given strong moral sentiments, does not necessarily therefore have to be tolerated wherever you have a whim to cause trouble. The qualifications 'illegally' and 'with the intent to frustrate' are important for distinguishing between, say, a protest march and a refusal to pay taxes. Both may be equally troublesome, but one surely would not wish to commit oneself in advance to the view that what goes for one (in terms of moral legitimacy) necessarily goes for the other. Perhaps the least obvious of Bedau's criteria is his qualification 'publicly', yet there certainly is a distinction between the Clay Cross Councillors who refused to collect rates (public activity), and those persons who, in the dead of night, defaced a cricket pitch in order to draw attention to their grievance. The latter acted illegally, non-violently and presumably conscientiously, as did the former, but they chose a clandestine form of operation such that they did not so much protest as publicise their cause. This distinction admittedly is a subtle one, and I am less committed to its significance than to that of other distinctions noted. Nonetheless, insofar as it can be discerned, the distinction should perhaps be noted.

Civil Disobedience 147

The above are recommendations for verbal distinctions, in line with usual usage, in order to pin-point and draw our attention to actual differences in the world. Any reader who imagines that I have been attempting to make substantive points by appealing to verbal habits (and there will be some), needs to re-read what I have written. One of the reasons that it has been important for me to make these distinctions is that in the remainder of this chapter I do not intend to say much about revolution or violence (physical). I do not want to be presumed to wish necessarily to make the same claims about them as I shall put forward about civil disobedience. If I were to pursue those issues, the conclusions I should argue for, broadly speaking, would be that violence (whether to individual or state) and revolution may be justified in human affairs, and that what ultimately justifies them is what alone ultimately justifies anything, namely an overall diminution of human suffering. But it should be noted that, insofar as my justification of democracy above is sound, it cannot be justifiable to engage in revolution in order to subvert democracy (as such, as opposed to a particular attempt at democracy), since the justification for both is of the same order. If democracy is the best form of government because in the long run it is the form most able to minimise suffering, then attempting to replace it by another form of government in the interests of diminishing suffering cannot be justified, whatever the actual errors of a democracy. That I do believe, and that, in a way, is why the issue of civil disobedience is of overwhelming importance in a democracy. In a case where revolution and physical violence against the state are ruled out, civil disobedience is the only remaining candidate for a means of correcting the state, when constitutional means have failed. (It is, anyway, other things being equal, a preferable way forward, since it is less harmful both directly and indirectly in terms of fears and tensions.)

But is even civil disobedience in fact morally acceptable? What of the arguments of those who claim that it is not? Consider first the Socratic view that we have an absolute obligation to obey the law. On the face of it, as I noted at the outset, this is counter-intuitive. It would justify complicity in the atrocities of concentration camps, for example, and make the very idea of the Nuremburg trials insupportable. That is hard to accept as either moral or reasonable. One might be willing to forgive evil done in obedience to the state, but surely not to justify it.

Wasserstrom has distinguished three variants of this view that we have an absolute obligation to obey the law.[7] The first is simply and precisely that civil disobedience, since it necessarily involves break-

148 *Injustice, Inequality and Ethics*

ing the law, is necessarily never justified. The second, weaker, view is that it can be justified by 'the presence of outweighing circumstances'.[8] The third is that it is usually obligatory to obey the law, on other grounds than merely that it is the law, but not always. That is to say, it may be claimed that, if it is illegal, it is *ipso facto* immoral, that, if it is illegal, that is a moral reason for refraining from doing it, which may only be overridden by other moral considerations, or that being illegal is not necessarily a moral reason for not doing something.

Wasserstrom's third position seems to me quite unconvincing, if I have correctly understood it. The suggestion appears to be that, before breaking the law, one should always *consider* whether disobeying it is in itself immoral or a bad factor, but it may sometimes be so and sometimes not. But the only way in which I can conceive that that could be true, assuming that we are not referring to the second view, which allows that something else may be worse than breaking the law, would be if we were to assume that some acts of disobedience in themselves involve moral wrong, while others do not. But what could this possibly mean? Wasserstrom seems to envisage something like this: acts of disobedience generally cost the taxpayer money and are consequently in themselves bad, but, on a particular occasion, an act of disobedience might not cost the taxpayer anything, and would therefore not in itself be bad. But despite the fact that the phrase 'in itself' seems to fit snugly enough, if that is what Wasserstrom means, he would seem to be saying no more than that disobedience as such is *not* bad, but costing the taxpayer money is. It would be a purely contingent point that disobedience generally is expensive and therefore wrong. And onsequently this position would be of no immediate interest to us.

We are therefore left with the theses that it is always wrong to break the law, and that it is in itself wrong, but may be less wrong than not doing so in certain circumstances. On what grounds might one attempt to defend the thesis that it is always wrong? Four different grounds have been suggested: that one has benefitted from the existence of the laws (the Socratic position), that by living under them one has consented to them (also suggested by Socrates), that if others behaved likewise the result would be chaos, and that morality and law are indivisible. The last mentioned position, that what is legally binding is morally binding, just isn't tenable. If it were, we should have very little reason to modify laws and very few grounds for criticising the practice of other states (past or present) on moral grounds. None of the issues discussed in this book would be issues, for whether abortion or civil disobedience were morally justifiable would simply be a matter of consulting the statute book and seeing whether they are legally permitted. Complacency would be the order of the day: that which we have legally enacted is thereby made good. The only frisson of excitement would come from the fact that, as the law about, say, capital punishment or homosexuality changed back and forth over the years, people would find themselves becoming and ceasing to be moral sinners, like birds springing in and out of cuckoo-clocks—a funny kind of morality, and of course it's nonsense. Law and morality are not co-extensive. Perhaps the law does, and should, seek to be moral rather than immoral (though, even then, many laws have nothing to do with morality), and perhaps we shall finally decide that it is immoral to disobey any law, but, if that is so, it is not simply because the law is the law.

Nor is the view that one must obey the law in return for benefits received under the law very persuasive. Indeed, it is rather like saying that one should be prepared to submit to brutality, if its perpetrators have hitherto been one's benefactors. Besides, one did not ask to receive benefits, and one may in fact not have received them. Similarly with consent, which is very seldom given except in the sense that one might argue that remaining in a state involves tacit acceptance of its laws. But one has so little choice as to whether one stays or goes in most states these days, that even tacit consent cannot be presumed. Besides which there does not seem any compelling reason to accept that, because by and large we do consent to our laws and do benefit from them, we thereby commit ourselves to abiding by any law that may emerge in any circumstances, even in a democratic state.

Possibly the most popular argument is the one that takes the form that one ought always to obey the law because of the unacceptable consequences of everybody acting on the assumption that, if they do not like a particular law, they are justified in breaking it. Now, it surely is true that there must be a general presumption in society that laws ought to be obeyed or, to put it another way, an *a priori* obligation to obey them. Other things being equal, one ought to obey laws, even if they are inconvenient to oneself, because otherwise a system of law cannot operate. But equally surely that observation is not really pertinent to the point at issue; for we are not considering whether people should feel free to do what they feel like doing, regardless of laws, but whether, in certain exceptional cases, civil disobedience may be morally justified. It is not necessarily the case that the system of law would break down and chaos ensue, if it were agreed that on certain limited conditions civil disobedience could be justified. It should also be noted that the fact that civil disobedience may be morally justified does not necessarily mean that it should not be legally penalised. We are considering the question of whether those who engage in civil disobedience should feel any moral shame for so doing, and not whether they should or should not still be subject to the law of the land, and therefore, perhaps, to some punishment such as a fine or imprisonment for their civil disobedience. That fact alone, as well as helping to ensure that the disobedience in question is conscientious, meets the practical observation that too much law breaking brings the law itself into disrepute, on its own ground, with the practical rejoinder that there will not generally be a temptation for every one to do likewise. So, one reply to this objection would be, 'So what, if everyone who was sincerely committed to civil disobedience on an issue did engage in it?' Indeed, according to the argument of the civil protester that is what they should do. As Wasserstrom says, 'Anyone who claims that there are actions that are both illegal and justified surely need not thereby be asserting that it is right generally to disobey all laws or even any particular law. It is surely not inconsistent to assert both that indiscriminate disobedience is indefensible and that discriminate disobedience is morally right and proper conduct.'[9]

If, then, we concede that the notion of a system of law presupposes that other things being equal it will be obeyed, or imposes a *prima facie* obligation on us to obey, but nonetheless deny that this obligation is absolute, the question remains: what could justify civil disobedience? At this point we need to introduce another distinction between civil disobedience that involves breaking any convenient law in order to frustrate government, and civil disobedience that is confined to breaking the law objected to or directly related to the government policy objected to. We also need to distinguish between protest relating to personal issues, such as abortion, internal political matters, such as income tax, and external political matters, such as nuclear arms protest, and between protest directed at substantive moral issues, such as capital punishment, and protest directed at procedural issues, such as proportional representation. My argument is that the line of reasoning that establishes that it may be morally justifiable to break a law is such that, at any rate on the face of it, it will only justify civil disobedience when it involves breaking a law which is either the issue itself or directly related to the issue, when it is a substantive issue, and when it is an internal political issue or a personal issue. That is to say, civil disobedience in this country as part of an international campaign for nuclear disarmament would not be justified, nor would it be justified as a tactic to support the policy of proportional representation (essentially because there are no directly relevant laws to be broken). On the other hand civil disobedience that involved breaking the current law on abortion, when abortion is at issue, or withholding income tax, when some tax matter is at issue, might be justified.

In principle a law is a bad one when it causes more harm than good or more harm than it need do; and one would be morally right to break it when doing so had less harmful consequences than not doing so, taking into account all the consequences of the disobedience in question, including both such things as the possible weakening of respect for law that it may contribute to, and the possible awakening of support for protest in others, leading ultimately, perhaps, to a change in the law. In practice, it is impossible to predict the consequences in this way, and for that reason many would argue that it is best to adopt the moral command 'Never break the law', just as we generally accept the moral command 'Never kill', though we know that it would sometimes have better consequences for mankind if we did kill a particular individual; because it seems on balance more dangerous to leave the matter as one for individuals to decide. But, just as further reflection shows that, though we do not want no rule on killing, we would be wise to qualify the rule in certain ways so that it becomes, for example, 'Don't kill except in self defence', so it would surely be preferable to qualify any rule about breaking the law so that it becomes 'Never break the law except in exceptional cases where your conscience cannot allow you to perform or refrain from the act enjoined by the law.' (Incidentally this no more amounts to the act-utilitarian view that one should simply make up one's mind in each particular instance whether breaking the law will increase human happiness, than the rule that one should never kill except in self defence, discussed above in Chapter 3, does. It is a quite specific rule, to be followed as such.) That formulation, it will be found, entails the limitations noted above on the kinds of issues where civil disobedience may be legitimate.

In full then, the claim that I would make would be as follows: a person is morally entitled to act illegally, publicly, and non-violently with the intention of frustrating one of the laws, policies or decisions of his government, when the illegality consists in breaking a law that is either at issue or directly related to the issue, and when his conscience will not allow him to abide by that law.

Before concluding this chapter we should briefly contrast and compare this view with three others, in order to shed further light on the whole problem. Robert Wolff offers a stark alternative with his anarchist view that there is no such thing as legitimate authority.[10]

Citing the student demonstrations at Columbia University in 1968, which he believes achieved much good at relatively little cost, he does not attempt to argue that they were therefore justified, but dissolves the problem by saying that, since the police, the legislature, the University Senate and so forth 'have no particular legitimacy or sanction',[11] it cannot be illegitimate to oppose them. Since he defines violence as 'the illegitimate use of force to effect decisions against the will of others',[12] he is also able to come to the amazing conclusion that, even where rocks are hurled and bodies laid prostrate, there is no violence. Consequently, and notwithstanding some sensible observations to the effect that different socio-economic groups define violence differently, or, as one might prefer to say, different people judge different things to be violent, it seems that only a verbal point has been scored. It has certainly not been established that student demonstrations of any sort are justified, whatever the motives or outcome.

Incidentally, we may note that the main reason that different people judge different things to be violent is the familiar one that people do not tie the meaning of the term down clearly. If it is allowed to float as a synonym for injustice, without any attempt to discriminate between physical, psychological, overt, covert, direct, or indirect violence, then of course people will cite widely different things as being violent. But the fact that, if the word is used broadly enough, it can become part of sterile ideological warfare, should not lead us to suppose that there can be a 'class' perspective on, or an ideological interpretation of, whether this man is beating up that man or not. It must also be observed that the phrase 'legitimate authority' is ambiguous. Some people might want to argue for the idea of an eternally and absolutely sanctioned right to authority being enjoyed by some persons or group, on the model of the supposed divine right of kings. More usually today, people simply mean authority that has been or can be justified. In the previous chapter an argument was put forward for democracy, and, assuming it to have been an adequate argument, it follows that a democratic state exercises legitimate authority in the second sense, and violence against it is consequently illegitimate. Wolff's belief that it is not seems to depend upon playing on the ambiguity, for it is true that the police and other authorities have no divine right to authority. The crucial points would seem to be these. There are various democratically enacted laws in the United States. At Columbia University in 1968 certain people broke various such laws, and some of them used violence in the normal sense of physical violence. Were those actions justified? To that question Wolff has no answer, beyond reiterating his creed to the effect that anything goes.

Mention should also be made of the contributions to this topic of Herbert Marcuse and John Rawls, in view of the estimation in which both are held, although in truth the former at least has little to contribute. He seems to adopt the utilitarian position, allowing that revolution (a term which he uses liberally to include violent and non-violent internal disobedience) may be justified by considerations of freedom and happiness.[13] But he fails to discriminate between defining happiness and judging whether people are happy on the one hand, and estimating the price of happiness on the other, assuming that all are matters of straightforward calculation. This confusion leads him all too simplistically to suppose that the revolutionary just needs to do his sums on happiness, and then revolt or refrain as the case may be. But what we ought to do, even on utilitarian terms, is not simply a matter of predicting empirical consequences. In principle, in order to calculate whether people will or will not be happy given various circumstances, we need to have a clear grasp of what happiness is, some way of knowing how happy people are, and some way of knowing what will make them happier. None of these is a simple matter of calculation. One also has to determine whether any policy that would bring more happiness would justify revolution, or whether only the policy that would ensure the greatest possible happiness would. The situation becomes even more complicated when one regards freedom as equally valuable, as Marcuse does and utilitarians proper do not. The point of making these observations is to show that, for all his following, Marcuse is far too slap-happy to be taken seriously in his contribution to the issue of civil disobedience, and also to suggest yet again that it is not as simple and straightforward an issue as some would have us believe.

Rawls argues that civil disobedience is justified, though not necessarily to be recommended, on three conditions.[14] They are, that one has been subjected to more or less deliberate injustice over a period of time, in spite of having made the appropriate and normal complaints through the political process; that the injustice involves a clear violation of the liberties of equal citizenship; and that it would not prove unacceptable in terms of chaos and social disorder, if others placed in exactly similar circumstances did likewise. Implicit in the first two points made here are some of the points that have already been made relating to the limitations on the kind of issue that may legitimately lead to civil disobedience. (Rawls clearly accepts that civil disobedience should be confined to breaking laws directly related to what is at issue.) Beyond that, his points, though with one exception plausible, seem more akin to practical safety tips than principled points. It certainly seems generally wise and desirable that people should be slow to revert to civil disobedience, but can one really say that it is not justified, unless one has submitted to injustice for a period of time? The exception is Rawls' interesting third condition, for surely this cannot be accepted even as a practical guideline. It compares well with the view of many people that striking should be legal and morally acceptable, but that strikes that hurt others are morally outrageous. But strikes are designed to hurt. If they do not, they are not worth having, so, if people object to damaging or hurtful strikes, they should object to strikes altogether. Similarly civil disobedience, being a conscientious act intended to frustrate the government, is designed to cause trouble. If, in a particular case, everybody acting in concert with my civil disobedience would cause chaos, so much the better: it would achieve my object more quickly and would incidentally suggest that my object is that of most other people.

That point leads me to finish the chapter by stressing a point made above: recognising civil disobedience as morally legitimate is not a recipe for disaster in terms of civil disorder, partly because it is only justified on limited terms, and partly, here the point to be stressed, because 'morally justified' does not entail 'legally permitted'. People who feel they should stand out against, say, abortion laws, should feel no shame in their civil disobedience. But nor should they complain, if fined or imprisoned. The real moral that Socrates pointed is that acting conscientiously can be painful for the agent.

NOTES

1 See Plato, *Crito*.
2 John F. Kennedy, *New York Times*, 1 October 1962.
3 Kai Nielsen, 'On Justifying Revolution', in *Philosophy and Phenomenological Research*, Vol. 37, No. 4, June 1977.
4 *Ibid*.
5 Newton Garver, 'What Violence Is', in *The Nation*, 24 June 1968.
6 Hugo A. Bedau, 'On Civil Disobedience', in *The Journal of Philosophy*, 52:21, 12 October 1961.
7 Richard Wasserstrom, 'The Obligation to Obey the Law', in *UCLA Law Review*, Vol. 10, 1963.
8 *Ibid*.
9 *Ibid*.
10 Robert Paul Wolff, 'On Violence', *The Journal of Philosophy*, 66, 2 October 1969.

11 *Ibid.*
12 *Ibid.*
13 Herbert Marcuse, 'Ethics and Revolution', in R. T. DeGeorge (ed.), *Ethics and Society.*
14 John Rawls, 'The Justification of Civil Disobedience', in R. Wasserstrom (ed.), *Today's Moral Problems.*

12 Animals

> 'Nothing can be more obvious than that all animals were created solely and exclusively for the use of man.'
> 'Even the tiger that devours him?' said Mr. Escot.
> 'Certainly', said Doctor Gaster.
> 'How do you prove it?' said Mr. Escot.
> 'It requires no proof', said Doctor Gaster: 'it is a point of doctrine. It is written, therefore it is so.'
>
> Thomas Love Peacock, *Headlong Hall*

Recently there has been a certain amount of able and persuasive writing on the question of the morality of our treatment of animals.[1] But despite that, and despite the fact that, as I shall argue below, much of what we do, or acquiesce in allowing to be done, to animals is more indubitably wrong than many of the things we agitate far more about (such as treatment of women), and more resolvable than many of the issues we are more inclined to struggle with (such as wealth distribution), it is still seldom that one is taken seriously when one expresses moral outrage at the treatment of animals. In the public mind women's liberation is a saner enterprise than animal liberation. Perhaps we should take heart from the fact that there was a time when the rights of wealthy landlords seemed more important than the rights of slaves.

Possibly the difficulties attendant on opening people's eyes to the simple wrongness involved in our behaviour in this respect are inevitable. There is truth in the view that 'a liberation movement demands an expansion of our moral horizons, so that practices that were previously regarded as natural and inevitable are now seen as intolerable.'[2] In other words, it is not a case of pointing out the obvious, or even pressing home reason, that we have here. Rather, a way has to be found of giving reason a purchase, of getting people to set aside their inhibiting conventional sentiments. One has to effect the same kind of dramatic shift of assumption and outlook as an Athenian would have had to make to oppose slavery two thousand years ago. The Greeks, after all, were not brutal psychopaths, as some Nazis appear to have been, and they were not acting as moral cowards in the way that some Germans, faced with a nasty choice under Hitler, may have been, nor were they conscious exploiters in the way that many eighteenth-century slave-traders were. They were people who took slavery for granted, as we take our treatment of animals or the schooling of children for granted.

There are a number of factors that help to explain and reinforce our prejudices in this matter. No animal, not even an orangutang, *looks* as much like a human being as another human being; and like is, no doubt, attracted to like. And then, all too often, attempts to discuss the issue of our treatment of animals become bogged down in empirical arguments about how we do treat animals, or speculative arguments about how various animals feel about particular experiences, and therefore the point of principle is never reached, or else it is forgotten or ignored. Sometimes attempts to suggest that our treatment of animals is immoral are scornfully associated with the views of little old ladies, whose attitude to their cats may be suffocatingly mawkish and very possibly unkind, while it is certainly very often not extended to other less lovely creatures. Sometimes, the distinct, though obviously connected, issue of vegetarianism serves to deflect the argument. Sometimes a naked appeal to self-interest (the 'would you cuddle a snake' gambit) is enough to curtail the debate.

The above points, though they may serve to defeat an argument psychologically, actually all miss the crucial point. In what follows, I shall therefore attempt to keep distinct points separate. I shall concede that there is room for disagreement about which animals do suffer under what circumstances, and that killing animals is not necessarily wrong. I shall also suggest that the case for vegetarianism, if there is one, is a political rather than a moral one. But at the centre of my argument is the relentless insistence that to cause animals to suffer is in itself a moral wrong.

I am not primarily concerned to dwell upon the empirical details of our treatment of animals, but, just in case the reader is completely unaware, even in outline, of what goes on, a brief comment must be made. Every single day some rather curious things happen to thousands if not millions of animals for three main reasons: in order to facilitate large-scale food production, in order to advance consumer research (for example, research into the effects of potentially noxious cosmetics), and in order to advance medical research. It is activities in relation to these three areas, which by and large people neither observe nor care about, that count in the main for the cruel treatment of animals by man, and not the relatively isolated but more visible instances of cruelty to pets or particular farm animals—which, paradoxically, do usually generate a little steam in those who witness them. (This difference of response is presumably just another instance of our ability to close our minds to distant large-scale horrors, such as the butchery of the innocent in Kampuchea, which would mortify us, if face to face.) A relatively bowdlerised list of the sort of things we do to animals for these three reasons would include the following (and the point of the list is not to carry the case by generating emotional revulsion, but to indicate what we are talking about): keeping calves all their short lives in stalls measuring five feet by two feet, keeping animals without any kind of bedding such as straw, keeping them standing on grids (for ease of cleaning), keeping pigs pegged or penned flat to the ground, cutting the beaks off chickens and preventing them spreading their wings. Experiments are carried out on live creatures, including, of course, cutting them open without anaesthetic. Animals are variously physically brutalised, poisoned, and otherwise made to suffer, with the specific intent of observing what adverse effects they suffer. The very well-known fact that cancer is deliberately induced in animals must rank as one of the least distressing things that can happen to them.

Such is a skeleton account of the sort of practices at issue.[3] We shall come in a moment to attempts to suggest that they are necessary, or not resented by the animals. But first let us tackle the central issue. If it is agreed that some at least of what we do to animals is grim and ghastly, why should anyone be tempted to think that, in itself, that doesn't matter, whereas it would matter if human beings were concerned? That is the question of principle. The immediate response of many people is to say that it doesn't matter, or it matters less, precisely because they are not human beings. But that, being no answer at all, is perhaps the most outrageous response, resembling in its incomprehension the response from a slave-trader of 'because they're black', or from a Nazi of 'because they're Jews'.

A fundamental principle behind any adequate moral theory, as we have seen, is that different treatment needs to be justified by a morally relevant reason.[4] Speciesism, as Richard Ryder has aptly termed it,[5] amounts to making the fact that somebody belongs to a different species the proposed reason in question, just as racism involves making the fact that somebody belongs to a different race a morally relevant reason for discrimination. The question is why anyone should think that being of a different species (or race, or sex) is a morally relevant reason for differential (and in practice disadvantageous) treatment, and how the suggestion could be substantiated. Certainly cows are not human beings, black men are not white men, Arabs are not Jews, and chickens are not cows. What, if anything, is the difference between these differences, from the moral point of view? The moral argument against racialism or chauvinism consists in pointing out that the fact of a particular difference cannot be shown to have any bearing on the broad issue of considering interests. To justify distinctive treatment, something has to be added that limits the context to matters where acknowledged differences are seen to be relevant. For example, one might attempt to argue that women differ from men in being child-bearers and physically weaker, and that therefore they ought to take on less physically onerous roles. Perhaps this particular argument is rather poor, and, anyway, it could only be said to work on the level of generalisation, but at least it involves an attempt to locate a relevant reason for differential treatment in a specific respect. But despite the antics, assumptions and assertions of various individuals who for various reasons have not wanted to treat certain groups pleasantly, nobody has ever, to my knowledge, put up a convincing case for saying that their being members of the group in question is sufficient reason for ignoring their interests.

So what is it about animals, granted that they are not the same as you and me, that might allow us to ignore their interests, to use them as mere means to our ends, and to cause them to suffer, all of which are *prima facie* characteristics of immoral behaviour? There are some fairly well-worn responses to this question. It may be said that they cannot reason as human beings do, that they (generally) cannot walk on two legs, that they do not have a language. But these claims, even if they are true, and any other such claims, have two great difficulties to face, if they are supposed to constitute morally relevant reasons. In the first place, merely to point out the difference is not to establish it as morally relevant. Why, for instance, should we assume that the fact that a group (or groups) cannot talk is a morally relevant reason for ignoring their interests, in a way that having hairy bodies or creative talents is not? Secondly, as the reference to 'creative talents' hints, any such attempt to locate a morally relevant difference is liable to lead one either into inconsistency, or unacceptably awkward consequences. If it were to be agreed that lack of language constitutes a morally relevant difference, then what about young children? Do they too lose any claim to moral consideration? Even if, in response to that, appeal is made to the slippery concept of potentiality, there remain the congenitally dumb to be reckoned with.[6] Likewise, if lack of reasoning ability be the criterion, persons suffering from extreme forms of spasticity and other mental defects would have to be classified, from the moral point of view, alongside other non-human animals.

The fact is that if one believes that suffering is bad and that every being's interests should count equally (as almost all, if not all, moral systems presuppose), it is difficult to see how, in consistency and good faith, one can avoid extending moral concern to all those with interests and a capacity for suffering. If you believe that it is wrong to treat others merely as means, this presumably should apply to any being that may sensibly be considered as an end in itself.

The case for not discriminating between humans and all other animals, in respect of moral concern, may further be strengthened, if at this point we recognise the possibility that these considerations may not apply to all forms of animal life. It is possible that some forms of animal life do not have the capacity to suffer, and cannot meaningfully be said to have interests. Thus, it might be that the argument does not establish that prawns and amoebae should be categorised with humans, but that, instead of drawing a sharp line between humans and other animals, we should draw it elsewhere, and think in terms of higher and lower forms of animal life. What would justify that way of looking at the matter, if indeed it is justified, would be precisely the point that since some forms of animal life are beyond suffering and having interests, they are beyond morality. What seems indisputable is that the capacity to suffer is crucial to the notion of moral personhood. It is difficult therefore to do better than quote Jeremy Bentham at this point.

The day may come when the rest of the animal creation may acquire those rights which never could have been witholden from them but by the hand of tyranny. The French have already discovered that the blackness of the skin is no reason why a human being should be abandoned without redress to the caprice of a tormentor. It may one day come to be recognised that the number of the legs, the villosity of the skin, or the termination of the os sacrum are reasons equally insufficient for abandoning a sensitive being to the same fate. What else is it that should trace the insuperable line? Is it the faculty of reason or perhaps the faculty of discourse? But a grown horse or dog is beyond comparison a more rational, as well as a more conversable animal than an infant of a day, or a week, or even a month old. But suppose they were otherwise, what would it avail? The question is not, can they *reason*? Nor, can they *talk*?, but, can they *suffer*?'

Justice, in short, demands that we treat beings alike, when they are alike in relevant respects. As time goes by, we come to see that colour of skin, IQ, sex, and so forth are *irrelevant* aspects when it comes to moral concern. Why should we still think that one's species might be relevant? What is morally wrong is causing suffering and ignoring interests. Since that is what is wrong, the capacity to suffer and the having of interests must constitute relevant respects for including beings in the moral category.

At this point some may be driven to resort to the plea that non-humans don't count morally, because they are not themselves moral. Nature, we shall be reminded, is red in tooth and claw. It is, indeed, quite true both that non-human animals do behave in violent and unpleasant ways to one another, and that at least most of them do not have a moral sense, as we understand it. (Though my cautious 'at least most of them . . . as we understand it' should be noted. On another occasion, I would be tempted to challenge the glib assumption that only man has a moral sense. Fortunately, even if I am mistaken, the main point of principle being argued here would not be affected.) That nature is red in tooth and claw, and can therefore be placed beyond the pale of moral concern, should, as a line of argument, cause a certain amount of embarrassment amongst humans. Are we so white? If beings who destroy and compete with each other thereby lose their claim to be treated morally, then the whole animal kingdom, including humans, must obviously fall together. The rather different point that only beings who are themselves capable of exercising moral concern should be part of the moral domain in any sense is, though popular, quite unconvincing. Certainly we cannot expect lions to act as moral agents, but no more can we expect babies, mental defectives, or psychologically disturbed criminals. We do not therefore assert that children, mental defectives and criminals have no moral claims, and can be used by us, as we see fit. No more should we take that attitude with non-human animals. We are back with the main point: what is crucial to mark a being out as entitled to moral consideration, from those who have the wit to give or withold it, is not a similar capacity, but the capacity to suffer and have interests.

At this point it is evident that we need to take up the suggestion that animals do not actually suffer, though I confess this seems a curious, unconvincing, last resort to me, for that animals can suffer I regard as being as certain as that stones cannot. It will be appreciated that the question of whether they do or not is not one that the farmer or animal researcher as such have any special claims to answer. Obviously these are people who, by and large, have the most first-hand knowledge of what various animals actually experience in objective terms, and they are better placed than most to make crude judgements about the overt behaviour of animals. The farmer, for instance, can vouch that the pig has voiced no complaint; the researcher can assure us that the rabbit did not anticipate the needle. But whether these animals suffer is an altogether more complex question, and one where working with animals is not a sufficient qualification. For the question of whether a being suffers could only be answered finally by one with a clear conceptual grasp of this generally hazily entertained idea, and with access to the inner minds of the beings in question.

When judging whether other humans are suffering we rely on three things: what they tell us, what we infer from our own experience, and what their visible behaviour suggests (again in the light of our own experience). If you insist that you are in a situation that would terrify me, of if I see you cringing, whining and running away from a place or situation, I infer, not necessarily correctly, that you are afraid. Very often our inferences are mistaken, particularly where mental suffering is concerned. The jovial exterior of a friend misleads us, and it is only when he commits suicide that we realise that he has been suffering. When it comes to non-human animals we have two problems. Firstly, they cannot talk to us, and, secondly, in consequence, we have never had it from the horse's mouth, so to speak, that they are roughly comparable to humans in the fact that they can suffer both physically and mentally. Nonetheless, it would seem a blatant example of the wish being father to the thought for anyone to persist in assuming that animals just cannot experience physical pain or mental torment, when one bears in mind what their behaviour seems to suggest, and the fact that their nervous systems are, in physiological terms, like ours. Why should one assume that throwing stones at a dog means nothing to it, when such signs as we have to judge by (it whimpers; it runs away; it becomes fearful of the stone-thrower) all suggest that it means more or less what it would mean to you? When I see a monkey cringing in the corner of a cage, apparently terrified, when I see an animal pinned to the ground so that it literally cannot walk, when I see an animal trying to stretch a wing that it has never been given the freedom to stretch, when I see a conscious animal being cut open—what conceivable contortion of thought will allow me to take it for granted that it does not suffer? To be sure, in each case it is only an inference that it does, but then, since I cannot feel your pain, it is only an inference on my part that you are capable of suffering.

There may be some respects in which (some) animals differ that have significance to this issue. For instance, a potent source of misery to many humans is their ability to anticipate and imagine events. Some, thinking perhaps of a pet dog who seems to look forward eagerly to his walk, may feel that non-human animals too have this capacity, and indeed they may be correct. Some people do claim that animals entering a slaughterhouse can sense death. Nonetheless, even if there are more similarities in this particular respect between different species than the more scornful might wish to concede, there does seem to be some difference. A society in which any human might be taken and operated on live, in the manner in which non-humans may be, would have the additional feature of a general sense of fear and anxiety, arising out of an awareness of a possible future which, perhaps, other animals do not have. But such qualifications cannot alter the fact that we have absolutely no reason to assume that animals, in general, are not capable of suffering.

Consider, in the first place, the very rationale and nature of animal research. The reason that this is carried on at all is to draw deductions about human beings. We don't smear guinea pigs with cancer-causing cosmetics for fear that, if we don't, even more unsuspecting guinea pigs may buy lipstick that poisons them. Animal research (whether for relatively trivial commercial purposes or more significant medical purposes) is carried out precisely because at least some animals are in various important respects, such as the structure of their nervous systems, like human beings. Furthermore, some of it is specifically designed to cause suffering, as, to take an extreme example, is the case with research carried out on monkeys to see how much anguish they can stand. I shall cite but one example here. It involves an experiment requiring that certain chemicals be injected into the brains of cats. 'With a number of widely different substances, recurrent patterns of reaction were obtained. Retching, vomiting, defecation, increased salivation and greatly accelerated respiration leading to panting were common features.' The injection into the brain of a large dose of Tabocuraine caused the cat to jump

from the table to the floor and then straight into its cage, where it started calling more and more noisily whilst moving about restlessly and jerkily . . . finally the cat fell with legs and neck flexed, jerking in rapid clonic movements, the condition being that of a major (epileptic) convulsion . . . within a few seconds the cat got up, ran for a few yards and fell in another fit. The whole process was repeated several times within the next ten minutes during which the cat lost faeces and foamed at the mouth.

This animal finally died thirty five minutes after the brain injection.[8] It is of course logically conceivable that it did not suffer.

The uncomprehending will try to shrug the example off as being an unusual and emotive one. The claim, however, was not that all animals are treated in that sort of way. I merely wished to produce an instance where the suggestion that animals 'aren't like us' (even though we are animals), and 'don't experience suffering', can be seen to be faintly ridiculous. But, for the record, on Ryder's conservative estimate of only 1 per cent of experiments with animals involving severe pain, that would still amount to no less than 150 animals going through such torment as the cat experienced every single day.[9]

My claim so far has simply been that causing animals to suffer is in itself morally wrong, and that there is undoubtedly a great deal of such suffering going on (even though we may legitimately disagree about whether particular animals, human or non-human, are or are not suffering in particular situations). We therefore ought, ideally, to stop inflicting such suffering on other animals. But, there are a number of other things, including inflicting pain or suffering on other humans, which, though in themselves morally wrong, may be morally justified as unavoidable, or the lesser of two evils. We must therefore consider the view that animal suffering is justified by the increase in our knowledge, or the greater economic efficiency that such treatment of animals produces.

If the argument above has been understood, it will be appreciated that one cannot claim, as a general principle, that it is morally acceptable to cause suffering to non-human, as opposed to human, animals for the sake of medical knowledge or increased food production. For such a position makes a distinction between species which is not justified, even if the need to cause suffering in the interests of knowledge is accepted. What one might try to argue is that, in the long-term general interest, some individual beings (human and non-human) may legitimately be made to suffer. But it is doubtful that this line of thought will prove particularly compelling. It seems to be established beyond serious question that the suffering we inflict on non-human animals in the interests of mass food-production is not necessary either in terms of diet and health or economic efficiency. Getting our protein through animal meat is inefficient and unnecessary, for instance. When it comes to cosmetics, the suggestion that the gains to mankind might justify cruelty to others seems frankly barbarous and obviously inadequate. The only argument that deserves to be taken seriously is that which insists that gains in medical knowledge may justify a degree of suffering for a minority. Possibly that is true. (It is not, incidentally, the kind of claim that can be demonstrated to be true or false, which explains why I leave it as a not altogether absurd hypothesis.) But

Animals 165

even if it is, the crucial points to remember would be, firstly, that this does not justify much of the wasteful and trivial medical research involving cruelty that actually goes on, and, secondly, that what is justified is the suffering of the few for the many. It might as well be you or I who experience the suffering, as the rabbit or the rat.

It is necessary now to say something about the question of killing animals and being a vegetarian. My purpose here is to indicate that these two questions have to be kept separate from the basic one of cruelty to animals, since accepting that it is wrong to inflict suffering on others has no necessary consequences in respect of killing or eating others. I shall not attempt to provide a certain answer to the question of the moral legitimacy of these practices, since the former at least has too many further ramifications to be taken up here. There are clearly some views about death which, insofar as a person holds them, would settle the issue of the morality of killing non-human animals without more ado. Some believe that no animal life should ever be taken deliberately. Some believe that human life is sacred, whilst other animal life is not. Some would distinguish between killing predators and killing peaceful animals. All such positions have at least a glimmer of an explanation behind them, although establishing that they are cogent positions to adopt would be another, more difficult, matter. What is certain is that killing has to be considered separately, since it can take place without the infliction of suffering, and the argument produced above has depended crucially on the issue of suffering. An attempt might be made to link the two, by arguing that if diminishing suffering and promoting happiness or a sense of well-being is the aim, then the more beings there are living, for as long as possible, enjoying a state of felicity, the better. Therefore, it might be said, we actually have a moral duty to increase and extend life, insofar as we can, from which it would follow that, other things being equal, we should not kill beings, even in old age. I don't myself find this line of argument very convincing, since I regard the essence of utilitarianism as being a moral requirement that we ensure as much happiness for all existing beings as possible, rather than that we should create as many happy beings as possible.[10] (For the same reason I reject the view that it is incumbent on people, from the utilitarian point of view, to have as many children as possible, in circumstances where to do so would not be counter-productive.) But in any case, even if there were an *a priori* moral duty to prolong life, there would still be cases of conflicting claims such as war, self-defence, fanatic lunatics, which would raise the question of whether killing might not be justified on occasion.

Can it then be morally legitimate to kill animals? In my view it may be, and such an admission can be quite consistent with the wider view that causing suffering to animals is in itself wrong, and not justified on the scale it takes place in our society. By the same token, I think we must concede that euthanasia in respect of humans, certainly negative (that is, not providing necessary life support) and possibly positive (that is, painless active killing), may be justified. (There is, as we noted above, a possibly important difference between human and non-human animals, in that we, the former, both call the tune and publish it. If we accept the practice of euthanasia in society, then we know that we do. Many people have argued that the attendant fears that people would have of being killed against their will are the main objection to legitimising the practice. That particular point would not effect non-human animals and so, it may be felt, the practice would be easier to justify in respect of them.) But if killing animals before their time is of questionable moral status, there are situations that provide no obvious problem. An outbreak of foot and mouth disease, for example, would surely justify the painless slaughter of cattle on straightforward utilitarian grounds. Faced with rats or poisonous snakes, with which we cannot negotiate and who pose a threat to us, we are justified in resorting to killing. Presented with animals in acute pain, whom we cannot help to recover, we are justified in killing. Perhaps, in certain circumstances, it is justifiable to kill animals in order to eat them.

I must make it clear that I do not wish to try and substantiate any of the specific claims just made, but merely to indicate that commitment to animal liberation does not entail the absurd position of assuming that I must submit myself to the jaws of the ravening lion. Nonetheless, some eyebrows may have been raised at the suggestion that one might even be justified in killing animals for food, since many animal liberationists argue, and popular opinion supposes, that one should also be a vegetarian. Possibly we should be, but if we should be, that must be for political reasons rather than simply moral reasons. For there is clearly nothing in the argument so far which suggests that it is morally wrong to eat an animal once dead, just as nothing but sentiment stands in the way of our eating human flesh. (To revert to the previous point, there may be circumstances in which it would be morally justifiable to kill a human being in order to eat—'morally justifiable', but not necessarily 'morally good'. One should not be taken to be advocating a practice, because one has the wit and imagination to conceive of a situation where a dramatic choice of inherently undesirable practices is forced upon one.) Two points deserve to be made, and commonly are made, in relation to this matter. Firstly, it may be said that to eat animal flesh (whether human or non-human, so far as this point goes) is to encourage further killing of animals. Secondly, it may be said that to refuse to eat animal flesh not only reduces the demand in a literal way, but also draws attention to the issue of the treatment of animals generally. The first point is obviously correct in general terms. If people at large could be dissuaded from eating animals, there would be less killing of them and less intense and cruel production of them. Nor is the counter-argument that, if animal liberationists feel this way about eating meat, they should also refrain from using shoe-leather, or doing anything else that involves making use of animal produce, very secure. For although a similar tactic could be employed in other areas, there seems little reason to believe that other uses made of the by-products of animals (dead or alive) are as significant in respect of causing suffering as food production and research. There is certainly nothing wrong with making use of shoe-leather that is produced from an already dead animal's skin. What is morally wrong, as we have seen, and what we should not do, is exploit or harm other animals, or use them *purely* as means to gratify our wants. Consistently with that, we may eat animals when dead, possibly kill them in order to eat them, but certainly not cause them any suffering in order to eat them. So, if there is a reason for being a vegetarian, it cannot be simply that one is morally opposed to causing animals suffering. It is, after all, too late to do anything about that, when the joint is on the table. The reason for being a vegetarian is that one thereby becomes an activist. To put it bluntly, the case for abstaining from eating meat (and other products based upon animal suffering) is to make a nuisance of oneself. If more and more people commit themselves to this tactic, the message spreads and it becomes harder for people to unreflectively accept our treatment of animals, harder to give dinner parties without making concessions to the liberationist view, and gradually a dent may be made in the great edifice of food production. However, there is a corollary: in being a nuisance, one is oneself causing a certain amount of pain and suffering, and that cannot simply be ignored. It is therefore impossible to conclude that vegetarianism is laid upon one as a moral obligation. It is a form of behaviour that has obvious relevance to the real moral issue, which is preventing the suffering of animals insofar as possible, but it is only one possible means to an end, and there may be occasions on which to insist on such behaviour would itself be to behave wrongly.

168 Injustice, Inequality and Ethics

NOTES

1 See, in particular, Stanley and Roslind Godlovitch and John Harris (eds), *Animals, Men and Morals: An Enquiry into the Mal-Treatment of Non-Humans*; Richard Ryder, *Victims of Science*; Tom Regan and Peter Singer (eds), *Animal Rights and Human Obligations*; Peter Singer, *Animal Liberation*.
2 Peter Singer in the *New York Review of Books*, 5 April 1973.
3 Further, more horrific, details may be found in Richard Ryder, *op. cit.*, and Peter Singer, *Animal Liberation*.
4 See above Chapter 9.
5 Singer, not overfond of the term, attributes it to Ryder, in 'All Animals are Equal', in *Philosophic Exchange*, Vol. 1, No. 5, Summer 1974.
6 On potentiality, see above Chapter 8.
7 Jeremy Bentham, *The Principles of Morals and Legislation*.
8 Quoted by Richard Ryder in Godlovitch and Harris, *op. cit.*
9 *Ibid.*
10 See above Chapter 3.

13 The Arts

'Allow me', said Mr Gall. 'I distinguish the picturesque and the beautiful, and I add to them, in the laying out of grounds, a third and distinct character, which I call unexpectedness.' 'Pray, sir', said Mr Milestone, 'by what name do you distinguish this character, when a person walks around the grounds for the second time?'

Thomas Love Peacock, *Headlong Hall*

Each year a certain amount of taxpayers' money is devoted to subsidising the arts. Theatres, art galleries and opera houses sometimes seem close to depending for their existence on subsidies rather than the paying customer. The Welsh National Opera company reveals that, even with capacity audiences, box-office receipts would cover only 25 per cent of their total costs.[1] (Though we should remember that subsidies come from other sources besides the taxpayer, notably business and industry, and that some parts of the arts world, such as the writing of fiction, are less subsidised than others.) Admittedly the amount of the national budget spent on subsidies for the arts is a small proportion of the total. Britain, according to figures for 1974, devoted 0.2 per cent of total expenditure to the 'creative and performing arts, museums, art galleries, etc.' which is miniscule in absolute terms, and small when compared to say, Belgium, which devoted 2.2 per cent to the arts.[2] On the other hand, in a country such as Britain, in which 29 per cent of people never read books,[3] let alone go to a theatre, the very existence of such a subsidy raises the question of whether taxes should be used for this purpose. True, no doubt, many people feel that flourishing theatres, museums and concert halls are a sign of a civilised country. But others feel that subsidising them amounts to an unfair hand-out to the already well-to-do, and is part of an inegalitarian switch: taxes paid by all are being used to bolster minority interests. (It is worth noting that this particular kind of problem is one that would not be solved by an equal distribution of wealth. Assuming that we all earn more or less the same and pay more or less the same amount into the common pool by way of tax, it is obviously important that the common pool should not be used so as to favour any one segment of the population.) Others again feel that for the arts to prosper is not just the veneer on civilisation, the icing on the cake, so to speak, but rather something of practical importance for its educational value. That is very often a view associated with liberal democracy (indeed it finds its recorded origin and apotheosis in classical Athens), but, as Paul Halmos has pointed out,[4] totalitarian states too, whether explicitly or not, recognise a practical value in the arts. Traditional Marxist-Leninist orthodoxy has it that art as part of the superstructure is necessarily a function of the technological base. But, contradictory as it may be, it also claims that bourgeois art is often used to advance capitalism, and further, Halmos suggests, in practice Marxist-Leninist leaders almost invariably attempt to control art in order to further their ideology. 'Herein lies an emphatically insistent testimony: art can be a most valuable asset or a most dangerous hindrance to the realisation of the socialist Utopia. The superstructure must be planned and strictly confined or it will crush the foundation.'[5] Many would concede the point that art has practical significance, but question the narrowness of traditional views of art. By all means subsidise art, it might be said, because art does indeed have educational value, but why should this mean money for Covent Garden Opera House, rather than cheaper television licenses?

At the time of writing the broad issue of state subsidy for the arts has a certain added piquancy, both because the amount of money involved generally has been severely cut by the government (along with everything else—this was 1981), and because the Arts Council, in administering finances, has had to make some judgements of priority within the domain of the arts. Should the ever popular, but hardly innovatory, D'Oyly Carte opera company take precedence over experimental theatre, or should it not? Should touring companies come before London based companies, or the reverse? Is it right that the Old Vic theatre company, long renowned and playing to full houses, should have had its grant withdrawn, while experimental theatre attracting very small audiences receives support? Should the National Theatre be accounted more important than the Festival Hall, museums than public libraries?

Another matter in which there has been considerable and longstanding interest, in contemporary society, is the question of censorship, both in general and in respect of art specifically. The Lord Chamberlain's office is less inclined to make the kind of objections that it once did to Oscar Wilde's *Salome* and Richard Strauss' *Der Rosenkavalier*, but the issue of censorship, whether for political, aesthetic or moral reasons, is not dormant. It fanned into flame as a major issue in 1966 as a result of the Moors murders. Ian Brady and Myra Hindley were charged with a series of shocking and gruesome acts of child torture and murder. Then their 'library' was found to contain some fifty books of sado-masochistic, pornographic or Nazi tendency. Was there cause and affect here? Brady himself argued, in the box, 'They cannot be called pornography. They can be bought at any bookstall.'[6] But should they be so readily available, or indeed available at all? The indefatigable Lord Longford set up his own committee on pornography, while Mary Whitehouse became a national figure with her campaign to clean up television. More recently the distinguished philosopher Bernard Williams was asked to head an inquiry into obscenity. It is probably fair to say that, through all this fairly ineffectual Canute-style resistance to the increasingly permissive society we live in, whatever managed to get itself classified as art was relatively untouched. There may be few who would go to the trouble that Walter Berns has done, to distinguish between what is acceptable ribaldry in great artists but obscenity in others.[7] But, whether through ignorance or design, many people do expostulate against scenes on television that are fairly innocent compared to some classic scenes in Chaucer or Rabelais.

There may therefore be some tactical advantage to be gained from defining art in such a way as to include one's own work or whatever turns one on. But in any case, it is evident that, in order to get a grip on these complicated and slippery questions to do with censorship and evaluation, we need to have a clear and workable definition of art.

I shall start by considering a fairly well-known view, which is representative of that school of thought that quite uncompromisingly sees art as something unique. This is the view of Clive Bell, and it is one that, despite its tendency to keep art in the domain of mystery, probably answers pretty well for many ordinary men and women. 'Either all works of visual art have some common quality or when we speak of "works of art" we gibber,'[8] Bell asserts confidently. Now, in fact, this is not necessarily true. There might conceivably be a chain, set or network of interconnecting factors, such that anything possessing a certain number of them, regardless of which, would count as a work of art. Something like that appears to be the case with games. There are connections between all the various activities we classify as games, from badminton to bridge, from rowing to monopoly, or from hopscotch to the hundred metres. But games can be very different from each other, and still remain games.

There is not a finite list of criteria that, taken together, are both necessary and sufficient to ensure that we have a game on our hands. However, we will concede this much to Bell: if we cannot pin down a conception of art, such that certain specific criteria have to be met for something to count as a work of art, then any claims that we choose to make about art will either have to be very general, or else will only apply in some cases and to some works of art. In just the same way claims about games either have to be on the general level of 'they can be fun', or else they have limited application. Not much that is true of rugby is true of cribbage. If we want to talk about art in a meaningful and constructive way, it must be a relatively specific concept. Talk about generalities (such as mankind, life or labour) is seldom of practical value. One other preliminary point should be noted. Bell himself is talking exclusively about the visual arts, and therefore his views, even if accepted, might not apply to literature or music. However, I shall ignore that point, partly because I am concerned with treating Bell as the spokesman for a view that could very easily be applied to other forms of art, if it can be applied to any, and partly because I shall argue that the view is best rejected.

Bell's central contention is that what constitutes art is 'significant form'. Significant form is form that is aesthetically moving. When an artist produces a work of art it will necessarily have significant form, which members of an audience may find aesthetically moving. It will 'necessarily' have the form, because that is how a work of art is being defined, but we only say that the audience 'may' find it aesthetically moving, because the audience will not necessarily discern the form. That is where art critics come in, in Bell's view. Ideally their job is to pinpoint or draw attention to features of the work, so that we, in recognising them, are enabled to experience the aesthetic emotion. This aesthetic emotion is unique in kind. Bell acknowledges that judgements differ about whether particular works are works of art, but claims, correctly, that that does not invalidate his theory, any more than the fact that different people find different things painful shows that we mean different things by 'pain'. It is quite possible that we should share Bell's conception of art, and still disagree about whether to classify particular works as art in that sense. One must also, surely, agree with Bell when he points out that we cannot easily define a work of art in terms of its power to inform or its descriptive accuracy, for we are disposed to distinguish between the good illustration or the admirable representation and a work of art.

Two points should be made at once about this account of art. Firstly, it may well be true that there is a unique emotional response that can be evoked by pure form. Secondly, we may well choose to call such form 'significant form' and works that have significant form 'works of art'. However, there are certain decided disadvantages in so doing.

Despite the splendid rhetoric of Bell's contrast between those who have 'made merry in the warm tilth and quaint nooks of romance', and 'the austere and thrilling raptures of those who have climbed the cold white peaks of art',[9] we have to ask how we can be sure that we know what he is talking about. We have to play Peacock to his Shelley. He is confessedly referring to an internal experience that has no other name and no other source. Who doubts that I can stare at a painting and feel something, let us assume something very powerful? But how do I know that this powerful response is caused by the form of the painting rather than anything else, such as the content, a memory it evokes, the warmth of the room or a combination of these and other factors? And how do I know that what I feel is what Bell feels? The simple answer to both questions is that I do not know. This by no means shows that what he says is ridiculous. There are many other cases where the same sort of problem arises: for example, I do not know that the experience you label 'painful' is similar to that which I have in similar circumstances. But in the case of the alleged aesthetic response there is room for considerably less certainty than there is in most parallel cases, such as the experience of pain. By and large, the same sorts of things produce pain. Everything that is observable suggests that having a nail driven through the hand would be much the same for you as for me. This is much less obviously so of people's reaction to alleged works of art. As I say, the fact that it is very unclear whether, when our reactions appear to be similar (so that we both say 'it's a work of art'), they really are so (so that we do both have a similar emotional response), and quite uncertain whether some form really does produce this unique response (as opposed to producing different responses, or even as opposed to different people investing the work with certain properties), does not show this theory to be false. But it must raise doubts about its usefulness.

There are also two more crucial questions. Why does Bell insist that this response to significant form is a more 'pure' experience than can be provided by other responses to the artefact, or, which comes to the same thing, what does he mean by that, and why should we value this experience? He himself takes its value for granted, stressing only that it has nothing to do with worldly matters or crude economic value. Yet he claims, 'even a mixed and minor appreciation of art is . . . one of the most valuable things in the world.' Indeed he says that it 'might prove the world's salvation.'[10] But it is very unclear either how this could be so or how one might set about defending the claim that it is. Since I do not know, and cannot know, whether the exhilaration I experience listening to the final movement of Beethoven's 9th Symphony is similar to the feelings you or Bell experience, or whether it is the product of significant form, and since I do not know what is meant by a 'pure' experience, why should I assume that my emotional state is 'one of the most valuable things in the world', and how might I suppose that it should save the world?

I must stress that the objection to this kind of view of art is not that it is wrong or false, but that it is obscurantist and unilluminating. Whether something is a work of art in this sense or not will be logically impossible to determine, and factually difficult to get agreement on, especially since Bell has allowed that a work may have significant form that people do not recognise. The value of art in this sense remains plainly and highly contentious. Attempting to answer questions such as whether certain television programmes count as works of art, whether art should be censored, and whether it should be funded by the state, will be well nigh fruitless working with this conception. Bell, in a more sophisticated way, has done something similar to those who break down all distinctions between music styles on the grounds that 'it's all music', or those who feel that the answer to all the world's problems is 'love'. Yes, it is all music, but different kinds of music are exceedingly different from each other, and what is true of one type is seldom true of another. There really isn't much you can say of music as such, in the broad sense. Equally, what the world needs now may well be love, but as a practical prescription, as a piece of guidance, that is worse than useless. It doesn't tell us how to recognise love, it doesn't tell us how to exercise it, it doesn't tell us why to try, it doesn't tell us what form love should take. Paradoxical as it may seem, art, in Bell's sense, may exist and may incorporate such works as are generally accredited as works of art, but still art in this sense is not worth dwelling on as a category for thought.

Leo Tolstoy may stand as representative for the kind of view of art that I wish to contrast with that of Bell, and for which I intend to argue on practical grounds. Tolstoy's view of art was essentially as follows. 'To evoke in oneself a feeling one has once experienced, and having evoked it in oneself, then, by means of movements, lines, colours, sounds or forms expressed in words, so to transmit that feeling that others may experience the same feeling—this is the activity of art.'[11] He goes on to suggest that 'the stronger the infection [that is, feeling evoked] the better is the art', judged purely from a technical point of view, but, taking the subject matter into account and seeing art in a moral framework, then it is better insofar as it contributes to communicating feelings that are more kind and needful for the well-being of mankind.

This conception has some obvious attractions. It is readily comprehensible, it makes aesthetic experience communicable, it answers to what many artists see themselves as doing (that is by no means a necessary condition to be met, but it is surely desirable), and it enables us to see why people should value art, and indeed fear it, as some, since the time of Plato, have done. Particularly is all this so, if we allow ourselves to add something. Tolstoy put forward his view in opposition to a number of others, including those that evaluated art in terms of its propensity to yield pleasure. Clearly, good art cannot be assessed solely by reference to pleasure potential, for not even the most lunatic of levellers wants to claim that 'This Is Your Life' is a work of art, by comparison with some little-known work of Schoenberg. But, on the other hand, we surely do expect great art to evoke feelings of satisfaction, and, at some level, pleasure. Why should we not add, as a further defining characteristic, that art is designed to evoke satisfaction? Tolstoy himself rather ignores the question of the artist's intention in seeking to evoke and transmit feelings to others, the question, if you like, of why an artist should be driven to being an artist. Because he would like to see more people coming together through the experience of art, he seems to assume in artists the intention to bring them together. But, as a general rule about artists, that doesn't seem quite right. Many have no conscious social purpose, and it is hard to see why the recluse, the single-minded or even the hater of humanity should not also be an artist. However, even these worthies would find it hard to deny that, insofar as their work is going to have an audience, they would hope that the audience would derive that satisfaction from it that comes from recognising the fitness of things or sensing a job well done. Artists, surely, necessarily want their work to give rise to that pleasure that is aesthetic satisfaction, or, rather, to be capable of it, even if they don't give a damn whether it actually finds an audience to please. Possibly it may be objected that this means that scenes of horror cannot be depicted in true works of art. The obvious rejoinder to that is that in such cases the content may give no pleasure, but still there may be the pleasurable recognition of the artistic conveying of the content to an audience. If the matter is pushed, and it be asked whether anybody could really take any kind of pleasure in Hogarth's depressing scenes or Picasso's *Guernica*, one might be driven to respond that perhaps there comes a point at which art becomes propaganda, social comment or something else. But even if there are some awkward borderline examples, it surely remains true that a work of art is, amongst other things, supposed to evoke a form of satisfaction in its audience.

That at any rate is what I understand by a work of art: a work in any medium, designed to evoke an experienced feeling and to convey it to others, in such a way that the work will also evoke in its audience a sense of satisfaction at the manner of its accomplishment. Further, I think it highly likely that works of art in this sense quite often, but not invariably, do in fact lead to some unique aesthetic response in people, as Bell maintains. But people differ in themselves, and therefore there may be works of art that some happen not to be able to appreciate. That commonsense suggestion is allowed for in a view, such as Tolstoy's, which enables us to distinguish between recognising a work of art and appreciating a work of art, as Bell's does not.

Art in this sense self-evidently has a value. It has a value in the pleasure it may give, in the greater communication and understanding between people it may promote, and in the content it may effectively disseminate. But it is not necessarily the case that it has enormous value, or that it has more value than a number of other things, or in particular, that it is so valuable that it should be protected by subsidy, or that it is too valuable for it to be permissible to interfere with it by means of censorship. Should it, then, be thus immune? Does it deserve heavy injections of taxpayers' money?

There are five frequently raised objections to state funding that need to be considered. Firstly, it is sometimes said that it is wrong to use public money on élitist interests such as the arts; secondly, it has been objected that public money should not be used to protect a class interest such as the arts; thirdly, it has been objected that money for the arts is money for the pleasures of the rich; fourthly, economic man has emerged to complain about directing the taxpayers' money to useless pursuits, and, finally, people have complained that to subsidise the arts is to use the money of all to finance the interests of a few.

The first four of these objections, notwithstanding their popularity, contain some very muddled thinking, so much so that, once the muddles are revealed or removed, the arguments in question wither away. Firstly, it is not the case that opera, literature, music, the fine arts and museums, whether taken separately or together, are the interests of a particular class or income group. No doubt there is a great deal of snobbishness involved in many ways in respect of the arts; certainly there is a great deal of money involved (though presumably even more would be needed to enjoy the arts without subsidies). But the fact, if it is a fact, that you might more often expect signs of acquaintanceship with a wide range of literature and music in upper class homes than working class homes, or that a large number of people attending the opera at Covent Garden have a lot of money (and need it to pay for their seats) is quite beside the point. Anybody who actually frequents opera houses, theatres, public libraries, concert halls, museums, or art galleries will know that in them class and economic boundaries are crossed into insignificance. Such generalisations as remain true (let us say, though I have no idea whether it is the case, 'more middle class people than upper class people attend the English National Opera') remain true because of other features of our society, and not because of the nature of art. There is nothing intrinsically upper class about art; it is not inevitably for the rich, and one of the arguments for subsidy (though, like all such subsidies, it benefits all equally, and not those who most need it more) is precisely to make it more generally accessible. There may well be factors contingently associated with class or finance that tend to alienate people from art: some art is inaccessible to certain people because they lack the kind of education that helps to make it comprehensible. Some people are inaccessible to art, as one might put it, because their background or their ideology tends to make them so. But the fact that, at a given time, for whatever reasons, an identifiable group or groups of persons do not care for art, is not a reason for stigmatising art as nothing more than a vested interest of the remainder. To argue against state subsidy on these grounds is rather like stigmatising health as an upper class fad, and consequently opposing a national health service.

Secondly, there is something pathetic in the view that the matter can be dismissed as a cultural conspiracy, and that concern for the arts is merely an élitist plot. Quite clearly, and quite as certainly and objectively as one can demonstrate that one car is faster than another, one can establish that Shakespeare is a greater artist than Noel Coward, or that Puccini's *La Bohème* is superior to a rock concert by Matchbox as a work of art, in the sense defined. (One could write an enjoyable book round that last remark alone. But I should at least make it clear that I deliberately chose to refer to Puccini's *La Bohème*, notwithstanding the fact that I think one could legitimately criticise it for sentimentality and aesthetic vulgarity in places; and that I am aware that most sensible pop music enthusiasts do not wish or attempt to assess the object of their enthusiasm as a work of art, in the sense defined. It is journalists and academics who seem driven to that rather curious idea. The point I am making is not one about superiority or social importance *tout court*. It is simply that a classic opus in the history of pop music, such as Elvis Presley's *Jailhouse Rock*, may be worth more to me than all of Mozart, and worth something to many more people, but it still isn't a work of art, while the *Marriage of Figaro* equally certainly is.) One must grant that there may always be borderline cases and room for argument and differences of opinion, but, given a clear and specific definition, there can be no room for claiming that anything and everything is a work of art, let alone good art, and, what is more, no obvious motive for doing so. It is obviously the case that, at any given time, those who either hold political sway or have cultural *auctoritas*, should the two be divorced, help to shape fashion, and that any typical candidate for status as a work of art is likely to have been endorsed and helped on its way by ruling and/or cultural élites of past and present. It is not, then, that such observations are false. They are beside the point. Whether the Tudors cunningly spawned him or not, we should be back where we came in: Shakespeare is a great artist. To care about and support the arts may coincidentally happen to suit the members of some élite, but it is not élitist in the sense of activity done for no good reason other than to support a particular power group.

Having a clear and reasonably specific definition of a work of art also helps us to deal with more general questions such as 'why subsidise opera rather than football?' With a broad, general conception of art, such as the view that identifies it with little more than leisure pursuits, one can fall into the trap of thinking that such a question is legitimately comparing like with like. In fact, of course, it is doing no such thing, and asking why we should subsidise opera rather than football is rather like asking whether we should put more money into schooling or give the milkman a pay rise. Obviously, at the end of the day such priorities have to be considered, although there is no very obvious way in which they can be definitely settled. But the more immediate point is that there is a difference in kind between a question such as 'why subsidise opera more than museums?', and a question such as 'why subsidise opera more than football?' It might be sufficient to reply to the latter by saying, because football is a recreational activity and nothing to do with art. What this boils down to is that there is a need to distinguish between arguments about whether art should be subsidised, and arguments about whether subsidy for the arts should be directed to more or less esoteric forms.

The Arts 179

To object to art on the grounds that it isn't useful, is to commit what I shall call the economic sin, which is very much the sin of our times. It is only true that works of art are not useful, if you characterise usefulness in terms of your own limited horizons, and they happen to be filled out with dollar signs. All that is true is that works of art as such have no use for some purposes and to some people. As to whether the view of life, the opinions and the natures of the sort of people of whom that is true are themselves worthy of any respect . . . ah, well that is altogether another question. Usefulness is not a property like squareness or hardness, that things either possess or do not. Usefulness has to be assessed by reference to purposes. It is clear from the definition of art alone that a work of art *may* be useful; indeed, given the definition, it seems plausible to suggest that many people will instantly see a use for society in the cultivation of art. But as to whether it is more important to communicate, experience and understand emotions in general, and to please the aesthetic sense in particular, or to build cheap and serviceable houses, for example—that is a matter of judgement. I would argue that in the long run our society would be a more acceptable and enjoyable one, if we were to take the arts as seriously as we currently take the lop-sided and extremist view that the only criterion of value is immediate economic return. But the immediate task is not to establish that, so much as to point out that the statement that art isn't a useful enterprise is, as it stands, more or less denuded of meaning. Consequently, there is no force in the argument that the state should not subsidise the arts, since they are not useful enterprises.

What is true, sadly perhaps, is that the arts are a minority interest. Although it is not true that concern for the various arts belongs exclusively to any one group, whether social, professional or economic, it is true that only a small proportion of the community is directly involved, or wishes to be, with museums, concerts, literature, sculpture, painting and theatre. The question that really needs asking, therefore, very simply, is whether there is good reason to see that society caters to this particular minority interest. Unfortunately, it is impossible to establish incontrovertibly a simple answer. In the nature of things we can only speculate about likely short- and long-term effects.

It is worth pricking the bubble of a familiar superstition that has it that the onus is on the advocate of the value of the arts to establish logical or, at least certain contingent, connections between involvement with them and some beneficial result. That is surely a quite unreasonable demand. I don't have to prove that it is logically or contingently impossible to cross a motorway on foot without being killed, in order to make a strong case against so doing on the grounds that it is dangerous. In the same way I don't need to establish that reading literature inevitably leads to greater sensibility, in order to make a case for literature on the grounds that it is a good way to cultivate sensibility.

It must be acknowledged that it may often transpire that circumstances in a community are such that preoccupation with the arts would, by anyone's standards, be a low priority. To subsidise art in Kampuchea at the present time, for instance, would be as monstrous as Nero's celebrated, if unhistorical, penchant for fiddling while Rome burned. The question is whether, in circumstances such as our own, this particular minority interest deserves support.

As I write, a part of the newly elected Labour Council in London has just effectively answered that question in the negative. They have proposed to stop the GLC grant to the appeal fund of the Royal Opera House, Covent Garden, thereby rescinding a promise made by the former Conservative administration. A spokesman explained the decision in this way: 'I do not see why the ratepayers who foot the bill for the arts should not have the arts taken to them. They should not be expected to go to the arts.'[12] He proposed that, in place of subsidising Covent Garden, a big festival should be held for Londoners in Hyde Park on May Day. Admittedly this case differs slightly from the norm we have been considering, in that it involves a local tax (rates), and in that the proposal does not set itself against art as such, but against a particular instance of it. Nonetheless, the issue is still about whether to use people's taxes to forward enterprises that many of them have no direct interest in, or to use it for purposes that will generally meet their approval (though one may question the assumption that the ratepayers of London want to spend their money on a big festival in Hyde Park).

This particular spokesman was clearly guilty of the mistake of assuming that the difference between opera at Covent Garden and a festival in Hyde Park is that the former is, and is exclusively, the interest of a mythical beast called the middle class, while the latter is the pet obsession of a no-less fictitious monster, the working class. He was also concerned to extend the definition of art, so that it includes things like public festivals. The answer to his specific argument is therefore fairly straightforward: you may call anything what you like, but that alone won't change things. You may lump opera and holiday festivals together under some general category (such as entertainment, which you might care to call 'art'), but that will not remove the transparent differences between them. What people want to do themselves is not necessarily all that they see reason to value, so the fact that many do not wish to attend opera does not show that they do not wish to preserve it. For that, and other, reasons the question of whether taxpayers' money is well spent is not simply a question of whether it is used to forward the lowest common denominator of activity.

What every individual has to decide is whether the existence of opera houses, museums, theatres, concert halls and libraries is relatively important in a community, regardless of whether the individual in question has any personal interest in making use of them. I should have thought that the answer was clearly, yes. Firstly, to support these houses of art is to preserve and nurture art, in all its forms, which, by definition has its own excellence. Secondly, as again follows from the conception of art being employed, we help to preserve and promote attempts to express and communicate with the affective side of our natures, and thereby to come to a greater understanding of feelings and emotions. Thirdly, the appreciation of the arts is one proven source of great and long-lasting pleasure for those who can learn to appreciate it. (That is not a tautology: there are interests that are capable of giving pleasure initially, but not sustained pleasure.) Fourthly, it is arguable that a society that could but doesn't take any interest in the arts at the level of the state thereby strengthens the sterile commercial spirit, as it has been suggested that the society that allows abortion may thereby breed a general lack of respect for life. If what one may rather grandiosely term 'things of the spirit' get no support from the state, then individual citizens may the more easily put aside such values in their preoccupation with the manners of the market. Certainly the record of history suggests as much, for time and again we see an emphasis on art combined with a vigorous, free, inventive and person-respecting culture, while the states that try to control art or ignore it are repressive, dour, and without light. The overall argument, in short, is that it is worthwhile taking active steps to encourage the arts (and appreciation of them) because, regardless of how many take immediate interest, and regardless of the fact that there is no proven direct correlation between sensitivity to art and the moral virtues of humanity, in the long term the phenomenon of art has subtle indirect consequences for society, which we ignore, as we are currently in danger of doing, at our peril.

There are two obvious rejoinders to this line of thought that need to be considered. Firstly, it may be conceded that we would like the arts to flourish, but it may be asked whether the state needs to subsidise them. Won't the cream rise to the top anyway? Secondly, going to the other extreme, it may be suggested that there should be state subsidy, but with it should go state control and censorship. As to whether the best amongst our artists would emerge and survive anyway, without the benefit of state subsidy, it is difficult to say. Certainly private patronage has proved every bit as effective as state subsidy in history; but it is difficult to assess their relative merits, because it is difficult to determine what effect an attempt at tight state monopoly of the arts in places such as Soviet Russia has really had. Would Shostakovich have been different, if financed by private patrons in the manner of Mozart? Would he have been a better artist? Would there have been more like him? Who can say? But surely the more important question is not whether the cream would rise to the top, but whether there would be an abundance of milk. Many of our great composers, writers, and painters have had very little direct support from the state, at any rate until they have become old and famous. But that is surely not the point. The argument is not that without our taxes the state could not afford William Walton or Anthony Burgess. It is highly likely that such men would have composed and written, respectively, in any society that gave them the freedom to do so. What is at issue is a climate of opinion. State subsidy is needed to generate a variety of artistic activity, and thereby to demonstrate that we take the idea of art, and what it stands for, seriously.

State control of art in the full sense is almost a nonsense. Because of what art is, the very idea of producing it in response to party dictate is ridiculous. One cannot help but be bemused at the way in which Russian composers have been reprimanded for failing to compose their music in satisfactorily 'revolutionary' terms, and then patted on the back when the offending passages have been restructured. There can be revolutionary art, in the sense of art that arises out of revolutionary ideology. But to count as art at all, it has to develop out of a sincere response to the world, or some aspect of it, and not out of instructions from others.

However, some degree of censorship by the state is obviously logically compatible both with the practice of art and even the valuing of it. The question to be faced here, therefore, is whether the value of art is such that any censorship ought to be resisted. The standard, and clearest, argument against any censorship remains that of John Stuart Mill.[13] He readily conceded that some of what is said, published or produced (whether art or not) might very well be harmful, either directly or indirectly or both; but nonetheless, he suggested, in the long term, society's best interests are served by preserving absolute freedom of expression. His central reason for thinking this is that truth is best served by freedom, and truth, in the fullness of time, is a prerequisite of social well-being. To put the point the other way round: error and ignorance of whatever sort, in whatever sphere, from technology to human relationships, to ideas about a God, must always stand in the way of man's ability to make a prosperous and happy society. Error and ignorance are best fought by creating a social climate in which all ideas are held tentatively, and may freely be challenged. To be sure, an individual instance of artistic expression, like any other individual expression, may harm society. But on balance such problems are worth putting up with, in the interests of the positive gains to be had in the long run from a climate of freedom.

But even Mill makes an exception of speech that incites people to violence in perilous times, as he may consistently do. And once that is admitted, it becomes reasonable to ask whether there might not be other candidates for exception. Marshall Cohen points out various phenomena that Mill did not even consider (largely for historical reasons) that might be thought to raise the question of exception, such as speech that interferes with the chances of a fair trial or speech in the course of advertising.[14] Why should somebody not legitimately add 'works of art that promote bourgeois values' (or 'works of art that promote Marxist values')? After all, if the general line of argument allows Mill-like liberals to declare misleading advertising to be obviously unacceptable, despite a premium on free speech, why shouldn't it allow a Marxist to declare the advertising of bourgeois values in a play to be obviously unacceptable? As far as the principle goes, the answer surely has to be that there is no reason why it shouldn't. Any attempt to distinguish these cases would have to resort to specifics. It would have to be argued that whereas it is clear that some instances of advertising involve falsehood and thereby do great harm, it is not at all clear that bourgeois values involve falsehood. But it is evident that in practice this line of argument will not prove effective with the committed Marxist.

All that can be said, is this. If the basic presumption is on the desirability of free expression, the onus is on those who wish to make exceptions to try and convince others that the exceptional case they are concerned with is clearly so harmful as to merit special treatment. In some cases, such as the publication of military secrets in time of war, the attempt to influence juries prior to a trial, and the dissemination of false advertising material, we are likely to agree, both on the fact that they are harmful and on the justification for making exceptions in these cases. In other cases, such as the view that a particular work exhibits pernicious political doctrine, we are unlikely to agree, either about whether it is pernicious, or about whether it is sufficiently harmful to merit censorship. We therefore do not have an answer to give to the question of whether such works should in principle be censored, but we do have the practical conclusion that, since the case is not made, the work should not now be censored.

The ground most commonly produced for censoring art, however, is not political. It is obscenity, and the harm that it is claimed a work of art may do, if harm it be, is usually in the line of moral-sexual depravity. But it is not at all easy to mount such a case with any degree of conviction. Reo Christenson is one philosopher who has tried to justify censorship on such grounds.[15] Firstly, he reveals that, according to one survey, three-quarters of the American people want some censorship, and he refers also to the opinions of those students of history who believe that cultures that have considerable latitude in respect of sexual behaviour lack creativity and remain at a primitive level, or decline. Secondly, he suggests that Mill's argument for freedom of expression is designed to meet the case of the dissemination of ideas, and not commercial entertainment. Putting the two together, he is able to conclude that promulgation of ideas involving sexual freedom is not protected by Mill's general argument, and could lead to the downfall of civilisation as we know it.

The argument is scarcely persuasive. That the majority want censorship is neither here nor there when it comes to considering whether there is good reason for it, though in a representative democracy it may have considerable bearing on what does actually come to pass. One can merely hope that in this case the majority, in forming their opinion, have not placed too much credence in the speculations cited by Christenson about the link between sexual freedom and social decline. For, at best, such evidence says something about a link between social attitudes to sex generally and the state of civilisation, and not, which is quite different, about the connection between the freedom to publish obscenity and the state of civilisation. A society that tolerates the freedom to publish obscenity, but hedges it round with all sorts of social restraints, is not at all the same thing as a society that behaves in a variety of obscene ways. The argument is not about whether we should all get into bondage and flagellation, but about whether those who wish to do so should be allowed to do so without being classified a criminals. A society that allows, and has a minority interested in obscene material is not, by any excess of rhetoric, a depraved culture. What would be needed to get this argument off the ground would be evidence of a decisive link between the existence of pornographic material and widespread sexual depravity in practice, which, as far as I know, nowhere exists. (Clearly, if this kind of argument could get off the ground, the next step would be to insist on clear and coherent accounts of what constitutes pornography, obscenity and depravity. The recently expressed view of one Conservative MP that there was no call on him to define such terms, since he could recognise pornography when he saw it, just as he could recognise an elephant when he saw one, won't do at all. We can all recognise elephants, because they are very distinctive creatures. The whole point is that pornography is not self-evidently distinctive. The MP should ask himself whether he would necessarily recognise a poltergeist, if he saw one. Furthermore, if it is true that he can recognise an elephant when he sees one (which I am beginning to wonder about), unless he has lost the power of speech, it cannot be true that he cannot give an account of one. What is it that he sees and recognises? Very well, then, what does he see and recognise, when his eyes come face to face with pornography? But I shall not pursue these conceptual questions, partly because, unlike the MP, I can recognise a real conceptual difficulty when I see one, and partly because the case for censorship of pornography does not seem to be able to get off the ground.)

Christenson's other point, that Mill's argument applies to ideas rather than entertainment, is a curious one. There would be considerable difficulty in defining a general term like 'entertainment' in any way that meaningfully separated it clearly from another general term like that of an 'idea'. At the level of practice the two would seem to be quite inseparable. Indeed the very objection that Christenson has to pornography seems bound up with the view that it puts nasty ideas into people's heads.

I cannot see any case for censoring art on any grounds, other than the extremely unlikely one that a work of art puts the safety of the state from external sources at risk. If one believes in freedom of expression at all, one must allow works of art to express seditious views in time of peace, for it is precisely such possibly damaging ideas that the general argument for freedom of speech is designed to protect. Objections on the score of obscenity would seem to have to rely solely on an intuitive sense that some things are just not to be borne, rather than any coherent account of the undeniable and unacceptable damage that is done by pornography. But my main purpose here has been to indicate the difficulty of mounting a successful case for censorship of the arts. One thing that is clear is that there is no simple matter of fact here.[16] When people talk about 'the corrupting power of pornography', do they mean to claim that it causes certain behaviour, or that it tends to lead to such behaviour? Or is it thoughts that it causes, or may lead to, rather than action? Is there evidence that it does any of these things? Might it be that pornography arises when people are of a certain sort rather than that it produces people of a certain sort? Would censorship be a better means of achieving the ends in question, whatever they may be, than voluntary restraint? Might pornographic material not serve cathartically? When people ask for censorship, are they assuming that a censor will prevent, or merely inhibit, certain practices? are they assuming that a censor can be found who knows best what should be permitted, or that anybody could fulfil the office of censor, since anybody knows what ought to be censored? or are censors supposed to be representative of the standards of the people? what people? is this a matter of morality or propriety?

These questions and many others do not have simple answers, if they are answerable at all. For which reason the case would seem to fall squarely under Mill's general argument. Works of art, whether pornographic or not, and whether seditious or not, being by definition well-wrought expressions in one medium or another of individual experiences and perceptions, should be uncensored. A social climate that accepts that (and extends it to the dissemination of ideas generally), notwithstanding the fact that it will have to put up with a number of offensive and troublesome consequences at times, keeps alive respect for the search for truth. That does not guarantee salvation, but what else can men of integrity do but put their trust in it?

NOTES

1 See programme notes for Welsh National Opera Company productions during 1981.
2 The figures are quoted from *The Book of Numbers*. Source: Euromonitor.
3 *Ibid.*
4 Paul Halmos, 'Art and Social Change', in *The Proper Study*, Royal Institute of Philosophy Lectures, Vol. 4, 1969–70.
5 *Ibid.*
6 Quoted in Pamela Hansford Johnson, *On Iniquity*.
7 Walter Berns, 'Beyond the (Garbage) Pale: The Case for Censorship', in Harry M. Clor (ed.), *Censorship and Freedom of Expression: Essays on Obscenity and the Law*.
8 Clive Bell, *Art*.
9 *Ibid.*

10 *Ibid.*
11 Leo Tolstoy, *What Is Art?*
12 *New Standard*, 13 May 1981.
13 John Stuart Mill, *On Liberty*.
14 Marshall Cohen, 'Concurring and Dissenting Opinions', in *The Public Interest*, No. 22, Winter 1971.
15 Reo M. Christenson, 'Censorship of Pornography? Yes', in *The Progressive*, September 1970.
16 Most of the following points in the text are outlined by F. E. Sparshott in his useful survey of the issues in *The Structure of Aesthetics*.

14 Education

I hate by-roads in education. Education is as well known, and has long been as well known, as ever it can be.

Samuel Johnson

As we enter the decade of the eighties, the philistines, it would seem, are upon us. One accepts that during a serious recession the arts, education and the social services may have to suffer alongside everything else. One even concedes that sometimes circumstances may be such that something like education may have to be altogether sacrificed to the interests of, say, food production. What is quite unacceptable is that in very difficult, but certainly not catastrophic times, all things should be assessed in terms of crude economic return. Closing down museums that do not pay, objecting that we get no material profit from investment in the arts, pointing out that teaching adults to read is a costly public service and therefore not viable, and demanding that universities pay more attention to what is currently wanted by industry, are ideas that baffle one more because of the ignorance that must lie behind them than because of the disastrous change that, from a long-term point of view, they would wreak in our society. In crude economic terms, museums *never* pay. They always have, and probably always will, cost hundreds of times as much to administer as they earn at the door. If this were an argument for reforming them or shaking them up, then they should have been closed down since the beginning of time, along with costly public services for the socially unproductive, attempts to open people's minds in commercially unproductive ways, and everything else that does not cater to a technical skill or to material production.

This issue of philistinism has little to do with party politics as such. Between the market mind of the right and the detestation of all that cannot be stamped 'authentic working class' of the left there is little to choose. The cultural sterility of the United States, supported by the pressures of the open market, is not in the end so very different from the cultural sterility of Russia, imposed by dogma, except that with the former there is a modicum of hope. In Britain the Labour party's distrust of middle class culture (as, in its present mood, it chooses to class the likes of William Shakespeare, William Walton and L. S. Lowry) is more or less matched by the Conservative party's distrust of anything too divorced from land and industry. It appears to be the mood of our times that tempts us to value only what is seen as an economically viable means to some further end, in a more or less endless chain. The present government, therefore, deserves no special censure for confusing a quite legitimate concern to cut out pointless waste and to cease paying out money that is not there with a random assault on anything that doesn't have an immediate material pay-off. Nor is it particularly surprising that it appears to have no conception of education as such, but holds instead to the unreflective and dogmatic assumption that schools are for training people for commercially viable roles with the minimum of fuss—a view that is fashionably summed up by reference to the need to provide 'social and life skills'.

In this chapter I shall attempt to put my bulk in the way of this clumsy bandwaggon, as it bears (down) upon schooling and education. But it must be said that it carries many willing passengers. Obviously, those who are committed to the ideal of the market economy and those who have no respect for the educated mind, for whatever reason, are going to support a cost/efficiency approach to schools. More sadly, they are unsuspectingly abetted by those educationalists who would like to reduce thought about schools and education to a matter of empirical research. In the interests of measuring, predicting and isolating teaching techniques, they have unwittingly conspired to distort and maim the enterprise of schooling, until the question, 'how should the school proceed?', which should open up a debate about one's philosophy of life, becomes comparable in people's minds to a question such as, 'how can we sell more of this product?' Some teachers, too, have to be judged guilty on this score, seeing their job as no more than the routine passing on of particular skills, and acting accordingly. Nor have philosophers done as much as they might to arrest this decline into technological totalitarianism, and to proclaim and explain the obvious truth that the value of education and the criterion of success in educating is quality of mind—something that cannot easily be measured and something that, though it may be fair to call it priceless, cannot be costed.[1]

Three factors have in the main contributed to this general failure to keep faith with education. The first is that people usually fail to appreciate the distinction between defining a word and analysing a concept. The second is that they usually fail to discriminate between schooling and education. And the third is that they do not seem to understand the problematic nature, at a very simple level, of the familiar demand that schooling should be useful and relevant.

To define a word usually, though not always, amounts to providing a synonym or a synonymous phrase, as when one says that 'consume' may mean 'spend', or that 'crucify' means 'put to death by nailing or binding to a cross'. (The exceptions come with words such as 'cubit', where a definition would need to explain that it is a unit of measurement amounting to about 18 inches, since it does not mean '18 inches', or 'good' where one has to explain that it functions to commend, rather than attempt to provide a non-existent synonym.) By and large, amongst reasonably sophisticated language users, the provision of the definition of occasional, unfamiliar words is all that is needed to keep communication going. If I say to a class, 'I want the black-haired children in the front row', no problem of definition will arise, unless perhaps there is a French child who needs the English 'black-haired' translating. There might more often be a problem of ascription, arising out of the fact that although the meaning of 'black-haired' is clear enough, there are borderline cases such that we are uncertain whether they count as black-haired or not. But a third and different kind of problem may arise if I say, 'I want the intelligent children in the second row.' Let us assume that everybody understands the verbal definition of 'intelligence' ('mental alertness' according to my dictionary), so I do not need to give a definition or translate it for the French child; but some people may have difficulty in grasping the idea or concept—in understanding what exactly is involved in this thing 'intelligence', 'mental agility' or call it what you will. Here we have a conceptual problem—a problem about what is really involved in an idea or what it amounts to, as opposed to mere ignorance of the meaning of a word. We know what we are talking about, but we don't know a great deal about what it is.

The failure to appreciate the difference between defining a word and offering a clear conception has had most unfortunate consequences in many ways. One of the most obvious is the tendency for empirical research to proceed when the terms have been merely defined, rather than when the concepts have been clearly articulated. That is as if one were to define the Snark by saying that it was a Boojum, and then set out to look for it. A more important consequence to dwell on here is that, by running the two together, people are able to dismiss philosophy as 'mere semantics' or 'just playing with words'. But when philosophers insist on the need to analyse the

Education 191

concept of education, they are not merely checking that we understand the English language. They do not want to be told that 'education' means 'the systematic training and development of the moral and intellectual faculties'. They want us to consider what that definition amounts to. They want us to work out what it entails. They want us to work out the ramifications and implications of this idea or this sense of the word 'education'. They want us, in short, to *think* about it.

If we were to do that, we would surely see that training a person to be an accountant, teaching a person to type, or initiating a person into ways of using a computer, are none of them in themselves educating; they are not even a necessary part of educating people. But this kind of thinking, which would show us in a moment that the 'relevant education' that many people call for isn't education at all, does not take place very often. And one of the reasons is that it is confused with knowing the meaning of words, and dismissed as a relatively insignificant business. But when people say that our education is out of date, and that it should consist of technological instruction and guidance about practical matters such as sexual behaviour, it is not words that they are playing with so much as ideas to which they are doing violence. Something of deep concern and potentially overwhelming is going on. Education as an enterprise, not as a word, is being taken away from us. The difference between those who counsel the provision of technological skills and social manners in schools, and those who urge the development of the mind in its broadest sense, is a substantive difference, not a verbal one. It is the difference between those who wish simply to give people control of the means to random ends, and those who wish to give people the ability to contemplate other means and to think about the ends of life as well.

No doubt those who go to the other extreme and disdain practical considerations entirely are equally at fault. But what is needed is a clearer grasp of what is at issue, and a clearer distinction between various different legitimate functions of schooling. Schooling itself is a very general term meaning little more than the institutionalised provision of instruction. It holds no conceptual problems, and by the same token, reveals no secrets under scrutiny. A great number of things might go on in schools without anything being logically amiss. There is nothing improper in itself about schools providing instruction in deep-sea diving, Sanskrit, airs and graces, bridge, mathematics, driving or philosophy. What is required is discussion and argument about what instruction it would be useful to provide for children in the light of various ends, considered to be desirable.

But one thing that schools have traditionally sought to offer, which it is not difficult to argue they ought to continue to offer, is education, and education is something rather special that makes certain logical demands on us.

Education, which is not necessarily the same thing as what passes for education in schools or the public mind, is essentially a matter of developing understanding of principles or, as Peters has well phrased it, the reason why of things.[2] (Just what principles and what reasons depend for a full answer on a characterisation of the kinds of logical distinction that are to be discerned in the domain of knowledge.) The educated mind is not judged by reference to the quantity of factual information it can regurgitate, its creative brilliance, its specialist know-how, or its ability to carry out specific tasks according to training. It is judged by the breadth and competence of its understanding of the nature of things generally. The question that every community has to face is whether, at a given historical moment, it wants and can afford education in this sense, as opposed to, say, producing trained technicians, blind followers of dogma or supremely gifted specialists. There can be no doubt that at the present time many communities cannot really afford education, perhaps because their limited resources must be directed to food production or perhaps because there are pressing reasons to produce citizens who are something other than educated. But equally, there can be no doubt of the worth of education for a community that can afford it.

Some will respond to that claim by asking why education is thought to have value. Is it useful? This brings me to the third point that needs clearing out of the way, before we can assess the value of education directly; there seems to be a popular misconception to the effect that use and relevance are properties belonging to things in the manner that shape and colour may be said to do. More figuratively, people attribute usefulness and relevance to pursuits, as if they were allotting cars to their owners. But, of course, nothing is, as such, useful or useless, relevant or irrelevant. What is useful or relevant varies from person to person, place to place and purpose to purpose. What is useful for your present purpose in this country, may not be to mine elsewhere. Not only do people tend to overlook this obvious point, there is also a marked inclination to relate usefulness and relevance to immediate practical purposes. A shovel is thought of as a more useful thing than a violin, notwithstanding the fact that in certain circumstances, such as a concert hall, it would be something of a handicap. A pursuit like carpentry is thought of as more relevant than the study of history, notwithstanding the fact that it has no relevance whatsoever, except for those who want to engage in some carpentry. Consequently, to ask whether education is useful or to insist that it should be (and/or that it should be relevant) is to betray deep confusion. To whom and for what purposes should it be useful? For the purposes of securing a particular job in the motor industry, being educated probably isn't particularly useful. On the other hand, education is decidedly useful, if we want a community of people with some breadth of understanding about the way things are. A popular view is that technical skills, mathematics and computer studies are useful kinds of thing for schools to teach, whilst the study of literature and history are relatively irrelevant pursuits. But if our aim is to educate, that distinction is meaningless, and if our purpose is to open minds or contribute towards a better society, the latter might well be considered more useful things to study. What has to be considered is not what group of skills and techniques will be useful for unreflective participation in a particular, inevitably impoverished, view of the future. What has to be considered is the advantage to society at large, in the long run, in trying to educate people, that is to say in trying to develop rationality, understanding and intelligence, rather than in trying to train people to perform particular tasks and to fulfil allotted roles in society.

It has been convincingly argued by, for instance, Samuel Bowles that while people tend to see schooling as a means of opening new doors and unlimited possibilities for all, in fact it serves to replicate existing differences of wealth, power and opportunity, or, at the very least, fails to alter them. 'On balance', Bowles suggests, 'the available data suggests that the number of years of schooling attained by a child depends upon the social class standing of his father at least as much in the recent period as it did 50 years ago.'[3] (Strictly speaking, the data cannot 'show' a relationship of dependence; they can only show correlation. But I am not at all inclined to dispute Bowles' interpretation of his findings.) Mass education has not proved a social leveller, or a means to fully equal opportunity, so much as a 'mechanism to ensure social control and political stability'.[4] Nor are current government strategy, Black Paper proposals, hard-nosed industrialists or so-called radical educationalists offering us alternatives that are likely to change that. Each of these alternatives is, in its own way, broadly speaking, a recipe for accentuating differences. Withholding finances to the point at which classes remain overcrowded at a time when we have too many teachers, and at which schools cannot afford essential equipment such as books, obviously hinders the schools in their task, and leaves the advantage with those from advantaged homes. Offering the majority something other than the familiar cognitive based curriculum, whether you do it for hard reasons ('the majority are not up to the traditional curriculum'), soft reasons ('movement and craft are just as good as science and literature'), or silly reasons ('brass bands and pigeon fancying are part of their real world'), inevitably deepens the divide between the many and the few. If choice is of serious concern to us, then we must strive to put everybody, from whatever background, as near to a position in which he can make informed choices as possible; that entails that we develop people's knowledge and understanding not of particular skills, but of abstract and general patterns of thought.

One error we have repeatedly made has been to look to schools primarily to be social reorganisers. Certainly they have failed to revolutionise social structures, but why should we ever have thought they would? Why should schooling be preoccupied with propping up the economy, fitting people to a world that may at any moment become outdated, or changing that world? Why should schools be organised with a vew to bringing about greater social equality? There is something agonisingly absurd about trying to tinker with schools in order to bring about changes somewhere else, and something objectionable about an indiscriminate reorganisation of schools in order to level elsewhere. If equality of wealth is wanted, as I have argued it should be,[5] then the distribution of wealth must be reorganised. Expending energy on finding ways to hold us all back equally at the starting gate, prior to a scramble for still unequal shares, is futile and monstrous. If people require more computer expertise in industry, then let industry provide the necessary training. Schools are there to prepare people in a general way for a meaningful and worthwhile adult life. The more open the society, the more that upbringing has to help people become flexible and autonomous, and the less specific the schooling can be. It may well be advisable that everybody should have some basic grasp of, say, mathematics, but it is plainly foolish to seek to make all of us mathematicians to any high degree or to make any of us only mathematicians.

In what respect, then, is education useful? It is useful in that it is education that carries most of us more or less well or badly through our lives. It is our education that, in addition to our home background and local environment, most affects our chances of being happy or miserable, our capacity for helping or hindering others, and how we live and cope with our lives generally. The socialisation we experience at home and school no doubt sets some kind of a limit within which we develop, but, in most cases, it is the quality of one's education that can develop positive characteristics for controlling and shaping one's life. It is the education that people receive that may strongly affect the quality of their lives in a free and open democracy. For what affects the quality of one's personal life is one's stock of expectations, and behaviour patterns, one's intelligence and rationality, and these develop out of one's social background and one's education. Schools should therefore seek to produce social, rational persons of intelligence and discernment. That would make schooling useful beyond a reasonable cavil.

'Social' involves no conceptual problems. Social behaviour, as opposed to anti-social behaviour, is behaviour in accordance with the accepted rules of the society in question. The question of whether a given society has acceptable rules of behaviour is quite distinct. But no society can conceivably avoid having some set of rules, whether they are formally articulated or not. Socialising people in this sense is not to be confused, however, with closing their minds on the rightness or acceptability of the practices in question. There is a difference between getting people to do such things as drive on the left-hand side of the road, tell the truth, or refrain from stealing and blowing their noses on other people's curtains, and getting people to assume that these are unquestionably correct ways of behaving. Because schools should also be concerned to develop rationality, there should always be in people a willingness to question the truth or acceptability of assumptions, but that does not make it inappropriate for them to nonetheless accept a set of assumptions about social behaviour.

By 'rationality' I refer to a disposition to seek good reason. The main aspect of the rational man is the urge to want to know why, to seek explanation and justification, and to have some account to give of his actions. But we don't only require of rational people that they are concerned about reasons; we also expect them to show some degree of competence in finding or producing them. Rationality, therefore, also requires a disciplined understanding. Insofar as there are logical distinctions to be drawn, whether between instances of things or between types of question, rationality demands that they are recognised. The rational man should see that for most purposes a duck is not a swan, and that whether either ought to be treated as sport is a different kind of question from whether some cultures do treat them as such.

Much in life, even at the most mundane level, depends upon judgements of value, and ultimately everything has to be traced back to fundamental value assumptions. These are not of the same logical order as various other kinds of judgements, as I have just indicated in reference to the question of the morality of duck-shooting. But what is the essence of the capacity to show discernment in questions of value? There is a widespread tendency to conflate the point that truth in this domain does not appear to be subject to public agreement with the claim that there is no such thing as truth or falsity in this domain. Thus some people argue that values are a matter of arbitrary commitment and that consequently the question of discernment does not arise, on the sole grounds that people do not agree about values. But the fact of the matter is that within any area we can in principle distinguish between work of quality and rubbish, as a direct result of understanding the nature of the activity in question. Good football is a matter for expert discernment, just as good literature is, and neither is to be distinguished from good science in this respect. But what is essential to a discerning judgement in these or any other fields is a good understanding of the activity involved. A full appreciation of the nature of the game of football is a necessary, though not a sufficient condition, of a sound judgement about the quality of a particular game. An essential part of education is to take steps to develop powers of discernment both by constantly demanding its exercise in all fields of activity, and by providing knowledge of various activities. Asking about the relative value of different activities, without reference to any particular purpose such as entertainment, brain-teasing or competition, is usually pointless, precisely because without a common purpose to compare them against, there is no agreed point of comparison. 'Is pop music as good as classical music?' is, as it stands, a meaningless question. But 'is one better than the other in certain clearly defined aesthetic respects?' makes sense, as does the question of whether one pop song is better than another, either in terms of what pop songs are supposed to be, or in respect of some extrinsic end.

The remaining question is, what constitutes intelligence? Clearly the word is a commendatory term implying good understanding. Intelligent people have to get things right. But what things? when? and how?

It is common for people to talk of a faculty of understanding, but that, since it begs the questions of what a faculty is and whether there are such things, is very misleading. Of course, somebody might use the phrase 'faculty of intelligence' and mean no more than 'intelligence'. But some people at least would seem to be suggesting by the phrase that there is some entity, some thing that one might in some sense locate or pick out, if not like an arm, at any rate like an electrical circuit. But is there any reason to presume so much? It seems far more plausible to suggest that ascribing intelligence to people is saying something about the manner in which they tend to understand.

'Intelligence' would seem to be a degree word and a dispositional term. To say that it is a degree word is to say that in principle it refers to an idealised conception, but that in practice it is applied to people who approximate to the ideal to any considerable degree. In other words, we may have our unsullied conception of what intelligence is, but no human being actually embodies intelligence without limitation or qualification. But, for simplicity, we classify the relatively intelligent simply as intelligent. It is a dispositional term inasmuch as to be intelligent is not to be in a perpetual state of intelligent thought and action. We do not assume that we have necessarily made a mistake, if a person whom we have classified as intelligent subsequently makes some mistake or misunderstands something. Even intelligent people frequently make mistakes at particular times or on particular issues, for a wide variety of reasons such as being carried away by some emotion, being ignorant of some information or being rather tired. An intelligent person is one who is generally prone to intelligent thought and action. What we have to consider is what makes thought and action or understanding intelligent.

The criteria that most obviously spring to mind would be speed of understanding, range, quality, coherence, practical functionality and discriminatory power, all of which, I suggest, are indepedently necessary and together sufficient conditions of what is thus shown to be the rather broad concept of intelligence.

Etymologically, deriving as it does from the Latin *inter* and *legere*, the word intelligence suggests something of being *quick* to pick up or apprehend a point. Probably most of us continue to conceive of intelligence as precluding undue slowness to see a point or understand something, although obviously rapidity of response need not be extreme and is in itself certainly not the same thing as intelligence. A second fairly uncontentious necessity is that intelligence should be displayed over a fairly broad field. People whose speed of understanding in the realm of chemistry is not matched by any understanding at all in a host of other areas, though possibly excellent chemists, can hardly be accounted intelligent people. Intelligence, then, demands at least reasonably quick and broadly based understanding. It must also surely be good understanding in the basic sense of thorough and complete in the ways appropriate to the matter in hand. An intelligent person doesn't just have information and views about, say, proportional representation and solar energy. He understands and can unfold the complexities of the arguments for and against the former, and he can consider alternative approaches to the latter. There should also be coherence between the various things that an intelligent person does understand. It would be a mark of a lack of intelligence to have a thorough understanding of some scientific explanation of an event, but to entertain some equally well understood, incompatible, supernatural explanation at the same time, or to subscribe to some dogma while holding certain beliefs in defiance of it.

But such quick, broad, well-grounded and coherent understanding does not quite capture the essence of intelligence. It is surely important also that it should not be confined to the non-functional and the impractical. This may perhaps be a contingent factor about our society at the present time, but whatever the reason, it is surely the case that we now tend to distinguish the learned or academic mind, which may meet the above criteria in respect of some purely theoretical pursuit, and the intelligent mind, which meets them in the everyday realm of social and practical life. Finally it must surely be added that intelligence demands understanding couched in terms of clear and specific, rather than blurred or general, concepts and categories. For understanding that is limited by blurred or general concepts cannot be particularly illuminating.

Schooling, as has been conceded above, may be called upon to fulfil many functions. But one function it has is to provide education. Education does not consist in imparting particular skills or particular types of behaviour, but in providing that kind of understanding that we recognise as intelligent along with the respect for reason implicit in the rational mind. The community will not be able to see any immediate cash return, perhaps, for the provision of this education. Nonetheless, to provide it would be one of the most useful things we could do.

NOTES

1 I have treated of most of the issues raised in this chapter, in much greater detail, in my *The Philosophy of Schooling*.
2 See R. S. Peters, *Ethics and Education*.
3 Samuel Bowles, 'Unequal Education', in P. R. and K. J. Struhl (eds), *Philosophy Now*.
4 *Ibid.*
5 See above Chapter 9.

Bibliography

Aristotle (1953) *The Nicomachean Ethics* (trs. J. A. K. Thomson), Penguin, Harmondsworth.
Aristotle (1962) *The Politics* (trs T. A. Sinclair), Penguin, Harmondsworth.
R. Baker (1975) '"Pricks" and "Chicks": A Plea for "Persons"', in R. Wasserstrom (ed) *Today's Moral Problems*.
R. N. Baldwin (ed) (1970) *Kropotkin's Revolutionary Pamphlets*, Dover, New York.
R. Barrow (1973) *Athenian Democracy*, Macmillan, Basingstoke.
R. Barrow (1975) *Moral Philosophy for Education*, Allen and Unwin, London.
R. Barrow (1976) *Commonsense and the Curriculum*, Allen and Unwin, London.
R. Barrow (1978) *Radical Education*, Martin Robertson, Oxford.
R. Barrow (1980) *Happiness*, Martin Robertson, Oxford.
R. Barrow (1981) *The Philosophy of Schooling*, Wheatsheaf, Brighton.
R. Barrow (1982) *Language and Thought*, Althouse, London, Ontario.
H. A. Bedau (1961) *"On Civil Disobedience"*, The Journal of Philosophy, 52:21.
C. Bell (1928) *Art*, Chatto and Windus, London.
D. Bell (1973) *Coming of Post-Industrial Society*, Basic Books, New York.
S. I. Benn and R. S. Peters (1959) *Social Principles and the Democratic State*, Allen and Unwin, London.
J. Bentham (1948) *The Principles of Morals and Legislation*, Hafner, New York.
J. Bentham (1958) *Anarchical Fallacies: Being an Examination of the Declaration of Rights Issued during the French Revolution* in J. Bowring (ed) *The Works of Jeremy Bentham*, Vol 2, Edinburgh.
W. Berns (1971) "Beyond the (Garbage) Pale: The Case for Censorship", H. M. Clor (ed), *Censorship and Freedom of Expression*.
S. Bowles (1972) "Unequal Education" in P. and K. Struhl (eds) *Philosophy Now*.
L. Bryson (ed) (1957) *Aspects of Human Equality*, Harper and Row, New York.
John R. Burr and Milton Goldinger (eds) (1976) *Philosophy and Contemporary Issues*, Second Edition, Macmillan, New York.
R. M. Christenson (1970) *"Censorship of Pornography? Yes"*, The Progressive, September.

200 Injustice, Inequality and Ethics

H. M. Clor (ed) (1971) *Censorship and Freedom of Expression: Essays on Obscenity and the Law*, Rand McNally, New York.

M. Cohen (1971) "Concurring and Dissenting Opinions" *The Public Interest*, No. 22.

A. Conan Doyle (1892) "Silver Blaze", Strand Magazine, December.

R. T. De George (ed) (1968) *Ethics and Society*, Macmillan, London.

J. Dewey (1937) "Democracy and Educational Administration", *School and Society* Vol 45, No 1162.

T. S. Eliot (1944) *Four Quartets*, Faber and Faber, London.

J. Feinberg (1973) *Social Philosophy*, Prentice Hall, New Jersey.

J. Feinberg (ed) (1973) *The Problem of Abortion*, Wadsworth, California.

A. Flew (1971) "Theology and Falsification: a Symposium" in B. Mitchell (ed), *The Philosophy of Religion*.

M. Friedman (1962) *Capitalism and Freedom*, University of Chicago Press, Chicago.

E. Fromm (1942) *Fear of Freedom*, Routledge and Kegan Paul, London.

N. Garver (1968) "What Violence Is" *The Nation*, 209.

B. Gendron (1975) "Capitalism and Poverty" *Radical Philosophers' News Journal*, 4 January.

S. and R. Godlovitz and John Harris (eds) (1972) *Animals, Men and Morals: an Enquiry into the Mal-Treatment of Non-Humans*, Taplinger, New York.

J. Glover (1977) *Causing Death and Saving Lives*, Penguin, Harmondsworth.

S. Goldberg (1979) *Male Dominance*, Sphere Books, London.

G. Grisez (1970) *Abortion: The Myths, the Realities and the Arguments*, Corpus Books, New York.

P. Halmos (1971) "Art and Social Change" *Royal Institute of Philosophy Lectures, Vol 4*, Macmillan, London.

S. Hampshire (ed) (1978) *Public and Private Morality*, Cambridge University Press, Cambridge.

P. Hansford Johnson (1967) *On Iniquity*, Macmillan, London.

R. M. Hare (1952) *Freedom and Reason*, Oxford University Press, Oxford.

R. M. Hare (1975) "Abortion and the Golden Rule" *Philosophy and Public Affairs* 4, No 3.

T. E. Hill (1973) "Servility and Self-Respect" *The Monist*, Vol 57, No 1, January.

T. Hobbes (1914) *Leviathan*, J. M. Dent and Sons, London.

S. Hook (1959) *Political Power and Personal Freedom*, Phillips, New York.

C. Jencks (1975) *Inequality*, Penguin, Harmondsworth.

I. Kant (1948) *Groundwork of the Metaphysic of Morals* (trs H. J. Paton), Hutchinson, London.

P. Kropotkin (1970) "Anarchist Communism: its Basis and Principles" in R. N. Baldwin (ed) *Kropotkin's Revolutionary Pamphlets*.

V. I. Lenin (1932) *State and Revolution*, The Little Lenin Library Vol 14, New York.

H. Marcuse (1968) "Ethics and Revolution" in R. T. DeGeorge (ed) *Ethics and Society*.

H. L. Mencken (1926) *Notes on Democracy*, Alfred A. Knopf, New York.
J. S. Mill (1962) *Utilitarianism* (ed) M. Warnock, Fontana, London.
J. S. Mill (1958) *Nature*, Bobbs-Merritt, New York.
J. S. Mill (1962) *On Liberty* (ed) M. Warnock, Fontana, London.
B. Mitchell (ed) (1971) *The Philosophy of Religion*, Oxford University Press, Oxford.
A. Myrdal (1972) "The Need for Equality" in P. R. Struhl and K. J. Struhl (eds) *Philosophy Now*.
W. N. Nelson (1980) *On Justifying Democracy*, Routledge and Kegan Paul, London.
K. Nielson (1977) "On Justifying Revolution" *Philosophy and Phenomemological Research* Vol 37 No 4.
J. R. Pennock and J. W. Chapman (eds) (1967) *Equality* Nomos IX Yearbook for the American Society for Political and Legal Philosophy, Leiber-Atherton, New York.
R. S. Peters (1966) *Ethics and Education*, Allen and Unwin, London.
J. Plamenatz (1957) "Equality of Opportunity" in L. Bryson (ed) *Aspects of Human Equality*.
Plato (1974) *The Republic* (trs Desmond Lee), Penguin, Harmondsworth.
Plato (1960) *Gorgias* (trs W. Hamilton) Penguin, Harmondsworth.
Plato (1954) *Crito* (trs H. Tredennick), Penguin, Harmondsworth.
P. Proudhon (1876) *What is Property?* (trs B. Tucker), Princeton.
A. Quinton (1973) *Utilitarian Ethics*, Macmillan, London.
J. Rachels (ed) (1979) *Moral Problems*, Third Edition, Harper and Row, New York.
J. Rachels and F. A. Tillman (eds) (1972) *Philosophical Issues*, Harper and Row, New York.
J. Rawls (1972) *A Theory of Justice*, Oxford University Press, Oxford.
J. Rawls (1975) "The Justification of Civil Disobedience" in R. Wasserstrom (ed) *Today's Moral Problems*.
T. Regan and P. Singer (eds) (1976) *Animal Rights and Human Obligations*, Prentice-Hall, New Jersey.
J. R. Richards (1980) *The Sceptical Feminist*, Routledge and Kegan Paul, London.
J. J. Rouseau (1911) *Emile*, J. M. Dent and Sons, London.
J. J. Rouseau (1913) *The Social Contract*, J. M. Dent and Sons, London.
R. Ryder (1974) "All Animals are Equal" *Philosophic Exchange*, Vol 1, No 5.
R. Ryder (1975) *Victims of Science*, David Poynter, London.
M. Scarf (1975) "The Foetus as Guinea Pig", *New York Times Magazine*, 19 October.
J. H. Schaar (1967) "The Case for Egalitarianism" in J. R. Pennock and J. W. Chapman (eds) Equality.
H. Selsam (1965) *Ethics and Progress*, International Publishers, New York.
G. Sher (1975) "Justifying Reverse Discrimination in Employment" *Philosophy and Public Affairs* 4, No 2.
P. Singer (1977) *Animal Liberation*, Granada, St. Albans.
P. Singer (1980) *Practical Ethics*, Cambridge University Press, Cambridge.

J. J. C. Smart (1973) *An Outline of a System of Utilitarian Ethics*, Cambridge.
F. E. Sparshott (1963) *The Structure of Aesthetics*, University of Toronto Press, Toronto.
K. J. Struhl and P. Struhl (eds) (1975) *Ethics in Perspective*, Random House, New York.
P. Struhl and K. J. Struhl (eds) (1980) *Philosophy Now*, Third Edition, Random House, New York.
J. J. Thomson (1971) "A Defence of Abortion" *Philosophy and Public Affairs*, Vol 1, No 1.
L. Tolstoy (1898) *What is Art?* Oxford University Press, Oxford.
M. A. Warren (1973) "On the Moral and Legal Status of Abortion" *The Monist* Vol 57, No 1.
R. Wasserstrom (1975) "The Status of the Foetus" *Hastings Magazine*, June.
R. Wasserstrom (ed) (1975) *Today's Moral Problems*, Macmillan, New York.
R. Wasserstrom (1963) "The Obligation to Obey the Law" *UCLA Law Review*, Vol 10.
R. Wertheimer (1971) "Understanding the Abortion Argument" *Philosophy and Public Affairs* 1, No 1.
L. Wittgenstein (1961) *Tractatus logico-philosophicus* (trs D. F. Pears and B. F. McGuiness) Routledge and Kegan Paul, London.
R. P. Wolff (1969) "On Violence" *The Journal of Philosophy* 66.

INDEX

Abortion, 4, 5, 21, 44, 54, 91–105
Achievement, 119–20
Anarchism, 45, 63, 151–2
Animals, xii, 5, 7, 102, 104, 156–68
Art, xii, 4, 55, 169–87
Autonomy, 30–1, 47, 71–2, 99

Beliefs, 38–40

Catholicism, 24, 36, 38, 40, 41
Censorship, 170, 171, 182–6
Choice, 70–5
Civil disobedience, 7, 44, 55, 141–55
Concepts, 3, 25, 27, 28, 57–66, 110–11

Democracy, 4, 5, 55, 59, 121, 129–39, 147
 (justification of), 138–9, 142
Discrimination, xi, 1–11, 23, 41, 54–5, 72–5, 82, 83, 87, 142
Dogmatism, 23–43, 46, 49, 50, 138, 142–3

Education, 2, 44, 87, 188–98
Equality, xii, 6–7, 11, 106–27, 193–4
 (of opportunity), 6–7, 108–9, 115, 193–4
 (of wealth), 106–27
Euthanasia, 4, 10, 22, 102, 104, 166

Fairness, 79, 115, 116, 123
False consciousness, 36–9, 65–6
Feminism, 37, 56–66, 67–76 (*see also*) 77–90, 91–105
Foetal research, 92, 104
Foetus, 4, 7, 91, 95–100
Freedom, 17, 34, 35, 40, 44–55, 71, 72, 113, 129, 131–2, 141, 182–4, 185
 (of association), 134
 (of expression), 134, 182–4, 185
 (of speech), 44, 52, 53, 134, 182–4
 (of thought), 44, 52

Freudianism, 24, 26, 31, 32, 36, 40, 41

Happiness, 12, 13, 16, 17, 18, 19, 20, 21, 25, 51, 52, 153

Impartiality, xii, 6–7, 72–4, 77, 79, 83, 84, 113
Intelligence, 4, 8, 9, 50, 196–8
Intention, 18, 19
Interest, 50, 100–2, 159–61

Killing, 5, 10, 14, 15, 16, 20, 53, 54, 91, 93–5, 100, 102, 103, 104, 166–7

Language, relationship to thought, 35–6, 42, 56–66
Law, obligation to obey, 147–50

Marxism, 26, 31, 32, 34, 35, 40, 41, 42, 56, 110, 135, 142–3, 170
Merit, 116–20, 121–7
Motivation, 18, 125

Nature, 47, 68–70, 75, 93, 116, 137
Needs, 38, 109–10, 111–12, 114, 116, 123

Obscenity, 4, 184–5

Personhood, 4, 10, 96–100, 102, 159–61
 (respect for persons), 49–50
Philosophy, xi, 2–5, 28, 44, 92, 190–1
Potentiality, 99–10
Poverty, 34, 110–12

Racial Discrimination, 1, 58, 59, 77–90
Raising consciousness, 36, 37, 65–6
Rationality, 23, 26–31, 39–43, 195
Reasons, relevance of, 7–9, 28–9, 73–4, 158–61

Referenda, 130, 133–4
Relevance, 192–4
Respect for persons, 49, 50
Reverse discrimination, 65, 66, 77–90
Reward, 88, 89, 106–27
Rights, 92–3, 101–2, 103, 137

Schooling, 4, 77, 87–9, 188–98
Self-awareness, 102, 104
Self-regarding activities, 51, 52, 53
Sex role stereotyping, 54, 67–76
Sexist language, 57–66
Significant form, 172–4
Slippery slope argument, 52, 98, 133
Social importance, 120
Social and Life Skills, 189
Social levelling, 193–4
Socialisation, 195
Speciesism, 104, 156–67
Subsidy, 169–70, 176–82
Subsistence needs, 110–12
Suffering, 147, 157–61, 161–5
Supply and demand, 118–19

Talent, 87, 117–19, 120, 121
Truth, 182–3

Universities, 83–7, 108, 124
Unprovable propositions, 24, 25, 26, 31, 32, 48–9
Usefulness, 179, 192–5
Utilitarianism, 10, 12–22, 42, 51, 53, 54, 101–2, 103, 153, 163
 (act), 14, 15, 16
 (hedonistic), 14
 (ideal), 14
 (rule), 14, 15, 16, 20

Value judgements, 195–6
Vegetarianism, 165–7
Violence, 35–6, 142–6, 151–3

Wants, 38
Wealth, xii, 5, 6, 78–9, 106–27
Wisdom, 30
Words, contrasted with concepts, 42, 58–66

For Product Safety Concerns and Information please contact our EU
representative GPSR@taylorandfrancis.com
Taylor & Francis Verlag GmbH, Kaufingerstraße 24, 80331 München, Germany

www.ingramcontent.com/pod-product-compliance
Lightning Source LLC
Chambersburg PA
CBHW070401240426
43661CB00056B/2487